FAMILY LAW

Family Lawyers
The Divorce Work of Solicitors

JOHN EEKELAAR, MAVIS MACLEAN
and SARAH BEINART

·HART·
PUBLISHING

OXFORD – PORTLAND OREGON
2000

Hart Publishing
Oxford and Portland, Oregon

Published in North America (US and Canada) by
Hart Publishing c/o
International Specialized Book Services
5804 NE Hassalo Street
Portland, Oregon
97213-3644
USA

Distributed in the Netherlands, Belgium and Luxembourg by
Intersentia, Churchillaan 108
B2900 Schoten
Antwerpen
Belgium

Hart Publishing Ltd is a specialist legal publisher based in
Oxford, England.
To order further copies of this book or to request a list of other
publications please write to:

Hart Publishing Ltd, Salter's Boatyard, Oxford OX1 4LB
Telephone: +44 (0)1865 245533 or Fax: +44 (0)1865 794882
e-mail: mail@hartpub.co.uk
WEBSITE: http//:www.hartpub.co.uk

British Library Cataloguing in Publication Data
Data Available
ISBN 1 84113–185–7 (cloth)
1 84113–186–5 (paperback)

Typeset by Hope Services (Abingdon) Ltd.
Printed and bound in Great Britain on acid-free paper by
Biddles Ltd, www.biddles.co.uk

We wish to dedicate this book to the memory of
Kathleen Funder
a gifted and dedicated researcher and dear friend.

Preface

The enactment of the Family Law Act 1996 provided an occasion for widespread discussion about the state of the family and family life in modern Britain. It also brought about an intensive reappraisal of the role of the legal process in relation to family matters. Debate, and change, in this area of the law had been going on for a long time. Indeed, the immediate post-war period saw a number of investigations into the way divorce law should operate, and significant changes occurred during the 1970s. So the fact that the role of the legal process should be under scrutiny was not unusual. What did seem different this time, however, was the intensity of the feeling that the legal process had not simply gone wrong, or was in need of improvement, but that it was somehow in its nature completely inappropriate as the mechanism for dealing with family disruption and conflict.

As the debate progressed, we began to feel increasingly uneasy. It was not that we thought there was anything wrong with the direct challenges which were being made to what was perceived as a legal hegemony. No social institution has a monopoly of virtue. Yet we were concerned that perceptions may have been formed on the basis of insufficient evidence. If significant change was to be brought about, we felt that we should at least understand rather better what it was we would be departing from. It was concerns such as these which led us to seek funding for research into the way in which solicitors do divorce work. An important part of this work is, of course, the relationship between solicitor and client, but we conceived of our inquiry in somewhat wider terms than that. It was intended to obtain a picture of the way solicitors organised and carried out their work when it related to divorce and similar matters. A more complete study would have included their child welfare (public law) work, but resource constraints meant we had to exclude that part of the work of family law solicitors from this study.

We must record our thanks to the Nuffield Foundation for funding the project. We profited much from helpful advice from Judith Sidaway. Work such as this relies totally on the willingness of the people being studied to co-operate in the project, and our subjects were generous with their time and goodwill in participating in it. Our thanks to them. We must specifically thank the two who read the text in draft form and Professor Gwynn Davis, who did the same. Their comments have been enormously helpful. We do not expect they have spotted all our errors, though we hope they have minimized them as far as possible.

JOHN EEKELAAR
MAVIS MACLEAN
SARAH BEINART

Oxford,
August 2000.

Contents

1

The Policy Context

THE FAMILY LAW Act 1996 put on the statute book a revolutionary mechanism for obtaining divorce. Either the husband or the wife (or both of them together), no less than three months after having attended an information meeting, could file a statement alleging that their marriage had broken down, and nine months after that (or fifteen months, if there were children of the marriage under sixteen, or the other party requested such an extension) either would be entitled to apply for an order of divorce. When the Law Commission originally suggested this kind of framework for divorce in 1990,[1] it saw its main advantage as lying in the elimination of the need to make allegations of fault as a condition to obtaining divorce, and considered the waiting periods as being "primarily" designed to provide "convincing proof that the marital relationship is indeed irreparable".[2] Although the Commission also thought that divorcing in this way would give the parties an opportunity to think about using mediation services as a way of resolving matters that were in contention between them, and adopted a positive attitude towards mediation, it also stated that "there are dangers . . . in relying too heavily on conciliation or mediation instead of more traditional methods of negotiation and adjudication". If mediation was to be used, the Commission insisted that it should be purely voluntary.[3] John Major's Government adopted the Law Commission's scheme, and a new framework for divorce was enacted in the Family Law Act 1996, though its implementation was put on hold while the significantly new structures to be put in place were

[1] Law Commission, *The Ground for Divorce*, Law Com No 192, 1990.
[2] Law Commission, *The Ground for Divorce*, para. 5.25. At present proof of irretrievable breakdown is established on the basis of (usually uncontested) allegations of adultery or of unreasonable behaviour. If the couple are willing to wait long enough, it may also be established after two years' continuous separation if the other party consents, or after five years' continuous separation if the respondent does not consent. Most divorcing parties prefer to use adultery or unreasonable behaviour, because it is quicker.
[3] Law Commission, *The Ground for Divorce*, paras. 5.34–5.

further explored. But in enacting the scheme, the Government moved mediation to the centre of the stage. This can be seen from the very title of its 1993 Consultation Paper: *Looking to the Future: Mediation and the Ground for Divorce: A Consultation Paper*.[4] Its final proposals were announced in a White Paper bearing the same title.[5] In that White Paper the Government conceded that mediation should not be compulsory, but insisted that it should be "encouraged". Mediation was now seen as having a role in saving marriages, and enabling the couple to "take responsibility for the breakdown in their marriage".[6] It was described as providing an alternative to "negotiating matters at arms length through two separate lawyers and to litigating through the courts" by providing a "constructive framework for using the period between initiating the divorce process and the making of the final divorce order for profitable reflection and consideration".[7]

The Summary issued by the Lord Chancellor's Department during the Major Government explaining the proposed scheme in the Family Law Act 1996, entitled *Marriage and the Family Law Act 1996: The new legislation explained* asked: "Does the present system pay enough attention to children?" and answered: "It is widely accepted that wherever possible children whose parents are divorcing should be able to maintain a close relationship with both parents". The brochure then goes on to say that "A system which encourages an acrimonious legal battle makes it less likely that such relationships can be maintained in the years ahead and serves rather to increase the trauma for the children". This perception that the lawyer-based system produces acrimony and conflict underpinned the strong advocacy by the Major Government of mediation as being preferable to "litigation", or even to "arms-length negotiation through lawyers". Since such conflict is seen to increase legal costs, this view of the legal process explains section 29 of the Family Law Act 1996 which seeks to divert clients who seek legal aid in family proceedings away from lawyers and towards mediators. In general terms, this provision requires such clients to attend a meeting with a mediator before their application for legal aid can be considered. If the mediator considers that the matter is appropriate for mediation, state funding for assistance by lawyers may be refused.

---

[4] Cm 2424 (1993).
[5] *Looking to the Future: Mediation and the Ground for Divorce*, Cm 2799 (1995).
[6] White Paper, 1995, para. 5.21.
[7] White Paper, 1995, para. 5.8.

The White Paper also developed the idea that the party who wishes to initiate the divorce should first attend an information meeting. This had not been part of the Law Commission's original scheme. The idea was introduced in the 1993 Consultation Paper. The meetings were envisaged as being occasions for providing general information about the law, the relevant procedures and the availability of counselling services.[8] The White Paper took this further, now suggesting that the meetings should provide information about the consequences of divorce and the effects of divorce on children.[9] This represented a movement towards using the information meetings as a means of dissuading the couple from divorcing, and this was confirmed by the attitude taken towards them under the Blair Government. A Home Office document of 1998 suggested that the meetings might be broken down into two stages. The first would be an individual meeting which would concentrate on "information which would help parties to consider whether their marriage really is finally over; marriage support services available to help; help for survivors of, or those fearful of, domestic violence; the decisions which have to be faced; and the impact of divorce on families, especially children, if the decision to divorce is finally taken". The couple would also be encouraged to meet a marriage counsellor. Later, there would be a separate group presentation giving information about finance and property issues and "the helpfulness of mediation".[10] That is a perfectly reasonable objective, though the absence of any reference to the "helpfulness of legal advice" (which must surely also be true) suggests that the information is to have a particular "spin". Such information goes well beyond simple facts about legal principles and procedures and the availability of certain services. It is to be presented so as to suggest to the recipient what is the most responsible course of action to take.[11] The implementation of these reforms, however, has been preceded by projects piloting the information meetings and the operation of mediation. It was expected that they would be brought into operation during 2000.

---

[8] Consultation Paper, 1993, paras. 8.1–4.

[9] White Paper, 1995, para. 7.4.

[10] Home Office, *Supporting Families: A Consultation Document*, 1998, para. 4.29.

[11] See John Eekelaar, "Family Law: keeping us 'on message' " 1999) 11 *Child and Family Law Quarterly* 387.

B THE REFORMS DELAYED: REPRIEVE FOR THE LEGAL PROCESS?

Not surprisingly, the new scheme was expected to change significantly the pattern of professional intervention in divorce. One commentator wrote:

> For the first time since the Matrimonial Causes Act 1857, the management of divorce looks as though it may slip from the grasp of lawyers. If the legal profession acquiesce in this revolution, not only will practitioners and judges have to be content with a far less dominant role in the process of divorce, but academic lawyers will also feel the draught as whole areas of knowledge around divorce cases cease to be within the discourse of law.[12]

The revolution to which Roberts refers has, however, not yet occurred. In June 1999 the Lord Chancellor announced a delay in implementing the scheme.[13] Divorce remains primarily a legal process, and most people going through it consult a lawyer, though they are more likely to do this if they have children We have some information from our previous work drawing on two national samples screened out from the general population in 1981 and 1994 about the proportion of those experiencing divorce who sought legal and other forms of advice, and on what subjects advice was sought. In 1986 we found that 61 per cent of the sample of 274 men and women who had divorced within the previous five years and who had no dependent children had seen a lawyer, compared with 87 per cent of divorcing parents.[14] The childless divorcees seldom received legal aid (only 9 per cent) whereas 63 per cent of those with dependent children did so. Seventy per cent of those with children were not required to pay their legal costs at the time of the legal intervention, though in some cases a statutory charge might be put in place. The conclusion we drew then was of the relative simplicity of childless divorce. The only significant transaction was the sale of the house or transfer of an interest in it, and in only 6 per cent of cases was a solicitor consulted about any other assets. In contrast, divorcing *parents* faced considerable problems which needed resolution within a legal framework. This conclusion was strengthened by our later

---

[12] Simon Roberts, "Divorce reform Green Paper: A coherent and radical vision" (1994) 24 *Family Law* 204.

[13] Lord Chancellor's Department, Press Release, 17 June 1999.

[14] John Eekelaar and Mavis Maclean, *Maintenance after Divorce* (Oxford University Press, 1986), p. 92.

research on divorcing parents.[15] Based on a sample interviewed in 1994, we found that, of 155 formerly married parents, 19 per cent had taken no professional advice; 74 per cent had seen a lawyer; 53 per cent had received advice *only* from a lawyer; 7 per cent had received advice from a lawyer and a non-professional adviser such as a friend or relative; 1 per cent had seen a lawyer and a mediator; 8 per cent had seen a lawyer and a counsellor; 3 per cent had seen a lawyer and a social worker. (For 4 per cent the response was not sufficiently clear to code). The proportion of divorcing parents who saw a lawyer in 1994 (74 per cent) was lower than the proportion of divorcing parents who had seen a lawyer in the earlier study (87 per cent). This may be due to changes in the eligibility criteria for legal aid, or to increased use of other forms of advice.

The importance of the legal profession to people who divorce was recently underlined by the results of a major survey conducted by Hazel Genn for the Nuffield Foundation in 1997 and 1998 in the context of developing government initiatives on access to justice.[16] The study sought to discover what proportion of the population experienced a "justiciable event" (defined as one which raised legal issues, whether recognised as doing this or not by the person concerned) of a "non-trivial" nature, and, if so, what they did about it. On the basis of the information obtained, it was shown that, over the previous five years, some 8.3 per cent of the population over eighteen, amounting to 2.4 million people, experienced a "justiciable" problem concerning relationships and family matters, and some 4.7 per cent of the population over eighteen, involving 1.7 million people, experienced problems related to divorce.[17] This compares with 7.3 per cent who experienced employment problems and 15.3 per cent (the highest category) who experienced problems concerning faulty goods. About one in five who had experienced family problems reported violence or abuse.[18] Of particular importance in our context is the finding that, where divorce or separation problems arose, the person experiencing the problem was more likely than in the case of any other problem, to seek advice from a solicitor or law centre both in the first instance (61 per cent) and at any time (82 per cent).[19] A further study involving a sample of

[15] Mavis Maclean and John Eekelaar, *The Parental Obligation* (Hart Publishing, Oxford, 1997), p. 133.
[16] Hazel Genn, *Paths to Justice* (Hart Publishing, Oxford, 1999).
[17] Ibid., p. 32.
[18] Ibid., p. 47.
[19] Ibid., p. 89.

fifty-seven divorced families showed that 89 per cent had consulted a lawyer at some stage.[20] These figures are consistent with our findings showing that about four out of five people who become caught up in divorce use a lawyer at some stage.

Despite the present degree of involvement of solicitors in the divorce process, this is taking place in a context in which official thinking is still dominated by the view that the way lawyers deal with divorce generates conflict and cost. In the words of the 1993 Consultation Paper: "Litigation and arms length negotiation often heightens conflict, reduce communication and exacerbate the stress arising from marriage breakdown".[21] Throughout the Consultation Paper, this picture of the legal process is contrasted with the alleged advantages of mediation.[22] Philip Lewis has analysed the assumptions made about lawyers and the legal process in the Major Government's Consultation Paper and White Paper[23] about divorce reform and compared them with the relevant research evidence available.[24] He identifies the following assumptions being made:

1. Arms length negotiation between lawyers often reduces communication . . . and often increases tension and conflict.
2. A translation problem between client and lawyer causes misunderstanding and anger in the other client about what is being said and how it is said.
3. Negotiating through lawyers is associated with getting the "best deal" at the other's expense.
4. Lawyers only give legal advice.
5. Negotiation is dyadic; only the parties are involved.
6. Lawyers will "unpick" or "interfere" with agreements reached through mediation without their involvement.

Lewis found that, although some of the assumptions were supported in part, the evidence represented a much more varied picture. The assumptions ignored the following evidence: that "there is often very

---

[20] Gillian Douglas, Mervyn Murch, Alison Perry, Kay Bader and Margaret Borkowski, *How parents cope financially on marriage breakdown*, Report to the Joseph Rowntree Foundation, November 1999.

[21] Consultation Paper, 1993, para. 1.14.

[22] For an analysis of the Consultation Paper, see John Eekelaar, "Family Justice: Ideal or Illusion? Family Law and Communitarian Values" in M.D.A. Freeman (ed.), *Current Legal Problems, vol. 48* (Oxford University Press, 1995).

[23] Above notes 4 and 5.

[24] Philip Lewis, *Assumptions about Lawyers in Policy Statements: A Survey of Relevant Research* (Lord Chancellor's Department, 2000).

little communication and a lot of tension in the first place"; that "private negotiation is far from desirable in all cases"; that while sometimes parties are misrepresented to each other, "sometimes too solicitors are used as scapegoats for views actually held by one party which they do not wish to take responsibility for putting forward"; that "actually not all clients, and perhaps not even a majority, will see increased hostility and attempts to overreach"; that legal advice is "more varied" than assumed; that lawyers "at least sometimes . . . are used not just to give advice or negotiate with the other lawyer but also to solve problems by dealing with third parties on the client's behalf"; and that solicitors are generally reluctant to overturn existing agreements. Lewis concludes that: "I am left reading this research with a sense that the authors see many matrimonial solicitors, perhaps a majority of them, as having done a good job in difficult circumstances; some, however, could have done appreciably better".

The view that the handling of divorce by lawyers increases conflict and cost has persisted under the Blair Government, which has continued to advocate the superiority of mediation. In its comprehensive review of family policy in 1998, it stated:

> When marriages run into difficulties and cannot be saved, government should ensure that the divorce process does not make the situation worse for the family as a whole by, for example, encouraging litigation or making children pawns between parents. This is why it is important to reduce conflict on divorce and strengthen mediation as an alternative to "arms-length" negotiation through lawyers over divorce proceedings.[25]

In a speech to the UK Family Law Conference in June 1999, the Labour Lord Chancellor, Lord Irvine of Lairg, re-iterated the perception of the previous government's 1993 Consultation Paper that the alternatives on offer were between mediation and *adjudication*, as if any case which was not resolved by mediation would go to trial before a court. He said:

> The Government is determined that as many people as possible know what mediation offers and are given the opportunity to benefit. The agreements reached in mediation have a rational basis. They are the result of constructive negotiation between those concerned. People are able to see that scoring points and settling wrongs, real or imagined, will not be helpful for the future and that, in order to ensure the best arrangements for their own future, and that of their children, it is better to discuss problems and reach

[25] Home Office, *Supporting Families: A Consultation Document* (1998), para. 4.41.

sensible agreement which both parties regard as acceptable. *Parties are more likely to adhere to agreements they have made themselves rather than orders that have been imposed from outside.* A mediated agreement will be their agreement. Both parties will feel more committed to keeping their part of the bargain.[26]

The implication seems clear that only in mediation will parties reach agreements "they have made themselves" and that not to use mediation leads to orders "imposed from outside". However, as will be seen, negotiation between lawyers very rarely leads to orders 'imposed from outside'.[27] By presenting mediation as producing "rational" agreements after "constructive" negotiation, the Lord Chancellor implicitly characterises the alternative, which is lawyer-based negotiation, as being irrational and unconstructive, and expressly refers to it as involving "scoring points and settling wrongs, real or imagined". We have to say that we do not recognise that description as representing the process which we saw family solicitors operating.

During the same speech the Lord Chancellor referred to the preliminary results of the pilot projects concerning the proposed information meetings. As we stated earlier,[28] the government had stated that one of the purposes of the meetings is to explain "the helpfulness of mediation".[29] Despite that, one of the results of the pilot projects showed that 39 per cent of the people who attended the meetings were more likely to want to go to a solicitor afterwards than if they had not attended the meeting. Only 7 per cent attended mediation.[30] One might have thought it encouraging that people were responsible enough to wish to seek legal advice when informed about the potential problems which might arise in matters which could affect them deeply. However, the Lord Chancellor described this finding as "disappointing". "For a policy which is intended to promote harmony and reduce acrimony", he stated, "it has to be accepted that these are outcomes which must give

[26] Speech to the UK Family Law Conference, Inner Temple, London, 25 June 1999. Emphasis supplied.

[27] See also John Eekelaar, "Family Justice: Ideal or Illusion? Family Law and Communitarian Values" in M.D.A. Freeman (ed.), *Current Legal Problems, vol. 48* (Oxford University Press, 1995).

[28] Above, p. 3.

[29] Home Office, *Supporting Families: A Consultation Document*, 1998 paras. 4.31–33.

[30] Lord Chancellor's Department, *Information Meetings and Associated Provisions within the Family Law Act 1996: Summary of Research in Progress,* June 1999. This research will be considered more fully later (see p. 48).

any responsible decision maker pause".[31] Since, as observed above, the Lord Chancellor *takes it as given* that lawyers disrupt harmony and promote acrimony, it is not surprising that he announced the postponement of the launching of the new divorce scheme until further results were available.[32] The determination to reduce the role of lawyers in divorce could not be made more evident.

C THE JUDICIARY LEND A HAND

The judges have also shown concern about the apparent failure of lawyers to contain costs of litigation generally. Lord Woolf, who later became Master of the Rolls, headed a comprehensive review of civil procedure, resulting in an Interim Report in 1995 and a Final Report in 1996.[33] These proposed a radical extension of judicial control over the preliminary stages of civil litigation. Claims below £15,000, the bulk of cases (an estimated 80–90 per cent of those above "small claims" limits),[34] would be placed on a "fast track" which would shift control over the course of the litigation from the parties to the court. There would be timetables, and the court would monitor progress of the case to ensure compliance and have power to impose penalties on the parties for unreasonable conduct of litigation. The system was brought into operation in April 1999. The reforms have been consistently questioned by Michael Zander,[35] who has argued, first, that merely to speed up cases risks compromising the quality of legal service; second, that judicial case management can increase costs, largely through requiring additional work to be done in anticipation of a court hearing in cases which would have settled without such hearing anyway (front-loading); and, third, that the proposal to exact penalties for delays overlooks the reasons for such delays, which usually lie in the "ordinary

[31] Speech by Lord Irvine of Lairg LC to UK Family Law Conference, Inner Temple, London, 25 June 1999.

[32] Lord Chancellor's Department, Press Release, 17 June 1999.

[33] *Access to Justice, Interim Report to the Lord Chancellor on the civil justice system in England and Wales.* The Right Honourable Lord Woolf (Lord Chancellor's Department, June 1995); *Access to Justice: Final Report to the Lord Chancelor on the civil justice system in England and Wales.* The Right Honourable Lord Woolf (Lord Chancellor's Department, July 1996).

[34] Lord Chancellor's Department, *Modernising Justice*, CM 4155 (1998), p. 40, note 20.

[35] See Michael Zander, "The Government's Plans on Civil Justice" (1999) 61 *Modern Law Review* 382.

problems of real life." The Government has attempted to control costs
in fast track cases by imposing a system of fixed costs which could be
ordered to be paid by the losing party to the winner. The sum would be
related to the value of the eventual award.[36] This would not, however,
affect the amount the lawyers could charge their *own* clients, though it
might be hoped that they would not fix them at a higher level than that
which could be recovered from the other side should they win. Zander,
however, considers this to be mere "wish fulfilment".[37] Nor does it
cover pre-trial costs. The system was introduced in April 1999, though
more consultations were taking place about the way pre-trial costs
might be controlled.

It remains to be seen how these reforms work out in practice. They do
not cover family cases, but there had been precedents for this form of
judicial case-management in procedures regarding children introduced
under the Children Act 1989[38] and also in schemes for pre-trial review of
financial and property disputes (which are termed claims for "ancillary
relief") operating in divorce county courts, of which there were over
eighty by the end of the 1980s.[39] The most ambitious experiment for processing applications for ancillary relief in the family jurisdiction, however, was initiated in the Principal Registry of the Family Division in
London in October 1996, though it subsequently extended beyond there.
This "Ancillary Relief Pilot Project" requires the court to fix a "first
appointment" for directions to be held no earlier than ten nor later than
fourteen weeks after the filing of the application. Thirty-five days before
the appointment each party must file and simultaneously exchange a
sworn financial statement in a form set out in regulations (Form E).
Then, not later than seven days before the first appointment, each party
must file with the court and serve on the other a questionnaire setting out
what information they seek of the other party; a schedule of documents
sought of the other party and a statement of the apparent issue between
the parties. The object of the first appointment is to define the issues and
save costs. The district judge will decide the extent to which the ques-

---

[36] See *Controlling Costs: A Lord Chancellor's Department Consultation Paper* (May
1999), para. 9.

[37] (1999) 61 *Modern Law Review* at p. 386.

[38] See Joan Hunt, "A moving target: care proceedings as a dynamic process" (1998) 10
Child and Family Law Quarterly 281; J. Brophy and P. Bates, *The Guardian ad litem,
Complex Cases and the Use of Experts following the Children Act 1989* (Lord
Chancellor's Department Research Series 3/99, March 1999).

[39] For an account of these, see John Eekelaar, *Regulating Divorce* (Oxford University
Press, 1991), pp. 29–30.

tionnaires need to be answered and give directions as to other matters, such as to valuations and other expert evidence. This is meant to speed along the preparation of the case, so no further information may be sought without the permission of the court. Unless it is not appropriate, the district judge will fix a time for a Financial Dispute Resolution (FDR) hearing, which is "to be treated as a meeting held for the purposes of conciliation" and "to guide the parties towards a settlement by exploring common ground and dispelling unreal expectations". Whatever is said at this hearing cannot be used at a later hearing which, if it takes place, will be before a different judge. The judge at the FDR is empowered to make Consent Orders as appropriate.[40]

This scheme has generally been held successful, and in 1999 the Lord Chancellor announced that from 2000 a modified version of it would be extended throughout the country.[41] Yet it is unclear how far, if at all, it will reduce overall legal costs. The evaluation of the scheme by the consultants KPMG,[42] which made comparisons between courts operating the pilot scheme with a control group of courts which were not operating it, found the following:

1. A higher proportion of cases (85 per cent) had achieved "final order" under the pilot scheme by the end of the survey than in the control courts (72 per cent). However, virtually the same proportion (86 per cent; 82 per cent) had settled *by consent*.

2. The average time from application to final order was 208 days for the pilot, compared with 226 for the control.

3. The average *costs* (for the parties) of the pilot cases were higher both for the legally-aided and non-legally aided cases. However, KPMG warn that, owing to difficulties of data collection, these figures are unreliable and they believe that there is no evidence of significant difference in costs.

It may be remarked that the first two findings make the same point, for, as it seems that cases are concluded somewhat faster (by some three weeks) in the pilot courts, it would follow that more of them would have reached a conclusion during the course of the research. It does not follow that the cases in the control group would not have

[40] *Rayden and Jackson on Divorce and Family Matters* (17th edn, Butterworths, London, 1997) 774.

[41] Speech to the UK Family Law Conference, Inner Temple, London, 25 June 1999.

[42] KPMG, *Ancillary Relief Pilot Scheme Study: Final Report* (LCD Research Series, No. 8/98).

reached a conclusion (indeed, it is hard to conceive that they would not have done). Whether they would have done so *by consent* is not known, but it is worth noting that, of all the cases which were resolved, just as many were resolved by consent under the "old" procedures as under the pilot scheme. A major assumption behind the whole scheme is that by bringing cases to resolution *more quickly*, savings in costs can be achieved. The KPMG report asserts that improvement in the time taken to reach "settlement" (that is, conclusion of the case) reduces costs.[43] However, it offers no evidence to substantiate this crucial assumption, and it is a matter to which we will return when we consider our data. In fact, what evidence the KPMG report did produce on costs suggests that the costs to the parties using the pilot scheme were slightly higher than those who did not. The fact that the report dismisses this finding as being insufficiently robust only demonstrates that the study was not able to demonstrate whether or not they were higher. A fuller sample with more complete data might show the costs of the pilot scheme are indeed higher. That could occur if use of the scheme put pressure on the solicitors to make elaborate preparations for the appearance in court ("front loading") and to obtain counsel's opinion. But in any case, the data sources used by KPMG for this purpose will give only incomplete information about true costs. This is for two main reasons. First, the study only included cases where an application to the court had been made both in the pilot courts and the control courts. If it were to be the case that the pilot scheme leads to more applications being made to court than would otherwise be the case, the scheme would clearly raise costs, but this would not show in the data collected. It is intuitively likely that a scheme which is designed to encourage the use of courts in the settlement process will increase the number of applications. The other reason is that the greater use of judicial time inherent in the pilot project is an additional burden on public resources. It seems important, therefore, that the new procedure is carefully monitored when it applies nationally as from 5 June 2000.[44]

It is clear that very costly litigation can occur when one or both of the parties take advantage of the complex appeal structure. In *Piglowska* v. *Piglowski*[45] the combined assets of the parties amounted

[43] KPMG, ibid, para. 12.4.1.
[44] Family Proceedings (Amendment No 2) Rules 1999. See Gold (2000) 150 *New Law Journal* 133.
[45] [1999] 3 All ER 632 HL).

to some £128,000. The costs of both parties stood at £16,000 when the district judge made a final order, but the appeal process was pursued to the House of Lords, by which time the costs exceeded the value of the assets. The House criticised the judges below for giving leave to appeal, and indeed the Court of Appeal for allowing the appeal, against a very straightforward decision. The judges, it seems, must have borne a high level of responsibility for the excesses of this case.[46] "To allow successive appeals in the hope of producing perfect justice", said Lord Hoffmann, "is to kill the parties with kindness". However, he also stated: "Speaking entirely for myself, I do not think that costs in these cases are capable of being properly brought under control until the courts or the Legal Aid Board impose cash limits which are directly related to the value of the assets in the dispute".

D EMPIRICAL EVIDENCE ABOUT LAWYERS AND DIVORCE

Lawyers who deal with private law family cases therefore appear to be seen as being excessively litigious, processing cases too slowly, and too expensive. Of course, there are always anecdotal accounts of delay and expense, but the existing research evidence tells a different story. In his pioneering examination of English solicitors' strategies published in 1992, Richard Ingleby[47] argued that there was a continuum between negotiation and courtroom litigation, which, following Marc Galanter, he calls "litigotiation". Although Ingleby saw courtroom litigation as being merely the ultimate conclusion of a process which incrementally invokes the court as a means of bringing about a conclusion, he notes of his research data that "it is striking that there was not one contested hearing about the final (financial) settlement in the whole sample. There were applications for such hearings and agreements at the door of the court, but in no case did the parties actually have their dispute directly resolved by a judge".[48] Not only that, he found that most cases were resolved at the bottom end of the litigotiation scale – furthest from the courtroom or its threat. Ingleby gives a set of reasons for this.[49]

[46] This was also true of *Tee* v. *Tee & Hollman* [1999] 2 FLR 613, where a county court judge allowed the parties to argue on the basis of trusts law when the matter fell under the matrimonial jurisdiction, leading to wasted costs of some £100,000.
[47] Richard Ingleby, *Solicitors and Divorce* (Oxford University Press, 1992).
[48] Ibid., p. 89.
[49] Richard Ingleby, *Solicitors and Divorce* (Oxford University Press, 1992) pp. 159–61.

1. Many clients already have some idea as to how they want the dispute to be resolved, or there is little to argue about. Contrary to the government view, noted by Lewis above, solicitors were reluctant to disturb these. "The notes of conferences and the correspondence between solicitors reveal an expressed preference for 'amicable' solutions".

2. There are financial advantages to solicitors for non-contentious resolution. "There are a number of arguments to suggest that the financial interests of solicitors lie in the rapid turnover of cases rather than their extension".

3. "The amounts of time necessary to prepare every case for trial are simply not available".

4. Pressures arise out of reasons of collegiality between solicitors, where good relationships are valued; it also enables solicitors to keep control over outcomes, which would otherwise pass to barristers and judges.

5. Disputes are easier to resolve before they become inflamed by threats of litigation.

6. Solicitors would wish to use the court only when confident they would be successful. The risks of litigation act as a deterrent.

7. There is a perception that agreed solutions are more durable.

We shall consider later how far some of these observations are borne out by our data. But the general thesis that lawyers were disposed towards settlement at the earliest stages possible is massively supported by the research of Davis, Cretney and Collins published in 1994. They colourfully remark:

> Indeed, some solicitors gave us the impression that they regarded trials of the ancillary relief issue in much the same light as they viewed the white rhino – a possibly mythical creature which was outside their immediate experience.[50]

The same has been found in a study of American divorce lawyers by Sarat and Felstiner, who found that the desire for settlement "was . . . a recurrent theme throughout conversations between lawyers and clients. In those conversations the lawyers' message is overwhelmingly pro-settlement. They consistently emphasize the advantages of infor-

---

[50] G. Davis, S. Cretney and J.G. Collins, *Simple Quarrels* (Oxford University Press, 1994), p. 40.

mal as opposed to formal resolution".[51] In Britain, the bias towards settlement is strongly supported by the stance of the Solicitors' Family Law Association, a widespread network of specialist family law solicitors supported by the Law Society. Its pamphlet *Need a solicitor for a family dispute?*[52] begins thus: "Do you dread becoming tied up in a hostile battle? SFLA solicitors encourage everyone to agree that divorces, separation and family disputes are not contests in which there are winners and losers but searches for fair solutions. They avoid using language that implies a dispute when no serious dispute necessarily exists. They avoid stirring up personal emotions . . . The aim is a fair settlement rather than expensive litigation". The SFLA Code of Practice proclaims at the outset that:

> the solicitor should endeavour to advise, negotiate and conduct proceedings in a manner calculated to encourage and assist the parties to achieve a constructive settlement of their differences as quickly as may be reasonable whilst recognising that the parties may need time to come to terms with their new situation and should inform the client of the approach he intends to adopt.

Yet the belief that lawyers inflame conflict has persisted. Why should this be? One explanation may lie in anxieties raised by observing an increase in the numbers of applications for ancillary relief and orders made as a result of such applications. This was an abiding concern of the Lord Chancellor's Advisory Committee on Legal Aid during the 1970s and 1980s. In its Annual Report for 1982, the Committee noted that while in 1974, one "ancillary relief order" had been made for every three decrees nisi of divorce, by 1981 the ratio had fallen to 1:1.5,[53] and assumed that this indicated an increased litigiousness among divorcing couples. Yet, as pointed out previously,[54] the implication of increased conflict from a higher number of ancillary orders cannot be made. It ignores increases in home ownership and in property values, which means that divorcing parties have more issues to settle on divorce; and, crucially, it overlooks the fact that the parties' agreement can only be insulated against subsequent attempts to seek variation by

---

[51] A. Sarat and W. Felstiner, *Divorce Lawyers and their Clients* (Oxford University Press, 1995), p. 191.

[52] "Need a solicitor for a family dispute? 10 Good Reasons why you should choose a member of the Solicitors Family Law Association" (SFLA, nd).

[53] 32nd Report of the Lord Chancellor's Legal Aid Advisory Committee, 1982 (HC 189, 95–104).

[54] John Eekelaar, *Regulating Divorce*, 1991, p. 33.

its incorporation in a consent order. Indeed, the rise in ancillary orders could reflect a *higher* rate of settlement as parties increasingly use this mechanism to achieve a clean break between them. This interpretation is consistent both with the experience of district judges, who claimed in 1990 that the settlement of issues had greatly increased, and with the statistics which show the high proportion of orders made by consent. In 1993, of 90,412 ancillary orders made on divorce, 63,385 (70 per cent) were made by consent.[55] In 1998, of 61,620 ancillary orders, 47,803 (77.6 per cent) were by consent.[56] In 1998 Gwynn Davis and his colleagues examined 301 court files from four separate courts and found that 69.4 per cent of ancillary relief orders had resulted from applications submitted *with the consent of both parties*: a further 7.3 per cent were settled at final hearing, without requiring adjudication by the judge. Only 4.6 per cent were adjudicated.[57] Put another way, the *settlement failure rate* was under 5 per cent. It is important to remember that this represented the proportion of settlement failures *of all cases*; that is, it includes cases where settlement was unlikely from the start, where, for example, one of both of the parties was determined not to compromise.

This must be contrasted with settlement rates resulting from mediation, which is usually only resorted to where parties have some disposition to settle. But even here settlement failure is high: a major study found that "all issues" were agreed in only 39 per cent of "comprehensive" mediations, and 19 per cent of child-related mediations.[58] More recently, a group led by Professor Gwynn Davis is examining for the Legal Aid Board the new pilot schemes for providing publicly funded mediation. Provisional findings[59] revealed that in those areas where section 29 of the Family Law Act 1996 (see p. 2) has been implemented for piloting purposes, most referrals concern children issues, rather than financial ones. Since section 29 requires an interview with a mediator in most circumstances prior to the possibility of the grant of legal aid, the amount of "intake" activity (i.e. initial interviews with media-

---

[55] *Judicial Statistics, Annual Report 1993,* Table 5.9 (HMSO) Cm 2623.

[56] *Judicial Statistics. 1998,* Table 5.7 (Stationery Office) Cm 4371.

[57] Gwynn Davis, Julia Pearce, Roger Bird, Hilary Woodward and Chris Wallace, *Ancillary Relief Outcomes: A Pilot Study for the Lord Chancellor's Department,* University of Bristol, 1999.

[58] Relate Centre for Family Studies, *Mediation: The Making and Remaking of Cooperative Relationships,* University of Newcastle, 1994.

[59] Gwynn Davis, "Monitoring Publicly Funded Mediation" (1999) 29 *Family Law* 625.

tors) naturally increased significantly. However, this was accompanied by a "dramatic" increase in the number of cases deemed not suitable for mediation. For those referred under section 29, the proportion of cases deemed suitable was around 20–25 per cent in the early stages[60] and just under 20 per cent of referrals actually began mediation. About 90 per cent of cases which proceed to mediation concern a dispute about children. The proportion of cases reaching agreement to those not doing so was 3:2 in children matters, with a lower rate of agreement in financial and property cases. The overall rate of full agreement fell from 44 per cent to 37 per cent during the research period. This proportion is therefore close to that found in the earlier study. Nor is it clear that the cases counted as being successful outcomes did actually result eventually in a written agreement. One observation made by the researchers was that clients attending intake sessions primarily desired resolution to their problems, and were little interested in what was perceived as mainly a procedural step in the divorce process.

So the success of lawyers' present practices in avoiding court-imposed outcomes seems clear. We will consider our evidence on this matter later. Nevertheless, government policy has persisted in the idea that, where cases are routed through mediation, they will cost less than when they are dealt with by lawyers. The Consultation Paper issued under the Major Government in 1993 made this explicit, stating: "The average cost of a matrimonial bill paid out of the Legal Aid Fund in 1992–3 was £1,565. Many privately paying spouses will have paid more". This was contrasted with the "likely average cost of mediation" as being "of the order of £550 per case".[61] Yet this costing overlooks a number of issues. First, the legal aid figures cover *all* cases, including those which would have been difficult or impossible to resolve by mediation; the mediation figure includes only those which were apparently successfully concluded by mediation, ignoring those which did not. Also, mediation currently is normally used as a supplement to legal assistance, the cost of which should therefore be added. It also ignores the value of other kinds of input which lawyers can make, and which our research describes later in this book. A more sophisticated model which attempts to compare the costs of mediation with lawyer-negotiation has been proposed by Bevan and Davis.[62] In comparing

[60] Personal communication from Professor Davis.

[61] Lord Chancellor's Department, *Looking to the Future: Mediation and the Ground for Divorce*, Cm 2424 (1993), paras. 9.30 and 9.20.

[62] Gwyn Bevan and Gwynn Davis, "A preliminary exploration of the impact of family mediation on legal aid costs" (1999) 11 *Child and Family Law Quarterly* 411.

likely costs between a situation where mediation is routinely attempted and where (as now, outside areas where the new mediation pilot schemes have been introduced) an application is made for a legal aid certificate, they conclude that the average cost of cases under the mediation scheme could range from 65 per cent to 115 per cent of the present costs (in disputes involving "all issues") and 68 per cent to 105 per cent (in "child only" disputes), depending on what assumptions are made about various matters, in particular mediation success rates. These figures are very different from the wildly optimistic claims of the 1993 Consultation Paper, and suggest that, should mediation success rates fall below something like 60 per cent, there will either be no savings or average costs will increase. As we have just seen, a success rate of 60 per cent looks very optimistic, though the likely success rate of mediation will be affected by the types of cases referred; the larger the number of referrals, the lower the success rate is likely to be. But it is likely that even these figures lean too favourably on the side of mediation, because the baseline figure taken by Bevan and Davis for legal aid costs of cases presently dealt with by lawyers represents the average legal aid costs for those cases which raise disputes on all matters (children, finances, personal protection), and that represented only 11 per cent of all divorce cases in the sample from which it was taken. Such conflicts do not arise simultaneously in the average case, as our data show.

E   THE PUBLIC FUNDING OF FAMILY LAW WORK: THE LEGAL AID REFORMS

Apart from the attempt to sideline the legal process in family cases in favour of mediation, family law practice has been caught up in the fundamental reform of the whole basis of public funding of legal services which was started by the Major Government, and brought to completion by its successor. In 1996, Lord Mackay, Lord Chancellor under John Major, produced proposals for capping legal aid expenditure.[63] Despite his criticisms of these proposals, Lord Irvine, the Labour Lord Chancellor, has maintained the same goal of imposing rigorous controls over public funding of the justice system. Before considering the nature of these reforms, it is necessary to consider the way family law

---

[63] *Striking the Balance – The Future of Legal Aid in England and Wales* (1996) Cm 3305.

work received public funding at the time when we conducted our research.

There is usually no public funding of legal services for those seeking a divorce decree, but where the financial eligibility criteria of the applicant and the merits test for the case were met, there was access to publicly funded legal advice and representation in dealing with ancillary matters (that is, resolution of disputes over finances, property and children). It must be understood that "representation" in this context covers any work in which a lawyer engages which goes beyond initial advice covered by the Legal Advice (Green Form) scheme, and thus comprises any activities in relation to the other party (for example, negotiations) and third parties.

In 1996–7 the average costs of a legally aided case involving money or property issues, leaving aside the small number of high cost (over £5,000) cases, was £1,400.[64] The total cost of funding these cases was however now much higher than it had ever been, as the number of cases had increased. It is clear that family law work entails expenditure of large sums of public money. It has been estimated that in 1995–6 up to £550 million was spent in gross fees to solicitors in connection with family work.[65] According to the Legal Aid Board Annual Report for the same period, about half of this came from the public purse through the legal aid budget.[66] Of the legal aid monies spent on family work, solicitors' fees represented about 75 per cent of the total legal aid expenditure on family and children work that year (1995–6), which came to £393 million, including disbursements, fees to counsel and initial advice under the Green Form scheme.[67] It should be noted, though, that the Board appears to use a slightly broader definition of family work than the Law Society's research team, as the Board includes public law children cases. Family and children work accounted for a third of all legal aid expenditure during 1995–6, and comprised the largest single category. Thus, while income from family work is estimated to account for 10 per cent of gross fee income overall, it comprises

[64] Sarah Maclean, *Report of the Case Profiling Study: Legal Aid and the Family Justice System*, Legal Aid Board Research Unit (1998), p. 36. The overall average cost of legally aided matrimonial cases, excluding legal advice (Green Form) costs was £1,800 (p. 99).

[65] Personal communication from Judith Sidaway, RPPU of the Law Society.

[66] Legal Aid Board, *Annual Report for 1995/6* (HC 505, 1996), p. 2, adjusted to reflect gross fees.

[67] Sarah Maclean, *Report of the Case Profiling Study: Legal Aid and the Family Justice System*, p. 9, para. 3.3.

one-third of gross fee income paid out under legal aid. Despite this, lawyers consider legally aided work in family cases to be seriously underpaid. Compared with hourly rates for private client work of between £100 to £200, rates for local authority work are around £68 per hour, and they are £41 per hour for advice under the Green Form scheme.

The firms in the Law Society Panel Study[68] reported that around 60 per cent of their gross fee income from family work came from legally aided clients. This proportion varied with size of firm. Almost all the family work done by sole practitioners was legally aided (92 per cent), compared with between 60 per cent of that done by firms with between two and twenty-five partners. The extent of current demand for legally aided work undertaken as a proportion of divorce work in general can be inferred from Legal Aid Board data for 1996–7.[69] In 1996, 128,488 matrimonial applications were made, for 75 per cent of which legal aid was granted, and 82,000 Children Act (private law) applications were made, 82 per cent under legal aid. In 1996, 73,443 legal aid certificates were granted, falling back slightly from the peak year 1993. In 1992 when just over 160,000 decrees were granted, approximately 117,000 grants of legal aid were made to women, 77,000 for financial matters, (75 per cent of applications), 13,000 for a child custody matter (45 per cent of applications) and 27,000 for a combined matter (68 per cent of applications).

However, it is important to remember that legal aid in property arrangements following divorce does not always result in a transfer of money from state to individual. It is in principle a loan, repaid either immediately or on the later sale of capital assets, secured by a statutory charge over those assets (with an exemption for the first £2,500 of any lump sum or property adjustment order), which now bears a realistic rate of interest, to cover any costs of the case borne by the legally aided person. The sums recovered have been large, rising from £3.82 million a year in 1981–2 to £34.59 million in 1992–3.[70] The Legal Aid Board has noted that, while gross payments from the fund rose by a yearly average of 5.8 per cent from 1994–5 to 1998–9, recovery, through contributions and the statutory charge, increased by a yearly average of 9.8 per

---

[68] B Cole, *Solicitors in Private Practice: their work and expectations*, Research Study No. 26 (The Law Society, 1997).

[69] Legal Aid Board, *Annual Report for 1996/7* (HC 52, 1997), pp. 68–9.

[70] See Stephen Shute, "The Effect of the Statutory Charge on Legally Aided Matrimonial Litigation" (1993) 109 *Law Quarterly Review* 636.

cent over the same period.[71] The extent to which the charge operates can be appreciated from the fact that during 1996, when 63,000 grants of legal aid were made to women for a financial matter related to divorce, 8,840 charges were paid off, and 4,680 were cancelled for a variety of reasons, including repossession of the property, or negative equity. Thus, about two-thirds of charges seem to "work". Also during that period, 16,922 new charges were created. There were 101,871 charges outstanding, of which 85,494 were quantified with a value of £186 million, and the rest unquantified. Of the newly quantified charges, 7,359 were interest bearing.[72] So it seems that a statutory charge is created in about one-third of grants of legal aid for financial matters in matrimonial cases. When the charge is paid off (which seems to occur in two-thirds of cases), it is likely to meet the complete cost of the legal aid grant despite the £2,500 exemption because the average cost of a divorce-related money case (£1,400) is less than the average recovery of £2,000 to the Board.[73] In other cases, the legal aid monies may have been recovered immediately through sale of the property or from the other side as part of the settlement.

As mentioned above, the legal aid scheme has been subject to critical review for some years, and reforms had been outlined by Lord Mackay. One attempt to take pressure off public funding of legal work was the introduction of "conditional fees" in 1995 under the Courts and Legal Services Act 1990. In this system, a lawyer can agree to take on a case on the understanding that he will only charge the client a fee if the case is won, but this fee can include an additional element (a "success fee" or "uplift") to cover the risk that, had the case been lost, the lawyer would have received nothing. The client can meet the costs out of the monies won in the case, or, preferably, by an order that the losing party pay his costs.[74] He may be able to insure against having to pay his opponent's costs if he loses. At first neither the "success" fee nor the insurance premiums could be recovered by the winner from the loser, though this has been changed by the Access to Justice Act 1999.[75]

---

[71] Legal Aid Board, *Annual Report for 1998/9* (HC 537, 1999), p.6.

[72] Legal Aid Board, *Annual Report for 1996/7* (HC 52, 1997), p. 65.

[73] Sarah Maclean, above note 64.

[74] *Access to Justice with Conditional Fees* (Lord Chancellor's Department, March 1998), para. 2.1; Lord Chancellor's Department, *Conditional Fees: Sharing the Risks of Litigation* (September 1999), paras. 1–6.

[75] Access to Justice Act 1999, ss. 27 and 29; Lord Chancellor's Department, *Conditional Fees: Sharing the Risks of Litigation* (September 1999), paras. 15–28.

Conditional fees were originally limited to personal injury and insolvency cases. However, in a speech to the Law Society in Cardiff in October 1997, Lord Mackay's successor, Lord Irvine, announced plans to concentrate legal aid spending on low income clients and to entrust most civil cases to the conditional fee system and in July 1998 the range of cases covered by the conditional fee system was extended as far as possible under the 1990 Act to all civil proceedings, other than family cases. In December 1998 a government White Paper suggested that the conditional fee system might be extended to some matrimonial cases, especially where the division of property was in issue.[76] However, the extension of conditional fee arrangements to family cases would require identifying a winner in order to secure payment. Yet the Government had been critical of what it thought was a "winner/loser" culture among divorce lawyers. Conditional fees could operate either as a severe disincentive against settlement when a lawyer believes the case is strong, or an incentive to inappropriately premature settlement when a lawyer believes he has done "enough" to earn the fee.[77] The Government was persuaded by such objections, and the Access to Justice Act 1999 therefore states that criminal and "family proceedings" cannot be subject to an enforceable conditional fee agreement.[78]

Although it now seems that conditional fee arrangements are unlikely to be introduced in family cases, at least in the immediate future, reforms to the legal aid system generally will have a significant effect on family law work. From 1994[79] practitioners taking on legal aid work were paid prescribed rates. More significantly, in 1998 it was proposed that legal aid expenditure would be further controlled through a system of block grants made contractually between law firms and a new Legal Services Commission (LSC) on the basis of competitive tender. As the Government stated in its White Paper, *Modernising Justice*:[80] "This is a fundamental change from the existing legal aid scheme, under which any lawyer can take a case and submit a bill to the Legal Aid Board for payment. In future, lawyers and other providers will only be able to work under the scheme when they have a contract

---

[76] Lord Chancellor's Department, *Modernising Justice* (December 1998), para. 2.43.
[77] M. Maclean and N. Rickman, "No House, No Fee – Conditional Fee Arrangements in Divorce" (1999) 29 *Family Law* 245.
[78] Access to Justice Act 1999, s. 27(1), inserting s. 58A into the Courts and Legal Services Act 1990.
[79] Legal Aid in Civil Proceedings (Remuneration) Regulations 1994.
[80] *Modernising Justice*, para. 3.17.

with, or a grant from, the LSC". It was announced that all advice and assistance and representation in family matters would be provided under contract from the end of 1999. The White Paper maintains the preference for mediation, expressly stating that "in most family cases (except care, adoption and domestic violence) applicants will not be granted representation by a lawyer, unless they can show that their case is unsuitable for mediation".[81]

The Legal Services Commission was set up by the Access to Justice Act 1999, and that Act conferred on the Commission the power to enter funding contracts for the provision of legal services. It would operate under a "funding code". A Consultation Document issued by the Legal Aid Board in January 1999 entitled *The Funding Code; a new approach to funding civil cases* [82] outlined the proposed code. The definitive Code was published in October 1999.[83] The Code introduces a number of new concepts in the public funding of legal work. The first is a distinction between Controlled Work and Licensed Work. The former comprises work which the providers may undertake within the terms of the contract with the LSC; it is not necessary to make a fresh application for each case, though the contracts may control the number of cases to be started in any period. The provider is also subject to inspection by the Commission. The contract provides detailed instructions about the steps to be taken and the time spent on various stages of the case. [84] Licensed Work is that for which application must to be made in each case. But only recognised providers may make such applications. The other concepts relate to the type or "level" of service given. This is divided into seven categories:

1. Legal Help (equivalent to the old "legal advice" under the "Green Form" scheme).

2. Help at Court.

3. Approved Family Help (which in turn may be either General Family Help or Help with Mediation).

4. Legal Representation (which can be either Investigative Support or Full Representation).

---

[81] *Modernising Justice*, p. 37.
[82] Legal Aid Board, *The Funding Code: a new approach to funding civil cases* (Legal Aid Board, January 1999).
[83] Legal Aid Board, *The Funding Code*, October 1999.
[84] Legal Aid Board, *General Civil Contracts (Solicitors)*, October 1999, chapter 7.

5. Support Funding (which can be either Investigative Support or Litigation Support).

6. Family Mediation.

7. Certain other services authorised specifically by the Lord Chancellor.[85]

Only Legal Help, Approved Family Help, Legal Representation (but not Investigative Support) and Family Mediation are available in family cases. Legal Help is "controlled work" and is subject to various restrictions as to eligibility and cost. It should not normally exceed three hours in divorce cases,[86] though it may be extended in some circumstances. Since this may not be sufficient to cover all the preparatory work a solicitor might need to do (and our data shows what the nature of that work can be), it may be possible to obtain Approved Family Help. Since that is Licensed Work, an application will have to be made. Approved Family Help will be of two types; one is Help with Mediation, and the other is General Family Help, which will allow the lawyer to continue assisting and representing the client. If the client moves into mediation, Help with Mediation covers only "advice to a client in support of family mediation, help in drawing up any agreement reached in mediation and where appropriate help in confirming such an agreement in a court order". It does not cover the lawyer doing any other work for the client, for example, having continued negotiations with the other party.[87] Furthermore, it is envisaged that Help with Mediation will only be given in cases requiring "substantial legal advice in support of ongoing mediation"; for most other cases which move into mediation, it is thought that the advice given under the two or three hours of Legal Help available prior to the mediation would be sufficient.[88] If the client does not desire mediation and therefore seeks General Family Help, the client will need to comply with section 29 of the Family Law Act 1996, and attend a meeting with a mediator, unless the case falls within an exempted category, such as where there has been violence. General Family Help (that is, funding of further work by the lawyer) "may be refused if mediation, supported if necessary with Help with Mediation, is more appropriate

---

[85] Legal Aid Board, *A New Approach to Funding Civil Cases*, October 1999, chapter 7.

[86] Legal Aid Board, *General Civil Contracts (Solicitors)*, p. 120.

[87] Legal Aid Board, *A New Approach to Funding Civil Cases*, p. 104.

[88] *A New Approach to Funding Civil Cases*, p. 105.

to the case than General Family Help".[89] The Code goes on to say that "mediation beyond the intake assessment may be provided only where the mediator is satisfied that mediation is suitable to the dispute and the parties and all the circumstances".[90] Furthermore, General Family Help will only be given if "there is sufficient benefit to the client, having regard to the circumstances of the matter, including the personal circumstances of the client, to justify further work being carried out".[91] Should the solicitor wish to make an application to a court, Full Representation may be granted. But, in financial provision cases, funding will be refused if prospects for success are "borderline or uncertain, save where the case has overwhelming importance to the client or a significant wider public interest; or poor".[92] Once again, funding may be refused if mediation is thought to be more appropriate. As far as issues concerning the children are concerned, Full Representation will only be given if there has been a prior meeting with a mediator (unless exempted), and if reasonable attempts have been made to resolve the issue without recourse to proceedings. Even then it may be refused if the prospects of success are "poor". General Family Help (but not, at least initially, Help with Mediation) will be subject to the statutory charge.[93]

It is clear that these changes, which became effective on 1 January 2000, will have a major impact on the practice of family law for legally aided clients. The number of firms willing and capable of taking on controlled and licensed family work will diminish, and a number of small firms doing only a few family cases will no longer be able to take on legal aid family work. This may lead to problems in providing geographical coverage, and may also restrict service provision by ethnic minority solicitors who often work in small firms. How they will affect the actual practice of solicitors, to be described later in this book, is uncertain. One major feature will be the sharpening of the "watershed" when legal involvement moves beyond advice into assistance (or representation), which under the practice we observed was very fluid. Now a separate application will need to be made to go beyond advice even if legal proceedings are not yet contemplated. Furthermore, it will also be necessary at this time to consider mediation, and the client is likely to

[89] Legal Aid Board, *The Funding Code*, p. 26.
[90] Ibid., p. 27.
[91] Ibid.
[92] Ibid., p. 30.
[93] *A New Approach to Funding Civil Cases*, p. 106.

be required to attend a meeting with a mediator. The requirement to have this meeting, followed by the additional requirement of applying for Help with Mediation or General Family Help (depending on the outcome of the meeting) will certainly disrupt the continuity of legal assistance for many clients. It will prolong the process even further, and this will be exacerbated by the fact that another application will need to be made for Full Representation should it be necessary to make application to a court at a later stage. Apart from the disturbance caused by these administrative requirements, it is difficult to know how the role of the solicitor will be affected. This is largely because the tests set out in the Funding Code are broadly drawn and have a high degree of discretion incorporated in them. For example, General Family Help can only be allowed if there is "sufficient benefit to the client" to justify further legal work on the case; Full Legal Representation may be refused "unless reasonable attempts have been made to resolve the dispute without recourse to proceedings, through negotiation or otherwise". It is our hope that our account of the work of family solicitors which follows will give some idea of the nature of the cases with which they are presented, and how they deal with them, and that this will assist those making these decisions in understanding the context in which their decisions will apply.

F FUNDING-DRIVEN SUGGESTIONS FOR CHANGES IN THE SUBSTANTIVE LAW

Worries about the expense of the legal process have led to suggestions which could have a significant effect on the law itself. Two possible kinds of change have been discussed. These arose from the Lord Chancellor's interest in the possibility of achieving greater predictability in making financial arrangements after divorce, through enforceable nuptial contracts made before or during marriage for the allocation of resources on separation or divorce, and through moving away from judicial discretion towards tighter rules for property division on divorce. By making matters more certain, it was hoped that the opportunities for "wasteful" legal negotiation would be reduced. As Geoff Hoon, the then parliamentary secretary at the Lord Chancellor's Department said in relation to nuptial contracts:

> They provide an extra power which helps to avoid litigation. If such agreements are enforced, then there is no need for argument over weeks and

weeks over who owns what. So it puts an end to many cases going to court and the possibility of conflict, which must be good for both parties.[94]

Both these suggestions are presented in the Home Office consultation document *Supporting Families* of October 1998. It is suggested, without supporting evidence or arguments, that enforceable nuptial agreements could make it more likely that couples would marry rather than live together, and if a marriage was "shaky" such an agreement would give the couple greater assurance than they might otherwise have had. But it is also suggested, with more conviction, that such agreements could protect the interests of children of a first marriage when a subsequent marriage takes place. It is proposed, though, that such contracts would not be legally binding if the couple had a child, or where the contract was unenforceable under the general law of contract, or where one or both had not received independent legal advice beforehand, or where its enforcement would cause significant injustice, or where one or both parties had failed to give full disclosure of their assets beforehand, or where the agreement was made less than twenty-one days before the marriage. The goal of reducing the costs of divorce is not stated in this document, and it is highly uncertain whether making such contracts legally enforceable would achieve such a goal, since it would open up new areas for dispute.[95]

The rules proposed for property allocation are also set out, and it is suggested that greater certainty would lead to less litigation and a reduction in the costs of divorce for both the couple and the Legal Aid Fund. The overarching objective would be to do that which is fair and reasonable for the parties and any child of the family. The first principle guiding a court towards this objective would be to promote the welfare of any child under eighteen by meeting the housing needs of any children of the family and the primary carer, and of the secondary carer, and to facilitate contact and recognise the importance of the secondary carer's role. Nuptial agreements would be taken into account, any surplus would be divided to achieve a fair result "recognizing that fairness will generally require the value of the assets to be divided equally between the parties" and a clean break would be sought as soon as practicable. The judges of the Family Division have expressed scepticism as to whether changes in the substantive law will have much effect on costs, remarking that "the difficult question is whether the

[94] *The Times*, 18 May 1998.
[95] John Eekelaar, "Should section 25 be Reformed?" (1998) 28 *Family Law* 469.

excessive costs, whatever their overall scale, are mainly caused by the procedure set for ancillary relief or its substantive law. Our instinct is that the excessively adversarial climate has been mainly to blame".[96] In fact, with the exception of the strength with which the clean break objective is stated, these proposals in effect follow quite closely the existing practices as we observed them in earlier work on how solicitors approach financial arrangements after divorce.[97] In that study we presented solicitors with a hypothetical case, and observed how they approached it, as a package. They considered the resources available to the couple and their children and their needs as a whole. They described how, in negotiation with the solicitor on the other side, they would seek first to keep a roof over the heads of the children, then to see whether the primary carer would need maintenance, and how this could be managed while also meeting the needs of the other parent. This seemed to suggest a rather different perception of the lawyers' role in divorce cases from that which underlay many of the policy assumptions considered earlier.

G IN CONCLUSION: LAWYERS ON TRIAL

We have described in this chapter the different ways in which, especially over the last two decades, a picture has been built up in official thinking that there is something fundamentally flawed about the way lawyers deal with divorcing clients. It goes beyond criticisms of individual lawyers, or individual cases; beyond the perception that it is a system which has imperfections and can go wrong sometimes. The very fact of dealing with these issues through lawyers, and courts, and, by implication, through the application of legal norms, is held to be misguided. We have traced the connection between this perception and concerns that the legal process costs too much. True, objections about costs have not been the only ones levelled against the legal process. It has been perceived to be inefficient, long-drawn-out and, above all, generative of conflict. Yet somehow all these alleged defects are seen to come together in the all-embracing view that they increase costs. When mediators have claimed that the mediation process reduces conflict

---

[96] "Ancillary Relief Reform" (1999) 29 *Family Law* 159.

[97] E. Jackson, F. Wasoff, M. Maclean and R. Dobash, "Financial Support on Divorce: The Right Mixture of Rules and Discretion?" (1993) 7 *International Journal of Law and the Family* 230.

between couples, the Government sees this is a possible way of making savings in the legal aid budget. When the judges, concerned about the time taken to conclude some cases, produced their reforms, these have been seized on by the Lord Chancellor's Department as a further way in which hoped-for reductions in costs may be achieved. Sometimes the contents of the law itself have been seen as a reason why legal costs are, as is thought, excessive, and nuptial contracts or a re-structuring of the discretion are promoted as ways of reducing them.

We have seen that many of the assumptions upon which this negative view of the legal process rest are not strongly rooted in empirical evidence. Indeed, many of the means suggested, or implemented, by which cost-savings are sought, have not be subjected to rigorous analysis. It is not our objective in what follows to decry any of these means in themselves. We do, however, believe that they must be viewed on the basis of a sounder understanding of what the legal process is actually like in this area. We have tried to provide that understanding.

2

The Data Collection

B ROADLY DESCRIBED, OUR aim was to obtain more detailed information about what solicitors in family practice actually do. Of course, other studies, which we have mentioned, have had the same, or similar, aims. Those studies, however, with the important exception of Ingleby's work, described in the previous chapter, primarily rely on interviews with either the lawyers themselves or with their clients or with both. For practical reasons, it is difficult for a researcher to observe a case from start to finish, and probably impossible to do this with any reasonably large number of cases. Hence, researchers use interviews, perhaps supplemented by observing a few cases at the litigation stage. Despite the usefulness of the data acquired in this way, generalised responses to issues raised by an interviewer may conceal underlying matters which the respondent omits because they do not seem important to the respondent, or the respondent has forgotten them or because the respondent is uncomfortable with them. Generalised comments will fail to give a sufficient account of any one particular case. One way to avoid this is to present the interviewee with hypothetical cases, a technique used by a number of researchers in this area. While this, too, is useful in bringing the respondent to focus on issues pre-selected by the interviewer, this very fact could overlook matters which the interviewer would not have anticipated. It is also rather better at dealing with issues of substantive law rather than processes and practices.

We adopted two separate methods of acquiring data. One was by direct observation of the working day of the subject. The researcher simply sat in the office and observed (and recorded) all that happened. The purpose of this exercise was to acquire evidence of the business context in which the lawyers operated, how they prioritised and responded to issues as they arose, and the details of their interaction with clients. The data obtained in this way are described as "the observational data". The second method was by interview. However, the

interview took the form of the solicitor "talking through" a pre-
selected case from its inception to its current position. The solicitor
was requested to recover the relevant file or files prior to the interview
and to work through the file(s) in the course of explaining the progress
of the case. On the basis of pilot interviews done in this way we were
able to draft a schedule of events on which we could draw to prompt
the solicitor in case certain aspects were being overlooked. This aspect
of the research we call "the case study".

B THE METHOD

A full account of the methodology adopted is provided in the technical
report set out in the Appendix, and only a brief account is given here of
the methods employed. To obtain our observational data, we sat with
ten solicitors throughout a whole working day, totalling fourteen days
of observation in all (since some solicitors were observed by two
researchers). We took note of everything the solicitors did, including
their appointments with clients and with counsel and their actions in
court. These solicitors were approached through personal contact as
this level of co-operation requires a high degree of trust and confidence,
and we did not feel it appropriate to approach practitioners to whom
we were strangers. All were partners, aged between thirty-five and fifty-
five, four men and six women. In the course of the day we were able to
observe the work of assistants and legal executives also, but felt that it
was not feasible to subject more junior members of staff to the stress of
our observation. Even the partners admitted to feeling under stress, for
example when dictating letters as we listened.

   These factors meant that we cannot claim that the solicitors we
observed constituted a true "representative sample" of solicitors doing
family law work. However, it is not our intention to make such a claim
with respect to this part of the data. As we saw in the previous chapter,
family law work is carried out by a wide variety of firms, which take in
family work to differing extents. Rather, we wished to build up a picture of how solicitors *can* and, probably, *often do* carry on their work.
We do not know whether this constitutes best practice, though it was
likely that these solicitors had a high degree of commitment to family
law practice. All were members of the SFLA. But we must repeat here
what we have said earlier: this part of the study was not intended to be
a descriptive study *in the sense that* some quantitative surveys would

be. It *is* descriptive in the sense that it gives an account of the practical side of the work of family solicitors. But in as far as there are variants in practices, we are not able to say which kinds of practice are more extensive than others. We were not counting such things. It seemed enough for us to say that we are describing legal practice as it *can* and, on our observations, *often does* occur in solicitors' offices. Under the new legal aid arrangements in family cases which came into effect in January 2000, it is likely that the practices we saw will reflect common practices in firms with which contracts will be made.

But we did wish to guard against observing only firms which were likely to have too many unique features. We therefore sought a geographical spread, and included solicitors in the North West, the Midlands, and the South East, including London. We also sought a variety of practice settings, dealing with different types of clients. We visited a sole practitioner, a divorce specialist doing mainly private client work, one small specialist firm doing almost all legal aid work, one small specialist firm doing almost no legal aid work, the family department of a city office of a major national firm doing only private client work, the family department of a provincial firm with a number of branches doing mainly legal aid work under franchise, a family specialist in a small country practice with two branch offices doing mainly legal aid work under franchise, the family partner in a twenty-partner London firm doing almost no legal aid work, and two London specialist firms doing almost no legal aid work. The researcher shadowed each solicitor throughout the day, keeping sequential field notes which were then written up in full. As a check on our reliability as observers, two researchers observed the same solicitor on subsequent days in two cases, and coded each other's field notes. It was not feasible to tape record, as the solicitors hurried from meeting to meeting, and there was no opportunity to seek the relevant permissions or even turn on the machine. But our observation was carried out openly, and we explained to the solicitors the purpose of the research as seeking to understand what made up their daily work load. The solicitors explained our presence to clients in slightly differing ways, ranging from "this is x and she is sitting with me today" to "may I introduce x who is carrying out research on lawyers, do you mind if she sits in on our meeting?" One client asked detailed questions about the research and the issue of confidentiality and then agreed. In only one case when a divorce client was to make her first visit to the office and had been very distressed on the telephone, in order to minimise her distress, the lawyer asked the researcher to leave before she arrived. (That in itself was a feature of lawyer behaviour worth noting). But for most clients our presence was either irrelevant amidst their multitude of problems, or something they were willing to allow in order to help their solicitor, with whom all those we observed seemed to have a good relationship. We were also able to discuss cases with the lawyer at the end of the day, which the lawyers seemed to enjoy. We were therefore able to involve the lawyers in the research process, rather than simply gaining information from them, and both sides were able to exchange information.

The second branch to our research strategy, the case study, required a sample which was much more truly representative of family law practice. Here we felt we should be able to say something about what was *characteristic* about the way lawyers processed their cases. We were therefore careful to approach a more representative sample of local practitioners, in order to give a picture of the full range of practice from "cutting edge" to "behind the times" or even just plain poor. Forty solicitors for the case file interviews were selected from four areas in England and Wales. We worked from the Law Society Regional Directories, using a random start fixed interval method of selection of solicitors offering family work. If we compare our interviewees with the national picture of the family solicitor workforce, twenty were women, i.e., 50 per cent as compared with the national figure of 66 per cent. Sixteen (40 per cent) had been admitted since 1990, 35 per cent during the 1980s, and 10 per cent before 1980. Three were not yet admitted as a solicitor, and for three cases we lack this information. The national figures for the age distribution of solicitors doing any regular family work are 18 per cent under thirty-five, 27 per cent between thirty-five and forty-five, and 63 per cent over forty-five. But for those specialising in family work 43 per cent are under thirty-five, 30 per cent between thirty-five and forty-five and 22 per cent over forty-five. Our sample appears similar to the age range of the specialist family practitioners but to under-represent the older practitioners. Thirty-one, (i.e., 62 per cent) were members of the SFLA, of whom there are now over 5,000 members nationally.

Of the firms in which our interviewees worked, twenty-eight had a legal aid franchise for family work and seven were applying, so only 12 per cent were likely to be outside the contract system when the new legal aid arrangements came into force which restrict the provision of legally aided work to franchised firms. The firms without franchise included all the sole practitioners and a firm which did no legal aid work. Twenty-six of the lawyers we saw were partners, twelve were assistant solicitors and two were legal executives. Only three spent less than half their time on family work, and twenty-eight of the solicitors estimated that at least half of their own family work was legally aided. If we compare our solicitors according to the size of their firm with national figures, 7.5 per cent of our group were in sole practice compared with 3 per cent nationally, 32.5 per cent were in firms with two to four partners compared with 35 per cent nationally, and 47.5 per cent were in firms with five to ten partners compared with 29 per cent nationally. Of our group 12.5 per cent were in firms with ten or more partners compared with the national figure of 35 per cent. Our sample therefore favours the smaller firms. We believe this is due to the fact that we did not interview in central London where the larger firms predominate. We also checked to see whether there was any gender bias in dealing with male and female legally aided and private clients in our sample. Of the solicitors acting for women, 57 per cent were women, and of those acting for men 75 per cent were women. Fifty per cent of legally aided cases were represented by women compared with 56 per cent of private client cases.

We also wanted the cases selected to be representative of the different types of divorce cases which present themselves to lawyers. In order to achieve this, each solicitor was asked to have ready the file for the first divorce case opened after 1 March 1997, which had proceeded at least as far as a decree nisi. The interviews were carried out in late 1998 and early 1999, and were taped and transcribed by the researchers. Sometimes on arrival the solicitor would apologise for a dull file and try to offer a more interesting case, but we made it clear that the selection by date was essential and that routine cases were just as important for our work as the unusual ones. The interview, lasting about one hour, was based on this file, with the interviewer using the topic guide referred to above which had been developed in the pilots, and after transcription the data were recorded onto a schedule and coded for content analysis. We covered background information about the solicitor and the firm, and then talked through the case on the file. As the file remained in the lawyer's hands, the identities of the persons concerned were never revealed. The order in which issues arise in a divorce case varies, and we therefore recorded not only the chronology of the divorce, but also the broad themes arising, including the situation at first contact with the clients, issues arising in connection with the petition, financial issues (details of marital assets, the process of establishing financial information, advising or giving information to the client about finances, the process of negotiation, the involvement of other professionals, details of any hearings), children issues (establishing information about the children, advising or giving information about the children's situation, the process of negotiating the children issues, involvement of other professionals, details of any hearings), the current state of the case, the final bill, and the solicitor's impression of the case and the client. Where there was time, we also asked about the solicitor's attitudes to property division rules, nuptial settlements and to changes to the legal aid system. Time lines were prepared to describe the progress of each case.

Every research technique has strengths and limitations. The closest methodology to ours was that used by Ingleby, who obtained his data directly from files, monitoring the files of sixty matrimonial clients from five solicitors over a period of eighteen months in 1985–7. This was a powerful study, to which we are much indebted. One of our purposes was to see how far things might have changed since his research was conducted, given apparent fears about increasing costs. But we also had contact with a wider range of solicitors, and the oral accounts of the solicitors could give a wider perspective than the written record might do. The main strength of our methodology, we believe, is that the *combination* of the two techniques we have described enables us to achieve an accurate picture of the daily workings of a family law practice, albeit tilted towards what probably counts as the more committed end of the service provision, together with a practical account of the way cases characteristically work themselves through the system. The limitations are found in those inherent in resource constraints: we would love to have had the money, time and researcher-power to have spent longer in the lawyers' offices, and in more of them. We would add that, in the case study, the fact that we were hearing the lawyer's own account of the case means that we can give an account only of precisely that: we did not have, for example, the client's account. We cannot guarantee that the lawyer told us everything, or did not omit an embarrassing exchange or letter. But it seems unlikely that they concealed much, if anything. Past events were often springing back into the lawyers' minds as they worked their way through the files. It would have required a fairly obvious attempt to dissemble should any have wished to do so. Nor can we guarantee that a lawyer might have passed over a file, which would otherwise have been selected, because it was thought to contain information discreditable to the lawyer. Certainly in at least one case the lawyer had failed to follow the instructions, and simply took the case presently on the desk before him. But these seem to be minor concerns. We have to concede, though, that what we have is the lawyer's version of the events. We do not claim this to be objective truth. Nevertheless, we were able to compare these accounts with the scene presented by our observations of their daily work. We can therefore note the extent to which the accounts of the lawyers are consistent with our own observations, in so far as such comparison is possible.

In fact, we found such comparison indeed was possible. We have therefore decided to set out first the findings of the observational study, and then those of the case study. But these are preceded by a description of the structure of the legal workforce whose work we are examining.

3

Family Solicitors: The Workforce and the Work

BEFORE EXAMINING OUR data on the working practices of family solicitors, we must first describe the place of family solicitors in the legal workforce, and the nature of the work they do. First we describe the place which family law work has within this branch of the legal profession, and consider issues regarding the funding of this work. We then consider the evidence about the work that they do and what it is that their clients seek

A THE NATURE OF THE WORKFORCE

In order to obtain a picture of the place of family law within the work of solicitors in England and Wales, we used the following sources with the assistance of colleagues at the Law Society and at the Legal Aid Board Research Unit:

The Law Society's ongoing Panel Study of just over 500 solicitors' firms with up to 80 partners (referred to here as "the Panel Study");[1]
The Law Society's Omnibus Survey of just under 700 individual solicitors in private practice;[2]
Statistics published by the Legal Aid Board.

Family law firms

On the basis of the Panel Study, the Law Society estimated that in 1995–6, 75 per cent of firms with up to eighty partners conduct some family work. In this study firms were specifically instructed to include

---

[1] B. Cole and J. Sidaway, *A Study of Private Practice Solicitors*, RPPU Paper No. 24 (1997).
[2] B. Cole, *Solicitors in Private Practice: their work and expectations*, Research Study No. 26 (Law Society, 1997).

all work relating to children as family work. The Solicitors Indemnity Fund database for the same year suggests that there are over 6,400 firms in England and Wales doing this kind of work. But the importance of family work to the firm varies with the number of partners per firm, and according to region. Sixty per cent of sole practitioners and 60 per cent of large firms with over twenty-six partners do family work, compared with 85 per cent of firms with between two and twenty-five partners. Only 60 per cent of London firms are involved in family law, compared with 85 per cent in all other areas. This can be explained, in part, by the high proportion of sole practitioners in London and by the high level of commercial work carried out by solicitors in the capital.

Family work accounts for 10 per cent of gross fee income for firms of up to eighty partners. But there is considerable variation in the importance of family work to these firms according to the size of the firm. The smaller firms with not more than ten partners received at least 13 per cent of their income from family work. This figure falls to 7 per cent for the firms with eleven to twenty-five partners, and to only 2 per cent for the larger firms with twenty-six or more partners. The firms most reliant on family work are thus those with up to ten partners. There was also considerable variation among the sole practitioners, half of whom received less than 7 per cent of their income from family work, while 28 per cent received more than a fifth from this source. Very few firms (only 2 per cent of the Panel) earned more than half of their income from family work. Firms in the north of England were more likely to earn a higher proportion of their fee income from family work than elsewhere in England and Wales. Sixty per cent in the north earned more than 13 per cent compared with 10 per cent in the south, and only 5 per cent in London. A majority of firms doing family work found it to be profitable (58 per cent), but 30 per cent reported that they only broke even, and 12 per cent of firms considered family work to be loss-making. In sum, most firms do some family work, but many do very little.

Family practitioners

The Law Society's 1997 Omnibus survey of solicitors indicated that 25 per cent of solicitors in private practice regularly undertook some family work. In this study the respondents used their own definition of family work, and may have excluded public law children work. Size of firm was a strong predictor of the likelihood of an individual doing family work, with sole practitioners the most frequent participants (48 per cent). Those working in firms with two to four partners had a similar rate (43 per cent), but only 28 per cent of solicitors in firms of five to ten partners and 7 per cent in firms with eleven or more partners, regularly did family work. Age was also related to the likelihood of doing family work. Eighteen per cent of young practitioners (under thirty-five) did such work, compared to 27 per cent of those aged thirty-five to forty-five, 34 per cent of those aged forty-five to fifty-four and 29 per cent of those over fifty-five. Solicitors in the Panel were then asked what proportion of their fee-earning time was spent on family work. Compared with other types of work, family came fourth, accounting for 10 per cent of work time overall. Business and commercial work took up 23 per cent of their time, while commercial property and personal injury work each consumed 13 per cent. There was little difference between the amount of time devoted to family work by partners and assistants, but women spent more than twice as much time on family work as men (18 per cent for women compared with 7 per cent for men). This finding is related to the difference in earning capacity between men and women solicitors. Sidaway[3] comments that gender reduces the average earnings of a partner by almost £6,000 per year, and family work is one of the least remunerative types of work.

Specialisation

There is currently an awareness of the increase in specialisation within the legal profession as a whole, and this is clearly the case in family work. The Law Society Omnibus survey distinguishes between family specialists and generalists, defining as a specialist a solicitor who spends not less than half his time on family work. Of the 25 per cent of all solicitors in private practice who regularly do some family work (of whom 9,900 are men and 4,400 are women) it is estimated that 29 per cent were specialists according to this definition. Assistants were slightly more likely to specialise than partners (37 per cent of assistants specialised compared with 23 per cent of partners), but women were five times more likely to specialise than men and form two-thirds of the specialist family solicitor workforce (That is, 66 per cent of the 4,400

[3] Personal communication, 1998.

women and 12 per cent of the 9,900 men). Specialism decreased with age and increased with size of firm. Of those under thirty-five, 43 per cent were specialists, compared with 30 per cent of those aged thirty-five to forty-four and 22 per cent of those aged forty-five to fifty-five, and only 3 per cent of sole practitioners were family specialists compared with 30 per cent of those in two to ten partner firms and over half of those in firms with more than eleven partners. It appears therefore that the main contribution to family work is made by a group of around 2,600 women and 1,300 men who specialise in family work. The total membership of the Solicitors Family Law Association is currently around 5,000, and so, although the match between specialism and membership may not be precise, it is at least likely that there is a close relationship between them, and that these family practitioners are represented by an organisation with a clear set of aims and values, and which urges solicitors "to advise, negotiate and conduct proceedings in a manner calculated to encourage and assist the parties to achieve a constructive settlement of their differences as quickly as may be reasonable whilst recognising that the parties may need time to come to terms with their new situation".[4]

B THE WORK OF FAMILY SOLICITORS

What do we currently expect of solicitors who do family law work? Research studies have provided various accounts of the work that the researchers think they do, what the lawyers say they do, and of what clients want them to do, together with analysis of the pressures for change. Before presenting our account of what we observed, we will comment on the findings of previous studies. We have noted above the changing policy context in which family lawyers now find themselves. We suggest that these policy changes are rooted in underlying changes in family structure as well as in the law, and are associated with increasing specialisation in ways of working with families coping with divorce.

---

[4] SFLA Code of Practice, para. 1.1. See also Mavis Maclean, Judith Sidaway and Sarah Beinart, "Family Solicitors – the Workforce" (1998) 28 *Family Law* 673.

The changing nature of family law

It has been argued that the many changes which are taking place in family life are having an impact on the professionals who work with families, "both on their interventions and on their relationship with each other".[5] New demands are being made upon them by families who are experiencing both more numerous and more complex changes to their structure. Couples may live together, separate, re-partner either informally or with legal regulation of their changing status through marriage, divorce and remarriage. They may have both biologically and socially based relationships with children, as they move away from or take with them children from one relationship into a subsequent relationship in which the other partner may also have children either in the household or elsewhere, and in addition the new couple may go on to have children of the new relationship. At the same time other children of both new partners will be living elsewhere with their other biological parents and possible new partners and new children of these new partnerships. We have moved on from the earlier complexities of family structures based on serial marriage after bereavement to those attendant on serial monogamy in which both partners survive, and parenting responsibilities need to be managed in parallel between households. The allocation of financial obligations and property entitlements across households in a society where personal finances as well as relationships are becoming more complex through extensive use of credit and deferred entitlements is a demanding task, for which most individuals need and welcome professional advice and support. In the UK this has traditionally been provided by solicitors in the context not only of divorce but also succession, house purchase, and debt management.

Socio-legal scholars would now argue that there has been a change in the focus of family regulation away from monitoring the obligations between adults, towards a concentration on the obligations between parents and children, particularly on how they are to be managed when parents and children no longer share a common household.[6] The

---

[5] B. Bastard and L. Cardia-Vonèche, "Inter-Professional tensions in the Divorce Process in France" (1995) 9 *International Journal of Law and the Family* 275.

[6] Irene Théry, *Le Démariage* (Editions Odile Jacob, Paris, 1993); Mavis Maclean and John Eekelaar, *The Parental Obligation* (Hart Publishing, Oxford, 1997); John Dewar, "Family Law and its Discontents" (2000) 14 *International Journal of Law, Policy and the Family* 59. See also Amanda Drane and Sarah Phillimore, "A Change of status – Wave Goodbye to Marriage and Say Hello to Parenthood" (1999) 29 *Family Law* 653.

freedom of adults to make choices about their own living arrangements is increasingly accepted by the law and within society. Debate continues however about the degree of public responsibility for parenting as each child becomes involved in a wider social group of not only biological but also social parents, i.e., those in the child's household as well as those biologically responsible for the child. Although much of the rhetoric around the Children Act 1989 has stressed the individualistic nature of the responsibilities of parents, the state has become increasingly concerned to see that parents exercise this responsibility in a "responsible" way. Hence the concern to make sure that fathers pay for their children, that parents maintain contact with their children if they separate, that parents become actively involved with schools in the education of their children (reinforced by increased penalties for failing to assure the attendance of their children at school) and that they exercise proper supervision over their children outside school.[7] The rolling back of legal regulation from family matters has not applied to such matters, and also excludes areas of public interest, such as wherever physical protection is an issue, and wherever there may be a call on the public purse. There may therefore be an expectation on the part of government that lawyers should play a part in seeking to instil an ethic of "responsibility" into parents, and part of current governmental frustration with family lawyers may arise from a belief that the lawyers do not do this sufficiently.

For the lawyers traditionally concerned with achieving and formalising a change in the relationship between a husband and wife, there is now a marked change in the kinds of relationship transitions on which their advice is sought. The proportion of clients seeking advice with separation where there has been no marriage has increased greatly. If we look at cases attracting public funds (as they are documented) in 1997 53 per cent of the legally-aided cases involving relationship breakdown were divorces, compared with 43 per cent separation and 3 per cent judicial separation.[8] Thus the content of work done may change, but not necessarily the volume, as the law now regulates parental responsibility irrespective of civil status, and the complexity of the financial arrangements of the separating unmarried cohabitants may even exceed those whose rights are a little more clearly defined as a

---

[7] See the Crime and Disorder Act 1998, s. 8.

[8] S. Maclean, "Profiling Family Litigation: Pathways and Strategies in Legally Aided Cases", Paper to Law and Society Conference, St. Louis, USA, May 1997.

result of having been married.[9] There may however be a move towards less lawyer involvement in dealing with financial arrangements for children. There were 2,000 fewer legally-aided ancillary relief cases in the year following the Child Support Act 1991, according to the Legal Aid Board Annual Report of 1993, though this may also have been affected by changes to the eligibility rules. It is certainly the policy intention that there should be less lawyer or court involvement in arrangements concerning where and with whom children should live after a separation between their parents. This was demonstrated by the insertion of section 1(5) into the Children Act 1989 which states that "where a court is considering whether or not to make one or more orders under this Act with respect to a child, it shall not make the order or any of the orders unless it considers that doing so would be better for the child than making no order at all", although as Bainham[10] has pointed out, this was not meant to suggest that there should be no legal intervention if the welfare of the child required it. Applications to the court in this respect have fallen. Bailey-Harris and others[11] indicate that in 1990, the final year before the Children Act 1989 came into effect, there were 161,709 applications compared with 81,000 in 1996. There may, however, be a little more lawyer activity in relation to the rights of unmarried fathers seeking Parental Responsibility Orders (5,587 orders were made by the courts in 1996 and 3,000 agreements registered in 1996).[12]

Family solicitors and other professionals

There are also pressures on the role of lawyers from the emerging professional and para-professional groups of mediators, welfare officers, counsellors and information and advice workers. Relationships with and boundaries between court welfare officers and solicitors are well established and effective in the court setting, and the advice and information providers are as yet only a small group. It is the mediators

[9] Jane Lewis, *Marriage, Cohabitation and the Law: Individualism and Obligation* (Lord Chancellor's Department Research Series No. 1/990, February 1999).

[10] Andrew Bainham, "Changing Families and Changing Concepts: Reforming the Language of Family Law" in John Eekelaar and Thandabantu Nhlapo (eds), *The Changing Family: Family Forms and Family Law* (Hart Publishing, Oxford, 1998).

[11] Gwynn Davis and Julia Pearce, "Privatising the Family?" (1998) 28 *Family Law* 614.

[12] Lord Chancellor's Department, *Court procedures for the Determination of Paternity. The Law on Parental responsibility for Unmarried Fathers*, Consultation Paper (March 1998).

with whom the solicitors have been presented in policy documents and legislation as being in competition, in that a smaller role is prescribed for the lawyers for the future as mediation grows. According to the SFLA, the lawyers maintain that their practice is devoted to seeking agreement and that they see themselves as the intermediaries in the divorce process. Some argue that they already practise negotiation with both parties present, e.g., in round table conferences, and that they alone can negotiate the legal issues which must be dealt with by a court. From this point of view there is no need for any other profession to intervene in divorce. The strategy of the lawyers has been to stay in touch with mediation, and to participate in its development with a view to controlling and containing it. A number have acquired qualifications as mediators themselves. They suggest that mediators should deal with specific matters, preferably confining themselves to questions relating to children. In Scotland,[13] many clients, lawyers, and mediators share this view. In England and Wales also there has been some reluctance by the "not for profit" providers of mediation to extend their practice beyond child matters, which were the starting point for the development of their skills. Before the availability of legal aid funding for mediation there was little take up of all-issues mediation by parties, which deals with financial matters as well as arrangements for children.[14] For the Government, however, intent on seeing mediation as a substitute for much lawyer activity, it is important for the mediation service to be comprehensive rather than to act as a child-centred bolt-on or addition to current legal aid provision through the work of solicitors.

What clients seek

In considering competing professional roles in family work, it is important to consider what it is that clients seek when they encounter difficulties in family relationships. We had some information about this from our previous study.[15] We indicated in the previous chapter the extent to which divorcing parents in that previous study had consulted with lawyers and sought other sources of advice.[16] As regards unmar-

[13] Jane Lewis, *Mediation in Scotland*, (Scottish Office, 1999).

[14] J. Walker, P. McCarthy and N. Timms, *Mediation: The Making and Remaking of Cooperative Relationships*, Relate Centre, Newcastle, 1994.

[15] Mavis Maclean and John Eekelaar, *The Parental Obligation* (Hart Publishing, Oxford, 1997).

[16] Above, p. 5.

ried formerly cohabiting parents who were separating, 28 per cent had seen a lawyer, 22 per cent had seen *only* a lawyer, 2 per cent a lawyer and a mediator, 4 per cent had seen a doctor and 6 per cent a social worker. Although the proportion of separating unmarried cohabitants who saw a lawyer was much lower than separating married parents, the proportion was still rather high (nearly one-third), indicating that there are matters other than the divorce petition which trouble couples who stop living together. We asked those who had seen a lawyer what had been the subject of their concern. The results are set out in Table 3.1.[17] It is not surprising that the unmarried cohabitants were more likely than the married parents to discuss money and social security, as in our sample they tended to have lower incomes and were therefore more likely to be using the social security system. It was however disturbing to note that 12 per cent of the married women had asked their lawyer about both the children and their personal safety.

Table 3.1 *Matters raised with lawyers by separating parents*

	Married parents % N =155	Unmarried cohabiting parents % N = 55
Money	53	73
Property	57	53
Children	73	67
Personal safety	19	20
Social security	11	20

When asked which source of advice had been most helpful, 35 per cent of the total said the lawyer, and less than 10 per cent identified any other professional. Three per cent identified the mediator. Family and friends were named by 22 per cent. There was a gender difference, in that 38 per cent of the women and 27 per cent of the men found the lawyer most helpful. Of all our sample who saw a lawyer, 71 per cent of the married obtained legal aid, compared with 48 per cent of the unmarried cohabitants. Of the women, 29 per cent asked about personal protection, and 25 per cent about safety and children. (Seventy per cent of all legal aid certificates in family work go to women, and

[17] This information was not included in the data published in *The Parental Obligation*.

30 per cent to men). We can compare this information with that obtained in a larger study by Hazel Genn[18] who found that 66 per cent of the respondents seeking advice in divorce and separation situations wanted to know about their legal rights; 43 per cent wanted to know about procedures, 44 per cent wanted advice about how to solve the problem and 43 per cent sought advice about their financial position. The questions asked of the respondents led to a different classification of replies from the one we adopted. However Genn's finding that 53 per cent found the advice very helpful and that 28 per cent found it helpful as consistent with our finding which highlights the usefulness of legal advice.

There are three kinds of studies which give us further information about this. The first group is drawn from the work which is related to monitoring the changes made in anticipation of the implementation of the Family Law Act 1996. The second has been carried out to inform those responsible for training and quality assurance and offers analysis of the skills employed and the tasks performed by solicitors. Thirdly, we have more sociological work which springs from a wider interest in the work of professions generally, at a time of increasing de-professionalisation. Such studies often focus on professional-client relationships during a transformation of clients into consumers with charters of rights.

Research into current developments associated with piloting the information and mediation services for the Family Law Act 1996, preparatory to implementation, is currently in progress. Janet Walker is looking at trials of information meetings such as those which are intended to be compulsory preliminaries to the divorce process under the divorce scheme set out in the Family Law Act 1996. A summary of the research as it stood in June 1999 has been published by the Lord Chancellor's Department.[19] An initial caution must be entered about this research. Since it was not possible to anticipate the compulsory nature of information meetings before the implementation of the proposed divorce scheme, all the subjects of the research attended the pilot meetings voluntarily. As a consequence, it was estimated that only 10 per cent of the population of couples who would normally be divorcing in the chosen areas attended the meetings. Although most of these agreed to a further interview after the meeting, the sample size remains

---

[18] Hazel Genn, *Paths to Justice* (Hart Publishing, Oxford, 1999), pp. 30–1.
[19] *Information Meetings and Associated Provisions within the Family Law Act 1996: Summary of Research in progress, June 1999* (Lord Chancellor's Department).

very small and the reactions may not represent those of a 100 per cent sample. A variety of models for information meetings were employed. It was clear that people went to the meetings "with a range of agendas"; to receive advice; to find out about their rights; to save the marriage; to avoid solicitors; to check up on the divorce process and get answers to specific questions, and learn about options. One of the most frequent complaints was that the meeting failed to address the attendee's personal circumstances. There is clearly a tension between providing information and giving advice. Nevertheless over 90 per cent felt the meeting had been "useful". However, when asked about what steps they took after the meeting "a common response is that it has been too late to attempt marriage counselling, but too early to consider mediation. Consulting a solicitor is often considered to be the next step after attendance at an information meeting and many saw this as an inevitable course of action to take".[20] This has led to the suggestion that the information meetings might be broken into two stages, the first, held on a one-to-one basis, would concentrate on "information which would help parties to consider whether their marriage really is finally over; marriage support services available to help; help for survivors of, or those fearful of, domestic violence; the decisions which have to be made, the consequences which have to be faced, and the impact of divorce on the families especially children, if the decision to divorce is finally taken". There would also be "detailed information on all other important matters mentioned in the Family Law Act, including mediation, legal aid, the divorce process and other questions that may arise on divorce or separation, such as finance and child support". The second stage would be by a group presentation, taking place "at the time people need this information" designed to "to give couples information about children, finance and property issues and to explain the helpfulness of mediation".[21]

The "marriage saving" objective of the meetings will face considerable difficulty. First, people almost always attended the meetings without their partner, and it is hard to pursue that objective with one of the partners alone. Second, although the researchers say that it was "promising" that 13 per cent "took up" the offer to attend a meeting with a marriage counsellor, slightly under half did so with the hope of saving their marriage. The other half were seeking help with ending it, or simply finding out more about counselling. Since the sample

---

[20] Ibid, para. 4.3.
[21] Home Office, *Supporting Families: A Consultation Document* (1998), p. 35.

consisted only of people who voluntarily attended the information meetings, it is perhaps unlikely that a similar proportion of the whole divorcing population would take up the offer. The objective of encouraging mediation also seems elusive. Only 7 per cent had been to mediation by the time of the follow-up interview. Although 57 per cent said they would consider it in the future, if appropriate, it is unclear whether this would be acted upon. On the other hand, the meeting encouraged some people to go on and seek advice where they might not have done otherwise. Thirty-nine per cent said they were more likely to consult a solicitor as a result of the meeting than had they not gone to the meeting, in contrast with 17 per cent who said they were less likely to do this. No doubt others would have consulted a solicitor anyway, and the meeting would not have affected the likelihood either way. Two-thirds had already seen a solicitor. Although the research is unfinished, these indications show that while the provision of information is generally deemed useful to those who attend the meetings voluntarily, it is unclear whether having the information changes behaviour very much. Some of the information could be delivered by solicitors, or simply by making an information pack available through ordinary retail outlets, or through other information media.[22]

Our second category of research into the work of family solicitors was that of the detailed studies of the daily tasks currently carried out by solicitors for divorce clients, and the skills employed. These have been defined in different ways, and for different purposes. Transaction Criteria research, carried out for the Legal Aid Board[23] defines the tasks of the solicitor in divorce proceedings as follows:

1. Getting information from the client including general information, the present state of the relationship, housing and financial difficulties of the relationship breakdown, ownership of property, the financial situation of the other party, residence and contact for any children affected by the relationship: advising on these aspects of the case and the costs and funding for the case

2. Further investigation, research and action

3. Keeping the client informed.

This analysis was undertaken in order to help the Legal Aid Board define the tasks which must be performed adequately for the lawyer to

---

[22] Do-it-yourself divorce "kits" are, for example, available over the Internet.

[23] A. Sherr, R. Moorhead and A. Paterson, *Transactional Criteria* (Legal Aid Board, 1992).

be accredited, and awarded a legal aid franchise. These criteria are now widely used, and were developed with a view to making it possible for the services provided to be audited by a competent but lay assessor. As explained earlier, the award of a franchise is now essential if a lawyer is to provide publicly funded legal services.

Sherr[24] has produced a typology of skills used as well as tasks carried out in family legal practice. This work draws on previous work from the Law Society's Research and Planning Unit.[25] This typology is of skills, not tasks, as the work was concerned with the development of professional training, and in defining which skills needed to be taught. The list is as follows:

- Administration and management
- Interviewing clients
- Drafting
- Travelling
- Negotiation
- Advocacy
- Legal research
- Reading and assessing papers
- Interviewing witnesses
- Time with counsel
- Dead time, i.e., time not allocated under any other headings

Finally, we consider how socio-legal research has considered the role of lawyers in family cases. Between 1973 and 1974 Mervyn Murch interviewed about 150 divorce petitioners, asking them to describe their experience of the legal process.[26] Most had found their solicitor "approachable, friendly and supportive"; 14 per cent made an unfavourable report, and 10–12 per cent had changed their solicitor because they were dissatisfied. But 55.9 per cent were very satisfied, 17.6 per cent satisfied and 20.6 per cent fairly satisfied with the service

[24] A. Sherr, *Solicitors and their Skills*, Law Society Research No. 6, (1991).
[25] This includes J. Jenkins, E. Skordaki and C. Willis, *Public Use and Perceptions of the Solicitors' Services*, Law Society Research and Planning Unit Study No. 1 1989; G. Chambers and S. Harwood, *Solicitors in England and Wales. Practice, Organisation and Perceptions*, Law Society Research Study Nos 2 and 8 1990 and 1991, together with technical report from S. Witherspoon and N. Aye Maung.
[26] Mervyn Murch, "The Role of Solicitors in Divorce Proceedings" (1977) 40 *Modern Law Review* 625.

they received. Sixty-three per cent saw their solicitor as a "partisan", although only 28 per cent said they would prefer their solicitor to be a "fighter" rather than to adopt a more conciliatory approach. This suggests a tension in clients between the value they perceive in the support they receive from their lawyer and a desire not to inflame the conflict. In 1988 Davis[27] reported on interviews with divorced parties conducted from 1978–85 and noticed a variety of styles. Although he describes the solicitor, in contrast to the mediator, as a "partisan", he stresses that the solicitor is "more than just a partisan", providing advice, counselling and emotional support to clients throughout an emotional period. "It is important to recognize" he writes, "that the solicitor's partisanship enables him to provide a different order of 'support' from that which may be offered by mediators or welfare officers . . . Where the parties are at their most vulnerable – in conflict with one another and confronted with legal machinery which they do not understand – the only 'support' worth having may be that which is unashamedly partisan".[28] While 7 per cent of his interviewees thought their solicitor was "too aggressive" (those whom Davis styles "the gladiators"), most were able to reconcile partisanship with a conciliatory approach. ". . . it is possible for a client to regard his solicitor as being 'for my interests', and yet to acknowledge that he had 'stopped us from tearing each other apart' ".[29] More recently, Davis has suggested that the settlement culture in the courts may be developing a class of "hybrid" practitioners: "Solicitors are called upon to modify their partisanship, welfare officers find it helpful to familiarise themselves with legal precedent, and district judges abandon many of the basic tenets of adversarialism".[30] Michael King confirms this from interviews with solicitors over how they handle disputes about children.[31] He observes that solicitors, many of whom have now trained as mediators, have absorbed the rhetoric of concern over the welfare of children, and use their authority to appeal to this factor, and to the expectation that the parents

---

[27] Gwynn Davis, *Partisans and Mediators* (Oxford University Press, 1988).

[28] Gwynn Davis, *Partisans and Mediators* (Oxford University Press, 1988) pp. 89–90.

[29] Ibid., p. 113.

[30] Gwynn Davis and Julia Pearce, "The Hybrid Practitioner" (1999) 29 *Family Law* 547 at 553.

[31] Michael King, " 'Being Sensible': Images and Practices of the New Family Lawyers" (1999) 28 *Journal of Social Policy* 249–73; S.D. Sclater, *Divorce: A Psycho-Social Study* (Ashgate, 1999), p. l; Christine Piper, *The Responsible Parent: A Study in Divorce Mediation* (Harvester Wheatsheaf, 1993).

should behave "sensibly", as a means of pushing clients towards settling such disputes.

Simple Quarrels[32] describes in more detail the way solicitors manage individual cases involving the negotiation of money and property disputes. This research was based on interviews with solicitors and clients, and courtroom observation in relation to eighty cases from the point when application was first made to a court to the resolution of the issue. The sample therefore consisted only of cases which had proceeded to a point where the assistance of the court had been invoked, and did not therefore cover cases which did not proceed that far, or consider the circumstances which led to such applications being made. Nevertheless, the authors claim (controversially) that "there are many cases – perhaps the majority – in which the bulk of the negotiation follows an application to the court for ancillary relief; and certainly all legal aid cases go down this route".[33] Our methodology allowed us to look again at this issue. Davis and his colleagues found that 50 per cent of male clients had a favourable view of their lawyer, compared with 70 per cent of female clients . They state that "this may in part be a reflection of the issue being tackled. Many women were grateful for the support which they received from their solicitor in a realm where they had commonly been overridden by their husbands. They were also pleased at the final outcome. Men, at least in their own eyes, did less well. The relatively modest approval rating for solicitors amongst our male informants may reflect the unpalatable messages which several of the men in our sample had had to absorb".[34] In characterising the approach of solicitors, the authors preferred to contrast active as against responsive modes rather than conciliatory as opposed to litigious approaches.[35] This refers to the solicitors' methods of managing work load. Most solicitors adopted a reactive stance, since this enabled them to spread their work more easily, leading, however, to delay and a "piecemeal" approach. The research also dealt with matters relating to negotiation, which we will consider when we review our data.

We described in the previous chapter how Ingleby employed Galanter's concept of litigotiation, implying a continuum rather than a contrast between negotiation and litigation in matrimonial work, and

---

[32] G. Davis, S. Cretney and J. Collins, *Simple Quarrels* (Clarendon Press, Oxford, 1994).

[33] Ibid., p. 298.

[34] Ibid., p. 92.

[35] Ibid., p. 120.

showed how strongly their work centred at the "negotiation" end of that scale. Ingleby also coined the term "the solicitor as intermediary" to refer to the important role of the solicitor in dealing with third parties on behalf of the client. American studies have taken further the analysis of the complexity of lawyer-client relationships, drawing on medical sociologists' studies of doctors and patients[36] which tended to focus on the power imbalance and the social control mechanisms in operation between professional and client. Sarat and Felstiner[37] observed lawyer-client interactions in two American settings. They emphasise the ways in which lawyers maintain their status in the eyes of the client, and control over the process, by means of "law talk", claiming expertise in the workings of the local legal system, predicting which judge will make which kind of decision and so on. Their evidence about the way lawyers can urge clients to "stick up for themselves" (for example, by pointing out "you're going to have to live with the outcome") can be directly replicated in our evidence, as also is their evidence of the way lawyers guide clients away from legally or practically unrealistic positions. Mather et al,[38] who gave open interviews to 163 divorce lawyers in Maine and New Hampshire also deal with the question of client autonomy. They argued that lawyers used a variety of techniques to bring clients to choose the outcome favoured by the lawyer, ranging from trying to "educate" clients through advice and persuasion, making reference to courts, delaying, pointing out the higher legal costs of choosing a different course, and, ultimately, withdrawing from the case. Lawyers claimed they were more likely to withdraw from a case where a client made unreasonable demands than if the client made unreasonable concessions, the main reason being concern over appearing in an unfavourable light to their legal colleagues. Our data give a somewhat different picture of the position regarding client autonomy, which may reflect both our different methodology and the fact that we were scrutinising the negotiating strategy of solicitors rather than the courtroom tactics of advocates.

[36] D. Mechanic, "Medical Sociology" (1989) 30 *Journal of Health and Social Behavior* 147.

[37] A. Sarat and W. Felstiner, *Divorce Lawyers and their Clients* (Oxford University Press, 1995).

[38] Lynn Mather, Richard J. Maiman and Craig A. McEwen, "The Passenger decides on the Destination and I decide on the Route: Are Divorce Lawyers 'Expensive Cab Drivers'?" (1995) 9 *International Journal of Law and the Family* 286.

Finally, in 1998, Gillian Douglas and her colleagues[39] interviewed members of fifty-seven families with children who had been involved in divorce. Thirty-six per cent of the sample had reached a negotiated financial settlement through a solicitor. A further 33 per cent had managed to reach agreement without such negotiation, but used the solicitor to "draw up" the agreement. Five per cent had been involved in some kind of court proceedings (and had used solicitors), and a further 12 per cent were using a solicitor, but the matter was not yet settled. Only 12 per cent had made their own agreement without use of a solicitor (or a court).

Philip Lewis and Rick Abel[40] have developed a framework for representing the tasks lawyers perform for clients. Their starting point is that when behaviour is legalised and lawyers are involved, it makes a difference. Lawyers may augment or diminish inequalities between adversaries because one side is more effectively represented than the other, or perhaps only one side is represented at all. Furthermore, lawyers operate in settings that are not strictly adversarial, and even within contentious settings they perform a variety of functions. Lawyers provide knowledge about the law so that clients can plan their future behaviour (they may also misinform); they provide clients with knowledge about and contact with influential people; they speak for their clients, using rhetorical skills and technical knowledge to address adversaries, negotiation partners, judges and administrators. Lawyers present not only legal arguments but also say things their clients cannot say either because they lack eloquence or the courage or are too emotionally involved. Lawyers can engage in therapy and may affirm or challenge feelings and thus change goals and strategies. They may perform formulaic activities. Lawyers construct narratives: they collect stories from clients and put together a story about what happened. They transform their clients' objectives and strategies by telling clients what they can and cannot obtain from the legal system. In divorce cases lawyers translate raw client emotion such as the desire for revenge into entitlements to property settlement and support. Sometimes this translation also reflects the lawyers' own feelings about the appropriate legal response, as in John Griffiths' reports that Dutch lawyers

---

[39] Gillian Douglas, Mervyn Murch, Alison Perry, Kay Bader and Margaret Borkowski, *How parents cope financially on marriage breakdown*, Report to the Joseph Rowntree Foundation, November 1999.

[40] P. Lewis and R. Abel, *Lawyers in Society* (University of California Press, LA, 1995), pp. 292–7.

discourage non-custodial parents from seeking weekly visitation because they believe that it produces too much conflict.[41] They "cool out" the clients, explaining that they must accept less than they want and why, blaming this on rigid rules, arbitrary judges and so on. Although people see the law as something complex, in practice the translation process is often one of simplification. There is considerable controversy and little information about the extent to which lawyers intensify or moderate legal conflict, or encourage their clients to comply with or evade the law. Sarat and Felstiner[42] offer convincing evidence that divorce lawyers moderate the adversarial inclinations of their client, which are fuelled by strong emotions. Lewis and Abel conclude by lamenting the paucity of research on what lawyers actually do for their clients and a hope that their outline may stimulate others to pursue these issues. We will try to respond to this challenge.

[41] J. Griffiths, "What do Dutch lawyers actually do in Divorce Cases?" (1986) 20 *Law and Society* 135.

[42] See note 37 above.

4

Observing a Dual Profession

THIS CHAPTER SETS out the results, and an analysis, of the observations we carried out in solicitors' offices. It provided us with a groundwork, derived from the relatively small number of practitioners we were able to observe, against which we could set the data derived from the case study, which we give in the later chapters. The evidence provided in this chapter is presented in a rather different manner from that in the later chapters. Here we present something of a "snap-shot" view of the workplace setting against which the solicitor meets (and interacts with) the client, communicates with third parties and engages with the court system. Unlike later chapters, it does not follow events over any length of time; nor does it follow themes which have been pre-selected for special analysis. But from the immersion in the environment of the lawyers' practice certain features do emerge which seem important for the understanding of that practice.

A A "DUAL PROFESSION"

Within the small group of family specialists we observed, we saw two distinct professional sub- groups at work, divided by the character of their client base. One group was working with mainly low-income clients doing predominantly legal aid work, and a second group worked with private clients. Of course the classification by clients is not always clear cut. A number of middle class women without disposable income within the marriage find themselves applying for legal aid, even if only as a loan,[1] in order to pursue a divorce action which may result in a substantial property settlement. And a number of middle class clients who are not eligible for legal aid find legal costs a burden, and try to reduce the expense by doing as much of the work themselves, seeking no more than reassurance and some technical assistance from their lawyer. Clients in the public sector, financed by the

---

[1] See the discussion of the statutory charge, above p. 20.

Legal Aid Board seemed to be generally well served in that the solicitor tended to formulate a plan for furthering the clients' wishes as closely as possible within the legal framework, and to carry it forward not directly constrained by the clients' ability to pay, though indirectly constrained by the acceptability of the course of action to the Legal Aid Board. Solicitors with a legal aid franchise are further constrained by the need to keep below the local average rate of failure to obtain legal aid certificates in order to keep their franchise, a matter which will assume increasing importance after January 2000. This will have the effect of gradually forcing the failure rate down locally and increasing pressure on practitioners not to apply for legal aid (in its new form) in marginal cases. These practitioners often juggled work for twenty different clients during a single working day, keeping a mass of detailed information in play, often fearful of being negligent under pressure. The financial rewards were limited, and several practices were finding it hard to stay afloat doing legal aid work. These solicitors tended to hear the client's story, to identify the key issues, to devise a plan and then to act. When the practitioner was dealing with multi-problem families the work often resembled that of a social worker rather than the traditional solicitor's role of taking instructions and advising. Firefighting seemed to be the name of the game. In addition, the lawyer needed to balance the interests of any minor children with the interests of the client, and also the public interest which requires careful use of public funds.

With the private clients the lawyers seemed to be more willing for the client to set the agenda, and to do what the client requested. In middle-income cases we observed that this led on several occasions to the parties effectively making their own plan and needing the solicitor to do no more than formalise arrangements which were largely agreed. In the "big money" cases the client was even more likely to get what he or she asked for. But to us this seemed to be not always in their best interests in the long term. There seemed in some cases to be a disparity between the amount of lawyer time being invested in the complex technical legal and financial work carried out in tax planning, setting up trusts, preemptions and so on, and the amount of time spent on determining exactly what the client's long-term goals were and how to move towards them. Sometimes a great deal of work was in hand, when the client would have a change of plan and costly effort would yield little benefit. There may be an analogy with private medicine, in that the "trimmings" of elegant meeting rooms and instant attention are there and the customer sets the agenda, but at the end of the day this may not represent the most effective way forward. A cynical interpretation would be that the solicitor is simply maximising profits by being swift to act on instructions, but we found no real evidence to support this view. We would suggest rather that, in part, deference to a wealthy client may lead to a less critical response to their wishes. And even at this level of work the lawyers seemed to be driven towards doing more rather than less by the fear of being found negligent rather than by a direct profit motive. The medical world again offers a useful analogy in the concept of defensive medical practice, whereby it is thought that excessive testing and treatment procedures may be carried out by doctors fearful of negligence claims.

Throughout the full range of firms we observed we would suggest that the lawyers were reactive rather than strategic in planning their work. This confirms the observations of Davis and his colleagues (above, p. 53). The consequence was that, even had they wished to, lawyers did not seem to have the scope to "generate" work with the objective of maximising their income.[2] Planning for income maximisation seldom went beyond careful billing and some defensive practice, for example in the use of disclaimers, rather than in large scale creation of additional work. Our observations are consistent with the suggestions made by Ingleby (above, p. 14) that there is just not enough time available to string out cases for motives of profit. The level of overload experienced by all but two of the lawyers we observed precludes any strategy involving work creation.

The following observational data illustrate the distinctions described so far, and indicate that the classic formulation of the lawyers' task as taking instructions and giving advice is not always so clearly defined in practice.

B THE LEGAL AID PRACTITIONER

A day in the office

Tony is a family specialist in his early forties, admitted sixteen years ago, a member of the SFLA and a trained mediator. Two thirds of his

---

[2] For a strong statement of the incentives of lawyers to do this, see Adrian Zuckerman, "Reform in the Shadow of Lawyer's Interests" in A. Zuckerman and R. Cranston (eds), *Reform of Civil Procedure* (Oxford University Press, 1995). In *Simple Quarrels* (p. 53 above), at p. 263 the authors describe the charging system as a "tax on efficiency".

time is spent on family work, including child protection, and he also does some personal injury work, mainly for children. The firm has High Street offices in three neighbouring small towns in the Midlands. The office is modern and pleasantly informal, with a large box of toys in the waiting area. Another partner works from the office doing criminal work; there are two conveyancers and Tony has an assistant. The area has wealthy pockets, but is largely rural and most clients are on low incomes. A free legal advice clinic is run one evening a week, partly as a pro bono activity but also to bring in new clients. Most work is legally aided, and the firm has a franchise for family work.

The office day began at 9am with a call from the neighbour of a young single mother who was afraid that she was about to be evicted. Tony was cheerful, reassuring, ascertained the type of tenancy and suggested an appointment at the free clinic, asking that she should bring any documents she had. The encounter resembled a GP consultation, offering primary care: swift diagnosis, possible treatment options were identified, and the patient was required to come in to the surgery for the prescription. Great care was taken to take and give names clearly. The skill of speaking to people who were under stress not only by their problem but also by having to ask unfamiliar professionals for guidance is clearly well developed. The main work of the day was expected to be for a divorce client of long standing (Bob) with an associated child protection matter, a new divorce client (Mary) coming in from the refuge she had just moved to, and another divorce client (Agnes) seeking custody of a stepchild. Tony described his child protection work as time-consuming. It involved large numbers of telephone calls from the client and from the other professionals, including solicitors for the other parent and the local authority, social workers for both parents, the guardian ad litem, specialists involved in assessments of the children and the family, doctors, housing authorities, the Benefit Agency and the local police. Tony was acting for the father who sought the return of his children from the local authority. There was no conflict in practice between trying to serve the interests of the client and the best interests of the children as any work done has the position of the court as its outer boundary, and the court will clearly be concerned about the best interests of the child. Work on the case that day took the form of listening to what Bob wanted, attempting to further the chances of his getting his children back, gathering information, checking it with the accounts of others, arranging meetings to resolve matters at issue between social services and the parents, negotiating with creditors and the Benefit Agency and seeking rehousing. The case had been running for some months, and Tony had a good idea of the local authority's position . . . but on this particular morning a crisis had arisen over benefits being cut off.

During the flurry of phone calls in and out on this matter, Mary called on a mobile phone to ask Tony to look out of the office window in case her husband was outside before she came in to sign her divorce petition. She had seen Tony the previous day, and he had arranged for her to move with her children to a women's refuge. He looked around and reassured her (though later admitting he had no idea what the husband looked like: but there had not been anybody there!) and Mary came in with her sister. Her mother waited outside in the car with the children. Tony was careful to explain that the petition he had drafted included a strongly worded detailed statement about the violence, and was careful to check with Mary that this was acceptable. He explained that it was not put in to inflame an argument, but to protect Mary when she looked to the council for rehousing from any possibility of being deemed intentionally homeless. Mary took the point, said it was all true anyway, and signed. She and her sister then asked for practical advice about how to let the husband see the children without giving away her current address in the refuge. Mary then suddenly asked what her position would be if her husband "topped himself". Tony calmly assured her that for pension and benefit purposes she would be treated as a widow. He gave her his home number and told her to ring him over the weekend if she was worried. As she left, looking much more calm and cheerful, a call came in from an old client who was having problems with maintenance payments. This lady asked Tony whether she could put pressure on her former husband to pay the children's maintenance by withholding contact. He gently and carefully explained that this was not the best way forward. Instead he encouraged her to deal with the matter herself by giving the phone number of the local court family service and suggested that she should register her existing county court order in the magistrates' court. "There are forms to fill in and they must be sworn, but you send it to the court and they process it and send it to the magistrates to deal with the arrears. Then you are entitled to receive enforcement of the court order. If he applies to vary the order you may need me under the ABWOR scheme". By this time, about midday, Tony was expecting Agnes, who had been caring for her stepchild throughout her marriage, when there had been no contact with the mother. She had stayed in a very violent marriage for the sake of the boy. She was now seeking a divorce but was anxious to keep or stay in close contact with him. Tony described this as a difficult legal issue. Agnes did not keep her appointment, which Tony said was not at all unusual with stressed family clients, who changed their minds a number of times. Finally that morning Tony took a call from a former client who had contracted a marriage of convenience with an immigrant, and now wanted to divorce in order to be able to marry but could not trace the former spouse.

During the course of this morning Tony had taken ten incoming calls, four from clients and six from other professionals, dictated four letters to other professionals and one to a client, seen one divorce client for forty-five minutes, and dictated notes on all these actions and conversations for the files.

The afternoon was spent largely on a personal injury case with the mother of a child now nine years old who had been run over by a baker's van outside his aunt's house in another part of the country four years ago, and suffered lasting impairment as a result of head injuries. Although Tony thought he had negotiated a fair offer of compensation, because the case involved a minor, the matter had to go before a judge and therefore counsel's opinion had to be sought and the barrister was advising further investigation. Tony and the mother would therefore have to spend a day going to the site of the accident, searching again for witnesses at the expense of the Legal Aid Board, after the solicitor had already negotiated what he thought to be a good outcome. Although Tony was frustrated by this prolongation of the case, there was a more leisurely feel to the afternoon, simply because the matter being dealt with was in the past. This was in marked contrast to the other family matters being dealt with where crises were unfolding by the hour.

These cases were all legally aided, all at crisis point, and all involved multiple problems. The solicitor's role seemed to consist of fire fighting; reacting to crises, trying to fend off further disasters, and strongly oriented towards protecting the interests of children and vulnerable adults. Profit levels were low. The bank manager called that day to remonstrate over the increases in the practice overdraft. Stress levels were high . . . with weekend emergency help on offer.

The activities observed corresponded closely to those mentioned in Lewis and Abel's framework: the provision of legal and practical knowledge, speaking for clients to other agents, providing emotional support, identifying what the law can and cannot offer, and doing nothing to escalate conflict. This brief account, however, can only hint at the minute by minute pressure, the high emotional involvement, the provision of steady support and reassurance combined with advice and action and teaching the client how to act for himself. The image which comes to mind is a mixture of general medical practitioner and social worker with clout.

C   A "DAY IN COURT"

The observation summarised above deals with a day in the office. We now turn to court-based work, giving examples of activities in court. The lawyers we observed spoke of "a day at court" as something to be avoided at all costs. It took up a great deal of time which could be better spent. They complained of delays, hanging around, and of district judges who did not have time to prepare properly and get "up to speed". From our perspective, however, time spent in court looked very similar to time spent in the office, if a rather speeded up version. The solicitors were still eliciting further information, checking information and negotiating with the other side either directly or through counsel. There are clearly differences between directions hearings, at which the parties are given an indication of the outcome the court would like to see, and final hearings at which a judge will announce a decision. But our impression was of the court as a place where many decisions are made but few directly by the judiciary. The door of the court, or more often the cafeteria of the court, was the place where, as all the key players are present and prepared, negotiations can be brought to a conclusion through urgent discussion between lawyers, parties and welfare officers. Then in the case of an order or injunction the outcome will be carefully explained to the parties by the judge, who in the cases we saw relied heavily on the views of the welfare officers. Even where a party seriously questioned the welfare report this seemed to be regarded by the court as the expert view of the servant of the court, working with the welfare of the children as the first consideration, and beyond criticism.

Jane, who was a partner in a small firm with a legal aid franchise doing only family work, was observed going to court with Mr Purvis over a contact dispute. The client was clearly angry, and told us how he had learned about his rights from a fathers' support group. He was seeking to re-establish contact with his son who was living with a new partner whom he regarded as unsuitable as a role model for the boy. The welfare officer's report had proposed overnight visits once a month. Mr Purvis said that he had made it clear to the welfare officer that he lived in lodgings and his landlady would not allow him to have his son overnight, and that he wanted more frequent contact, on a weekly basis. His former wife and her solicitor were in the lobby, but avoiding any contact with Mr Purvis. Jane spoke to the other solicitor and to the welfare officer but could not achieve any movement. The parties went in to the district judge at about 11am, and Jane explained that no agreement had been reached. The judge sent everyone outside to try once more. Jane, over a cup of coffee, worked carefully and skilfully with Mr Purvis to find a way forward. Jane explained that everyone wanted him to have a good relationship with his son, and that was what they were working towards. But she suggested moving towards this a step at a time, gradually building up to more contact. Mr Purvis remained adamant. Jane then invoked the court. She said that the court wanted what was best for children, and what was clearly not best for the boy was for his parents to be involved in litigation. She said "I'm afraid that you'll polarise things and set Pete back . . . you risk him choosing against seeing you". To this Mr Purvis replied "If there's an order there is no choice". The welfare officer had been recommending contact for two days a month, and he wanted six hours a week. Jane almost reeled in her fish, but at the last moment he pulled away, rejecting the facts in the welfare report, and demanding a contested hearing, saying that if Jane's firm would not do what he wanted he would find a firm which would. As a result the parties went back in before the judge, Jane requested a hearing and a date was set. Jane was angry and frustrated at what she saw as her failure to reach a settlement when the difference was so apparently minor. There was no objection to contact in principle, but only a dispute over whether this should be overnight every other weekend or during the day every weekend. On returning to the office, Jane expressed her concern to her colleagues, but then set about finding a tough young male counsel to go to the hearing with Mr Purvis. We had observed Jane holding out strongly for her position, which she believed to be the position which the court would take, for as long as possible and then capitulating and accepting the client's instructions. This was a legal aid case. We will encounter such sequences again in our case data.

A second example is given to demonstrate how productive a day in court can be. The client, Maria, was in the process of divorcing her husband but in the meantime wanted him out of the house because he drank and abused her verbally though not physically. Tony's assistant, Claire, was taking the case, which was legally aided, with counsel. Claire met Maria at court and introduced the barrister, also a young woman, to Maria over a cup of coffee. The husband was not represented, but was accompanied by his wife's sister to "look after him and keep him calm". The lawyers feared that it would be difficult to get an injunction as there was no physical violence, but were ready to use the opportunity to deal with the money side at the same time. Maria asked the lawyers whether she should leave the house. She was anxious to get everything sorted out on the one day in court, and thought it should be possible because her husband is "sensible when he's not drinking" and that he loved her and she cared about him. Maria seemed quiet and capable, and obviously fond of her husband, but could not cope any longer with the stress arising from his drink problem, and did not want her six-year-old daughter to see her father abusing her mother. Both lawyers related easily to her, and together worked out what level of income she needed to be able to stay in the family home. The barrister, Patricia, went over to the husband on the other side of the court coffee shop with the suggested offer. She came back with an offer from the husband to give an undertaking not to molest, and had explained that if he breaks it he could go to prison. The money was being negotiated. Patricia summed up her advice as "close the joint account and divide, he will pay on the first of the month at least £65 per week, but in a good week (his earnings were variable) he would pay £100". Maria was anxious about the amount. Patricia went back once more and got agreement from the husband to pay £85 per week, to be used by Maria to pay the mortgage. The case was listed for 10am, and at 10.45 we were called in to the court where the judge sat, robed and formal. Patricia stated that agreement had been reached, stated the terms, and asked for time to draft the order. The judge refused, saying that she must "come back with the order". Patricia then asked if the order could just be handed in, but the judge said "no", as he needed to explain the serious nature of such an undertaking. He told us to return at ten minutes to one, just before the hour at which judges lunch.

Claire was called away by a call from the office on her mobile to other clients who were also in court (a case where her client, a father who was seeking a residence order, and who still lived in the family home, was being accused of abuse). By 11.30am Patricia had drafted Maria's order and tried to keep the parties calm. As we waited, Patricia raised the question of contact, and it became clear that Maria had not realised that the order would permit her husband to enter the house to see his daughter. This was amended so that he could pick her up elsewhere by arrangement. The husband was getting anxious. Claire was using the waiting time to good effect with the other client, but Patricia was unable to do anything constructive once she had drafted the order and was also restless. At ten minutes to one the judge was not ready, and we were asked to come back at 2pm. Patricia was angry and asked to see a district judge in chambers. We did so, but the district judge would not make the order because he was not satisfied that the county court judge had released the case. The district judge said he would deal with the matter at 2pm when this had been done. We went in again at 2pm and the district judge explained the nature of the undertaking to the husband, who agreed. This took four minutes. Claire copied the order on the Xerox machine in the lobby, whispering to her client that there was no power of arrest attached to it but if she was in trouble to call the police or Claire and it could be taken back to court. The order covered the payments for the mortgage as well as staying out of the house. The lawyers were both furious about waiting around from 11am, though Claire had made good use of the time on her other case. Attributing the time spent according to case for the Legal Aid Board would not be easy. But Maria had had lunch with her husband and her sister, had obtained the order she needed, plus the practical advice on going straight to the bank to arrange the payments plus the payment of the mortgage. What on paper appeared to be an application for an exclusion order, or a contested injunction, and led to a lot of wasted time at court, was in practice an amicable negotiation with skilled help on the issues of who would move out, the practical financial arrangements, and contact. In addition further work was done on another urgent case to good effect.

D   THE PRIVATE CLIENT

We referred above to this being a "dual profession", dividing sharply between legal aid work and work for private clients. This is illustrated by describing the morning's work of Richard, a young partner specialising in divorce work in the family department of a large firm where many clients were seriously wealthy and no legal aid work was accepted. In our description of the work of the legal aid practitioner, we observed how a solicitor's main activity seemed to consist of almost continual talking, face to face, on the phone, or to a dictaphone to clients, colleagues, other professionals and a range of third parties. But we had seen very little that could be termed "receiving instructions". Only Mr Purvis could be clearly seen to be giving a clear instruction, and this clarity was the result of his rejection of the advice of his lawyer and the court welfare service. But with the higher income and wealthy clients there did seem to be more evidence of a direct routing of requests from client to lawyers and these were generally acted upon, though sometimes reluctantly.

For Richard, the day began early, with preparation for a hearing on a contents dispute, and a meeting was planned for the afternoon with a very wealthy client on the financial arrangements for his divorce. The first case, the Smiths, occupied most of the morning. Although there was no current dispute over arrangements for the children, or the disposal of the family home, cars, or valuable jewellery and antiques, the couple were facing a court hearing over some kitchen china and bathroom fittings. A flurry of faxed correspondence between the lawyers resulted in a Draft Consent Order minutes before the hearing was due. Richard arrived in court at the last moment, informed the judge (a district judge sitting in the local district registry of the High Court) who then had to read the papers. (District judges are allotted only thirty minutes reading time in such cases, and sometimes find it difficult to deal with the papers in that time). The judge accepted the amendments and then brought out of his desk drawer scissors and sellotape with which to cut and paste. Richard then offered to have the document retyped and delivered to the court by the end of the day, an offer gratefully accepted by the judge who thought it would be much quicker than relying on court staff. Some judges now have a laptop computer and printer in court, and can type and print documents on the spot, but not in this case. There had been a remarkably fierce contest over various items, and clearly the solicitors on both sides had not in any way urged on the conflict, but were both accepting instructions from paying customers who were valued clients. Between dealing with this urgent matter, Richard had had a difficult time explaining to a client that even though he wanted to give the family home to his wife and take his name off the title deeds, he could not be automatically released from the mortgage. Clear technical advice was given to a middle class educated man who was not at a crisis point in any negotiations, and even so the information had to be repeated several times and confirmed in writing.

The afternoon was fully occupied by a meeting with a very wealthy client for whom a draft consent order was being prepared. The divorce was amicable, but the finances were so complex that the firm had a team of eight solicitors working on it, with an accountant from outside, who were dealing with company issues, setting up trusts, conveying properties and taking care of tax management. The atmosphere and organisation of the meeting was markedly different from meetings at the legal aid practice described earlier, where small children played on the floor, and the lawyer kept a look out for a violent husband from his office window. Here the client arrived, a businessman about to take charge of a meeting, ordering lunch, and appearing relaxed and in control. He was in a hurry, and impatient with some of the finer details of the tax implications of his plan raised by Richard, and was willing to forgo several hundred thousand pounds in order to simplify and speed up the transaction. But even in this meeting there was a moment of tension when the client suddenly refused adamantly to pay a very minor sum for his wife's mobile phone bill, and required the lawyers to deal with the problem. He gave his instructions clearly, advice was sometimes given by the lawyers and not always taken, and the work was swiftly done. It appeared that the client's wishes were immediately put into effect, though several times there had been reversals in strategy with the result that a great deal of work was done and then had to be done again. It seems as if the more familiar the client is in dealing with lawyers through his business activities, the less amenable he might be to professional advice on a matter as personal as divorce, and that during a period of emotional strain and mood swings it was possible that instructions were taken and acted upon when in the case of a client who was less experienced with lawyers there might have been stronger pressure from the lawyer to reconsider before taking action.

During the day Richard sent out four letters to other solicitors and clients, and several faxes to the other solicitors, was in court for twenty minutes, held a meeting with a client for two and a half hours, took three calls and made two.

But if we move from work with a very rich client, to private clients with lower incomes, the picture changes. The sub-group within the family solicitors who work with private clients in the middle income ranges seemed to us to be an endangered species. This is the population group about whom the Lord Chancellor expressed concern as being above the legal aid limits but not able to afford costly legal services.[3] They are often able to make a plan for the division of their assets, and then simply ask the lawyer to draw up a form of words to give effect to their wishes. The work resembles drafting a will, making sure that there are no technical hitches to accomplishing the client's requests. The two solicitors we observed doing this kind of work were happy to do this, but found it difficult to earn a living so doing. This group of clients seem to be those for whom the Family Law Act 1996 and mediation should work well, in that they do not seek conflict, but wish to make things as easy as possible for their children, are able to work out the kind of outcome they seek and are articulate enough to be able to mediate if conflict arises. All they seek from the lawyer is ratification of the Consent Order they have prepared. These clients seem the ideal candidates for the process envisaged under the Family Law Act 1996, whereby the parties are seen as rational actors willing to avoid wasting resources on unnecessary legal fees, but using the lawyers for the formalisation of their decisions. However, although we came across some such cases among those recited to us by our broad sample of solicitors, these cases were very much in a minority. (Cases 102, 303, 310 and 314). In Case 303 the solicitor thought she was being rather generous giving him half the house because, on the face of it, it had been a gift from her parents; but once the wife had explained the financial history, the proposed arrangement did seem fair and he did not advise against it. In Case 314 the solicitor said:

> "He asked for advice, but in general terms. I mean, he's not a helpless client who'd come to me and say: 'O, what do I do?' He'd come to me and say, 'This is what my wife wants. I think it's OK. Is it totally out of order? What do you think?' And it was actually very fair. Too fair". (314)

E THE CORE ACTIVITY: INTERACTION

Perhaps for lawyers in other areas of practice there is an assumption that the aim of the work is to win the case. But in family law there is no such overriding unitary objective. The lawyer aims to do the best for his client not just at the time of divorce but with a view to the future, and with an overriding concern for the welfare of any children

---

[3] Lord Irvine of Lairg, Speech to the Law Society's Annual Conference, Cardiff, October 1997.

involved. This long term dimension, and the concern about the interests of the third parties, shapes the practice of family law. The solicitor
working with a divorcing client appeared to us to assist the client in the
move from one household to two, perhaps taking a child, and trying to
hold on to sufficient resources to carry out this change. A common
phrase from solicitor to client was "So, how can we move things
along?" In carrying out this movement along the path towards life after
divorce, we observed the primary activity of the lawyers whatever their
client base, to be to "accompany and guide" the client through this
process. This involved constant communication and interaction with
the client and other persons involved in the process. When we broke
down the day into units according to the mode and purpose of activity,
we saw solicitors spending the day in contact with their clients, with
the other side, and with third parties, many of whom were non-legal
professionals. They were interacting, usually by talking to others
directly, by phone, or by dictating letters. This interaction constituted
the major activity as the lawyers carried out administrative tasks,
obtained information, gave advice, negotiated, and actively supported
their clients.

We recorded what we saw the lawyers do in the following categories:

1. Administrative work.
2. Eliciting, checking, or passing on information about the case.
3. Offering advice which in practice consisted of endorsing or rejecting
a goal or course of action identified by the client, or offering one or
more suggestions to the client with or without recommending a particular one.
4. Negotiating first with the client and then with the other side, by
making offers or trading or rejecting offers from the other side.
5. Offering help and support.

We had expected to separate out activity based in court from work in
the office (and in some cases visits by solicitors to home, or, in one case,
hospital, to see clients) but found in practice that the work in court
resembled the other activities of the lawyers so closely that it should be
dealt alongside out-of-court work. The activities which did not involve
contact with others were only a minor part of the day. Reading documents, which we had expected to be a major activity, in practice
accounted for a marginal part of the lawyers' day. Travelling was mini-
mal, as all the lawyers we saw were close to any court they had to attend.

Even drafting documents or reading the post were often done in conversation with colleagues. The picture on the ground is very different to the neat cut-and-dry segmentation of family law work laid out in the franchise contract.

Administrative work

All the solicitors we observed undertook administrative work with their clients, arranging meetings, providing, completing and getting signed the necessary documents, and acknowledging receipt of documents such as divorce petitions, affidavits, mortgage documents, contracts for house sale and purchase, pensions arrangements, and loans. Where the client was anxious or not familiar with this kind of paperwork, or in extreme cases unable to read or write English, the solicitor's help was essential in filling in complex forms. Where the client had greater educational or financial resources, the lawyer often dealt with more complex matters and again had a key role even at the level of administrative help. It might be thought that this kind of activity should not require the time of a highly trained lawyer. Alternatively it could be seen as using experience and expertise to guide a client quickly through the paperwork necessary to petition for divorce, to state arrangements for children, to clarify arrangements for contact or, less frequently, residence, and to prepare the financial affidavits and papers related to transfer of property or periodical payments. The work involved seemed akin to assistance with an income tax return, benefit application, or house purchase. It could be compared with the work of accountants for those with property, or with benefit agency staff for those on low incomes; and for transfer of property with the work of conveyancing lawyers. When considering the boundaries of the work of the family lawyer, it might be helpful to place it alongside these professions, as well as the mediators who are concerned with resolving the disputes which may arise in connection with the changes being made. We considered discussion of fees under this administrative head, and were interested to see lawyers at all levels of client income advising on how to keep costs down, particularly by not litigating about house contents. As one lawyer told us: "It's not worth litigating about anything under £6,000 . . . you might as well give each lawyer £3,000".

Giving Information and Advice

(i) Distinguishing information from advice

All our solicitors carried out an iterative process of seeking and veri-
fying information with all their clients, which was then communi-
cated selectively to the other side and to third parties. The solicitor
might be seeking documentary evidence in preparing a financial statement. "The facts in this affidavit are very woolly. I don't know what
the school fees actually are . . . do you get a copy of the actual fees?"
Written or oral statements were probed and checked but care was
taken to avoid appearing to doubt what had been said, and to appear
continuously supportive to the client. The phrases used included:
"would it be right to say . . . can I just check . . . we need to talk
about . . .". Feelings needed to be checked as well as facts. These
queries were often presented to clients as safety checks rather than as
a questioning of the clients' veracity, and justified by the need to prevent future problems with queries from the other side or from a court.
The SFLA code requires lawyers not to disparage the other side but at
the same time the lawyer needs to probe the accuracy of any contra-
dictory statements and to ask for the client's views of the other side's
statements and on the reports of experts, particularly the family court
welfare officer. Thus, the same point is addressed over and over
again. This might be seen as causing delay and pushing up costs . . .
or, alternatively, as constructive attention to detail. The careful
checking of all statements and documents, the probing for information which may not have seemed relevant to the client but is recognised by the solicitor as a result of his experience as important, often
appeared to be well worthwhile. For example, in a 'big money' case
involving a multi-million pound settlement, Richard identified both
inaccuracy of a plumbing bill and an unsubstantiated total in the documents of £3 million. This iterative process cannot be placed easily
within the traditional framework which sees lawyer-client interaction
solely in terms of taking instructions or giving advice. It seemed to us
instead rather to be part of a process of negotiation between lawyer
and client about the path to take within the parameters of the possible; whether the constraints are legal or practical. The lawyers'
experience is unique in covering both facets of the case. We did not
see the client telling his story for translation into legal terms, as

described by Cain.[4] We saw what looked more like an interview of the client by the lawyer. In the first interview the lawyer would ask, almost as a doctor would do, what it was that occasioned the visit. At that stage the response would either be a statement that the client was in a situation he wished to get out of, or had a preferred state of affairs in mind and was seeking a way in, or needed to respond to the action of the other spouse. The client might then seek advice or go on to state his plan for achieving his goal. When the client had no clear view of the future, the lawyer offered a diagnosis and a treatment plan, and proceeded like a doctor to take a history of the case. He sought the information which was useful to him and discouraged other information (often an account of the emotional side of the marriage). If the client had already identified the goal, the lawyer needed only to provide the treatment plan. In either case the lawyer proceeds by asking questions, eliciting information, checking this information, offering information, seeking further information and so on. The lawyer is in effect in a process of negotiation with his client, long before beginning to talk to the other side.

What kind of information did we see the solicitors give to the clients? We were particularly interested in the boundaries between the giving of information and the provision of legal and other advice in the light of the possibility of information meetings being introduced under the Family Law Act 1996. We wished to understand what kind of information is being given by solicitors, at what stage, and whether there might be a potential overlap in service provision. Alternatively the solicitors may offer very different kinds of information from that planned for the information sessions, either spontaneously or on request.

The first point we observed is that most clients at first meeting were clear in their minds that the marriage was over. (This was not always the case with the other party). This also turned out to be true in our case study. They were therefore not seeking information about how the marriage should be saved, and it is unlikely they would have welcomed it if given. This contrasts with the proposals about information meetings, which stress that one of their purposes is to explore ways of saving marriages. Generally the first type of information involved the solicitor explaining the stages through which the case was likely to pass, and stressing the next step to come. The information given ranged

[4] M.E. Cain, "The General Practice Lawyer and Client: Towards a Radical Conception" (1979) 7 *International Journal of the Sociology of Law* 331.

from "your wife's flat has burnt down" to complex details on trust law. Non-legal practical information was also offered, e.g. "two bedroomed houses in that area cost x" or "that house is in the catchment area for such and such a school". At first meeting a client might be quite stressed and upset. In these circumstances it is particularly difficult to take in information, and we noted on many occasions the way in which the lawyers repeated over and over again even simple information, confirming it in writing. Again this activity might be considered wasteful of professional time, but without such help these clients were unable to move forward. Information of a general nature was also given by the solicitors. But this was usually for a tactical reason, either to encourage a client to try a particular course of action (for example, "most people find it difficult to see their child in what was their old family home and find it easier to have the visit somewhere else") or to discourage a course of action by pointing out how the individual differed from the general course of events (for example, "many people do x but because of your debts/medical condition I would suggest we try y"). Specific information about the administration of their case was also given to all clients, e.g., "the date of your hearing is x", "your legal aid has come through", and so on.

At what point does the kind of very specific provision of information which we have described become advice? Our working definition included as information the straightforward statements given above, concerning dates, descriptions of procedures, or even descriptions of what the court was likely to do. Advice becomes the appropriate description when a course of action is under discussion, i.e. when the client puts forward a plan and the lawyer accepts or rejects the idea, or when a lawyer puts forward a plan or a modification of a plan, or when a number of ideas are on the table and the lawyer recommends one of these either in its entirety or in part. Giving advice by our definition would thus include explaining the likely outcome of a course of action, as opposed to describing the next steps in a procedure. This might almost be seen as giving information, but it occurs so frequently alongside recommending a course of action that it fits more closely within the category of advice. Similarly, pointing out which issues to focus on in making a decision is close to information giving, but again this always occurred alongside making a recommendation and thus cannot be separated from the advisory function.

(ii) Tactical advice

We saw what was clearly "advice" being given on tactics, i.e., the taking of strategic decisions. For example, Tony advised on making a full statement about incidents of violence in order to smooth the way for subsequent rehousing. We also saw a client advised to ignore harsh statements about his behaviour coming from the wife's solicitor, as now that he was seeking contact rather than residence, the court would discount these, and they had been only tactical by the other side. In addition, the client was advised to go for a contact order, just in case things became more difficult in the future even though no problems about contact existed at the time. Thus an order was being used strategically, to provide a framework within which a fragile agreement might be supported. In all cases when a choice must be made whether to follow the single course of action on the table or to make a choice, the lawyer gave advice to support a way forward. One solicitor advised her client to travel north for a hearing even though this would be difficult, as judges there were thought to be more traditional and generous in their treatment of women.

(iii) The client's view

We also saw the rejection of advice by clients, and insistence on taking another course of action from that suggested by the lawyer. We have described above Mr Purvis and his refusal to compromise over his application for contact. There were less dramatic examples of rejection of advice, for example, the "big money" client who was heard saying to the lawyer "let's keep it simple. . . I'm chucking it in . . . why don't I just transfer out . . . it's a concession worth £200,000 to her". A middle income client rejected a draft letter to the other side saying "No. Let's not be so aggressive. Let's write a letter saying OK". In both these cases the lawyer felt the client was selling him/herself short, but in all cases of such disagreements the client's view prevailed. No difference was observed between legally aided and private clients in this respect. We will return to the question of client autonomy when we recount the data from our case study.

(iv) DIY advice

We also saw solicitors advising clients to act for themselves without the intervention of a lawyer. Sometimes this meant giving them the specific information which would enable them to do so. For example, when a long standing client rang Tony asking how to enforce a child support order, she was given the number of the local family court service and told how to register the order in the magistrates' court for enforcement. We also observed solicitors advising clients as a matter of generally accepted practice to talk directly to their spouse, especially when they were still living under the same roof, and especially about the children. The contents of the family home were also a matter on which clients were advised to talk directly to each other. Even in one of the "big money" cases which was amicable, the client was advised to talk directly with his wife about sharing the contents of the family home.

Negotiation

As we have described, a great deal of the early exchanges of information and advice between lawyer and client could be categorised as their own internal negotiations which both precede and accompany negotiation with the other side. Given that so few matrimonial cases end up in contested hearings, and that two out of three property orders are made by consent, we expected negotiation towards settlement to be a primary part of the lawyer's work, but had not expected to see so much taking place between solicitor and client rather than between the two sides.

This internal negotiation between lawyer and client took the form of the lawyer trying to modify the client's expectations. Solicitors often referred to what the court would want to see. Using the court as an external authority with which the lawyer but not the client is familiar is an effective technique in most cases (but not all: see Mr Purvis). Where there were children, the needs of the children were used as a bargaining counter both because of the importance of their welfare to the court, but also in their own right. So, lawyers said " if a spouse is angry and says so to the child the judge will see this as you expressing your own need, putting your need before the child's . . . you need to know what the judge will think. He will put the children's needs before yours"; and, "we all want the same thing . . . we want you to have a good relationship with your children". In some of the big money cases the lawyer referred to other external authorities valued by the client, such as the client's own accountant and tax advisers. Whether this was because these were more salient to the client than fear of the court, we cannot say.

When a case reached the point of offers being made and considered, again solicitors would refer to other people in similar situations to encourage agreement. When an offer was considered generous, we never saw a client being advised to refuse, though if an offer appeared too low the client would be advised to continue negotiations. We were told that women sometimes do want to accept unrealistically low offers simply because they have had enough of the process and want it to be over, while men sometimes experience fits of generosity stimulated by guilt. In negotiation with the other side many of the same techniques were used, including reference to the need to settle to keep costs down, or to avoid CSA involvement, and to call on the views of other professionals. It was common to refer to the likely attitude of the court, but expressing the wish to avoid a court hearing was more common than threatening court action if the other side continued to resist advice. Occasionally we saw the lawyer rejecting an offer at the insistence of their client against their own better judgment, but this was rare. In addition to these negotiating activities, at the same time there would be continuing exchange of information, of documents, arrangements for meetings and so on. We were to see later in our case file interviews the impact of skilled negotiation over the full span of a case, where the ability to keep away from court had a major impact on keeping costs down. The case where costs were most disproportionate to the assets was one where one side had no legal advice (see below p. 141).

A final category of negotiation combined with advice seeking, took place with a wide range of third parties. These included expert witnesses, social workers, interpreters, court staff, the Legal Aid Board, police, the housing authority, refuges, the Benefit Agency, the bank manager, a client's employer, court welfare officers, guardians ad litem, the Official Solicitor, counsel, a pension adviser, an employee service, financial advisers, an immigration adviser, tax craftsman, accountants, Alcoholics Anonymous, and Gamblers Anonymous. In some instances the lawyer was negotiating for his client, particularly with the police, with the local housing authority and the Benefit Agency. In other cases the lawyer sought advice, for example, from an accountant and tax advisers, and advice agencies dealing with particular problems such as addiction. This kind of direct contact on the client's behalf with third parties is again akin to the activity of a social worker, or adviser . . . and markedly different from any activity which a mediator could undertake.

Help and support

Just as information work blended into the giving of advice, and advice into negotiation, so also the activity of negotiating often came very close to the giving of help and support. We have described how the information seeking and checking procedures were always carefully phrased to indicate ongoing support rather than lack of trust. We observed unfailing courtesy and support to clients, many of whom were distressed or angry and afraid, even when a client was making unreasonable demands which were beyond what any court would accept. For example, Tony offered his home number and availability over the weekend to Mary in the refuge, his assistant whispered to her client while her order was being photocopied that, although there was no power of arrest attached, she should call the police if she found herself in trouble or "if it's not quite so urgent phone me". We saw the heroic efforts by Amanda to help a woman wanting a divorce who was so seriously ill that the Official Solicitor's office was querying her ability to understand the nature of the divorce process and therefore whether she could go ahead with her petition. Another client was being very slow in getting her financial information together, and though finding this frustrating, the lawyer explained to me that she was lacking in confidence, had been badly treated by her husband, who was financially very acute if not dishonest. Valiant and successful attempts were made to support a woman being threatened with a custodial sentence for failing to comply with a contact order when the transport she needed for compliance was not available. Even the husband in a "big money" case was supported, with the lawyer saying "making an inventory of your house is very stressful even when you are basically in agreement . . . take time".

F CONCLUSIONS

We have described in this chapter a profession with a range of activity depending on the client base, but have identified here the two extremes:

the legal aid practitioner whose work in many ways resembles that of a social worker or general practitioner, and the private client practitioner who, when dealing with a "big money" case, looks more like the adversarial commercially minded stereotypes of the divorce lawyer, largely because he accepts his client's instructions rather than negotiating a strategy with him. In between we saw the private client lawyer with the rational actor client, for whom it may be that the writing is on the wall as the client can act for himself in all but a formal capacity, and when involved in a dispute could be helped by mediation. However, it is important to remember that the legal aid clients are by the far the most numerous category, and also the category with fewer alternative sources of guidance and support.

This latter part of the analysis has indicated that, despite the division of the profession according to the characteristics of the client base of each practice, this division should not mask the underlying commonality of the work of the lawyers. We have described the unifying element as being one of *interactivity*: that is, interaction with the client and with others involved in the case. This interactivity is constant and continual. Of course, it is not *continuous* throughout each case. Lawyers move constantly from one case, or even one crisis, to another, in the reactive mode identified by Davis (see above). But the lawyer stands, as it were, in the centre of a web of activity, one hand, metaphorically, on the client's shoulder.

We divided this activity into its component parts. First, administrative work; then information work, which included giving, gathering, checking, and exchanging information. This shaded into giving advice, which in turn was interlinked to negotiation, not only between the two sides but internally between solicitor and client, and also other third parties. This contact with third parties was not confined to negotiation, but embraced the seeking of advice, and other activity of direct benefit to the client, which shades into the provision of support and help.

We can therefore suggest the following adaptation of Lewis and Abel's typology of what lawyers do in the context in which we observed them:

1. Help to achieve change in legal status.
2. Help with the redistribution of resources in an equitable manner.
3. Help the transformation of one household into two bearing in mind both the welfare of any children involved, and the impact on the public purse.

These tasks are accomplished by:

1. Providing knowledge about potential adjudication and the practical experiences of others so that clients can plan ahead, perhaps needing to transform their objectives in line with what is possible both legally and practically.
2. Facilitating contact with third parties such as banks, utilities, and creditors.
3. Constructing narratives from the chaos of events and acts.
4. Speaking for the client, marshalling arguments and being unemotional in negotiation.
5. Offering support and guidance, both emotional and practical.
6. Carrying out formal acts.

5

Solicitor and Client: Support and Negotiation

W E CLOSED THE previous chapter by listing the kinds of tasks which our observational data showed that solicitors perform in assisting for their clients a change in legal status, redistribution of resources in an equitable manner and effecting a transformation of one household into two. These tasks involved providing knowledge, facilitating contact with third parties, constructing narratives, speaking for the client in negotiation, offering emotional and practical support and guidance and carrying out formal acts. This chapter now turns to our case studies to examine two major themes which emerge from these tasks. The first is the provision of *support* for the client, through reassurance, advice and sometimes practical action. The second is more complex. It relates to the representative role, where the solicitor plots a course of action for the client through the transition that is taking place. But the solicitor does not do this alone. It is achieved through a the process of *negotiation with the client*. The case studies confirmed that both of these functions were an essential key to understanding the way family lawyers deal with divorcing clients.

A SUPPORTING THE CLIENT

Reassurance

Of course most contact with clients takes place in the solicitor's office, but our cases threw up two examples of contact elsewhere. In one case, this was in a psychiatric ward (Case 104), and in another, at the client's home :

"It is difficult to bring four young children into the office". (100)

Such efforts enhance the feeling of reassurance which the solicitor can bring to a troubled client. The very fact of listening sympathetically to

a client might be counted as providing "emotional" support, and solicitors did occasionally see themselves as providing some kind of reassurance to people in emotional turmoil, even if it was only simply by
calming them down:

> "The husband had run off with a new women one week ago; a bolt from the
> blue. She was shell shocked . . . my advice was to take time; the mortgage
> would be paid by social security if you're on income support". (108)
> The wife "didn't know whether she was coming or going". (306)
> "Of course my client was spitting furiously . . . 'she can just fuck off if she
> wants the kids'. I'd calm him down and say: 'It's a bit short notice' ". (308)

Often merely outlining the legal position could provide reassurance,
and, as would be expected, this was commonly done:

> "They were both [eastern European] . . . she was very unsure what her rights
> were: I went through them with her . . . focusing on the fact that I thought
> the primary thing was where the children would live". (205)
> "He wanted advice on the processes of divorce as the wife was threatening
> to petition . . . also on finances". (301)
> "The wife wanted divorce and to know what would happen to the house and
> children". (304)
> "The wife didn't want divorce (though they were long separated) but wanted
> to safeguard her living in the house – the husband had stopped paying the
> mortgage". (307)
> "On first contact, the husband wanted advice on how secure the residence
> arrangement was". (308)
> "The wife wanted advice on divorce, and also on the housing situation –
> could she return to jointly owned matrimonial home?". (309)
> "The husband, who had left home, wanted to know how quickly he could
> get divorced – and what he could take out of the marriage". (311)

Practical support

Frequently, however, the support given was of a directly practical
nature. Although violence had been in the background in at least six of
our forty cases, we had only one case where the client initially came to
the lawyer to seek protection from physical abuse, and this was as
much to find out how the husband could be prevented from "snatch-
ing" away the child as for personal protection (Case 112), and in
another the issue of harassment arose after initial contact (Case 304).
In both cases legal measures were taken or threatened. We will have
more to say on the question of violence later (below, p. 85).

In some other cases the advice directly concerned the children:

"I think it was I who suggested the boy have therapy". (204)
In a case where the child was disturbed, the solicitor advised the wife "to use her contacts with school governors and to keep her GP informed so that if necessary they could obtain a medical report". (319)

Not surprisingly, however, the client's immediate worries will be financial, so the solicitor may check with the bank to see whether a joint account needed protecting (Case 100), or advise the client himself or herself to take protective action. Solicitors did not see themselves as financial advisers in the technical sense. In complex matters they would prefer to recommend that the client should seek specialist advice. But they were very ready to offer practical advice on how to get a grip on the household economy, ride out the crisis and prepare for longer-term solutions:

"The first thing is to advise clients to be in touch with people who may not be being paid, saying what has happened. My experience is that banks, mortgagees, gas board, everyone you can think of, is very much more sympathetic to the plight of divorce than people think and therefore if they're approached . . . they are very sympathetic: what causes the problem is if people don't contact them". (203)
On the solicitor's advice, the wife was investigating alternative housing – she looked at part-buy, part-rent schemes. She went to the housing association. The solicitor had suggested she do these things. "If I did everything her legal aid bill would be astronomical, so I said to her it's best if she did some. And she was able to do it, she just needed guidance on where to go". (302)
The solicitor wrote to the XY building society about the wife's interests, but as the mortgage was in his name, they said it had nothing to do with her. (307)
The solicitor sent the wife to seek independent financial advice. "I'm concerned about her poor pension position. She hasn't really told me what it is, except that it's poor. Also, I'm not sure whether we should gear the settlement so that she gets some money now which she can invest in a pension or annuity or whatever, or whether we might say . . . well, you live in the house and we can sell it in a few years and we'll get a larger sum then". (312)
The solicitor advised the wife to contact the DSS and YZ building society about taking on an interest-only repayment of the mortgage on the matrimonial home. She did so. (317)

This advice could extend to how to make ends meet in a situation where income had suddenly become very uncertain. Thus it might be necessary for the client to have a clear idea of expenditures, not only as a matter of prudent management, but to lay the basis for a financial claim against the other party:

"I had a very nice trainee who literally sat down and did a budget for my client". (100)

"I had to give her a lot of practical advice . . . I think it came from me it was best to have a sum each month that she knew was hers rather than having him pay the bills. I explained that to her . . . she was very childlike . . .". (204)

"I went through all her monthly out-goings with her, and what money she had coming in". (302)

At the end of the first meeting, the solicitor sent the client away with a list with three items on it: income, assets and expenditure. "That's a very useful exercise for her – she sees what she needs, and also for me. It's a very good cornerstone, starting point . . . what she needs for herself". (319)

In some cases it turned out that there were many other issues on which the client needed advice and assistance. For example, in a case which presented initially as merely being about contact, the client appeared very vulnerable:

"She was very dependent . . . she really needed to have her thinking done for her to some extent". (306)

"The client was not very assertive – I thought at the beginning she needed a huge amount of advice on inter-related matters because she didn't have any knowledge of the system here – housing, immigration, benefits, all sorts of things – the way the police might operate if he did take the child". (313)

Wives were mostly the beneficiaries of such practical assistance, since they were more likely to have found themselves in circumstances of crisis following a separation. But a husband could also be given practical advice which would protect his position:

"I asked him to do a budget for himself for his monthly incomings and out-goings, and a budget for her (his wife) and then compare the two. Because that's all that happens when you go to court". (311)

The solicitor advised the husband not to pay anything more into a joint savings account because the wife was living off it and (apparently) spending heavily. (322)

These examples show how advice merges into assistance. But frequently the assistance took the form of practical action by solicitors themselves. One, for example, searched the companies register to keep track on the husband's financial activities (Case 100); another organised the valuation of the property and ascertained the value of endowment policies, something that that solicitor always did for legally aided clients (Case 304). Checking on a husband's assets, by contacting pension companies (Case 314) or obtaining other forms of documentary evidence (Case 316) was common.

Such actions by solicitors of course add to costs, and solicitors showed themselves to be aware of this by recommending actions which the clients could undertake themselves:

> "If the client is confident, they can write letters themselves . . . it saves costs. . . if not, I write the letters; it depends on the individual; it's just a question of judgement". (203)
>
> "If I did everything her legal aid bill would be astronomical, so I said to her it's best if she did some". (302)

These activities were not only undertaken to try to obtain information about the other party which might be of use to the client. Solicitors for husbands often instigated inquiries with the object of ascertaining the extent of a husband's wealth, so they could know what kind of offer it would be reasonable for their client to make.

> The solicitor contacted pension companies to check up on information about client's (husband's) personal pensions. (314)
>
> The solicitor had extensive correspondence with estate agent over value of house which was owned by client (husband) so as to be aware what he might have to offer the wife; and similarly with the husband's accountants, to establish the value of the business in case the wife sought more capital. (318)
>
> "I felt initially that he wasn't being very straight. However, that's corrected itself because I've written to the various institutions now anyway, and they've confirmed to me what the position is. I always check anyway, because when it comes to the disclosure stage, we've got to have the information at hand". (322)

Violence

The term "violence" seems straightforward enough, suggesting physical assault, but within a domestic context may be taken to encompass a range of intimidatory behaviour. It is for that reason that the expression "molestation" is left undefined in the Family Law Act 1996 in the context of the provisions for granting non-molestation orders. The detection of violence or intimidation in domestic circumstances may be made more difficult by the apparent fact that "victims of violence frequently minimize the severity of violence against them, especially in professional/client encounters".[1] Thus Greatbatch and Dingwall have produced evidence that, when the topic is hinted at in mediation, mediators (and the victims) tend to minimise it.[2] We read our data as suggesting that this might also occur when the issue is touched on with lawyers. In one case this was very clear:

> "The husband was behaving very aggressively though actual violence was never mentioned. She didn't instruct me that there had been actual violence, although my suspicion was that she was understating it because she was firstly wanting to be conciliatory in her approach to him, and secondly I got the impression that she was scared maybe to go the whole hog and say it was happening for fear it would escalate further". (305)

The solicitors, too, appeared to try to "play down" suggestions of violence which sometimes surfaced, even if perpetrated by the "other side", suggesting that it was just "verbal abuse", or a "one-off" incident. They seemed unwilling to encourage the escalation of the conflict by, for example, resorting to special protective measure unless this was clearly needed. What they did recognise, however, was the atmosphere in which such events occurred, and in five cases referred to the husband as being "bullying" or "domineering". In such cases their reassurance of the wife about her legal rights, and practical advice, acted as a counterweight to the husband's dominance. A good example is provided in Case 302:

> "[After the husband's solicitors had suggested reconciliation be attempted] I consulted my client but she was certain that this [petitioning for divorce] was what she wanted to do. She felt that he had dominated her life for so long, that this was one thing she could take control of and do. She'd been depressed and wanted to take control of her life, and she felt that was the reason she was feeling like this". (302)

This could prepare the ground for a couple who were living together to separate, thus immediately reducing the tension. But sometimes the lawyer intervened more actively:

> "Things had got worse; she was crying on the phone; there had been a real deterioration. She was talking about an injunction, and the children were affected. So we wrote to him saying how difficult things were and that she would make an application to the court, which would consider the balance

[1] David Greatbatch and Robert Dingwall, "The Marginalization of Domestic Violence in Divorce Mediation" (1999) 13 *International Journal of Law, Policy and the Family* 174.
[2] Ibid.

of harm. His response was to phone and say he was moving out, and he did".
(113)

In another case (Case 106), the solicitor said:

"I did have to write one or two letters saying: don't come into the house and
lose your temper and push people around",

but immediately downplayed it by saying:

"I suppose that is domestic violence . . . but it was to do with the situation
. . . tempers were spilling over following the breakup". (106)

Various attempts at mediation were made, without success. Problems
still existed over contact but, as a result of separating that issue from
finances, the latter had been settled relatively amicably.

In Case 305, mentioned above, the solicitor, at the wife's request,
wrote a letter to the husband asking him to "review" his attitude to the
marriage. The letter referred to unjustified aggression and belligerence,
but not to actual violence. Not hearing anything for a couple of
months, the lawyer wrote to the wife, asking if the file should be kept
open. She made an appointment, then cancelled it. A further letter was
written three months later, and the wife replied saying she was reflect-
ing on the position. A year after her first visit she returned to the solicitor, the husband having left, and initiated divorce proceedings. While
we cannot be sure whether the solicitor's letter helped to extend the life
of this marriage by a year, it was a case in which the wife had used her
visit to the lawyer partly as a means of trying to get the husband to
mend his ways (as she saw it) but also to fortify her position. The case
eventually revolved around a contact problem, which was resolved by
consent.

In other cases more substantial steps were taken. In Case 112, the
wife came to the solicitor "in quite a state" after a serious violent incident when the husband snatched a child on a contact visit. The lawyer
spoke about the mechanisms for protection, (again minimising the
issue), and indeed gave advice about the whole financial position, but
the "wife did not wish to rush into anything". The lawyer urged discussion between the parties, but at the same time wrote a letter to the
husband "warning him off" and asking him to stay away from her.
Later each side made undertakings not to visit the other at their place
of work. Another warning letter was sent following a further incident,
and finally there were proceedings at which he gave undertakings not
to return to or attempt to enter the home for six months. This had

maintained the peace, and contact was in the process of being sorted out with the help of a court welfare officer. In Case 304 the wife, after initially seeking advice about divorce, came back four months later inquiring about an injunction after an incident to which the police had been called. However, legal aid was refused because the wife had refused to press charges. Violence did not arise although the case took a long time to settle because the husband was very reluctant to make disclosure. (See below, p. 163).

Case 313 shows another way in which the solicitor provided security for the client. This middle-eastern woman complained of aggression and threats by the husband, and, while willing to allow him contact with the three-year-old child, was unwilling for this to be unsupervised because she feared he would remove the child from the country. After a good deal of negotiation, the court made an uncontested residence and prohibited steps order, which effectively required the husband to return the child after each visit. It may be argued that such an outcome should have been reached without judicial intervention, but the lawyer tried hard to achieve this. The husband appeared to regard entering into such an agreement as an assault on his authority, but on the other hand did not contest the order, which seems to have provided the security the wife desired.

B NEGOTIATING A POSITION

The case studies therefore confirmed the observational data as to the way in which solicitors used the experience and information available to them to help the client properly evaluate her or his circumstances, secure as far as possible the client's immediate needs and those of the children concerned, and plan sensibly for the future. That future will usually involve coming to some accommodation with the other party. Before dealing with that party, we found solicitors having to agree with the client how to approach this task. This standardly gave rise to a process which could be described as negotiation between the solicitor and the client.

Separation, and divorce, do of course have long-term consequences, and it is almost inevitable that the terms upon which the parties arrange matters between them will raise conflicts of interest. Our key concern was to throw light on how solicitors handle, and resolve, these conflicts. While much attention has recently been given to the importance of the parties reaching agreement over these matters, partly to avoid protracted conflict, which is regarded as psychologically damaging to themselves and any children, the forces which determine outcomes are little understood. In this section we will focus on the interaction between solicitor and client which leads to the adoption of a *position*. This position is the preferred outcome for the client as represented by the solicitor. It may not be the final outcome, which will follow either from negotiation with the other party or decision by the court. The way that position is reached is the subject of this section. It involves a series of decisions by the solicitor which result from interaction with the client and which involve a number of elements. We call this the *decisional matrix*. One constituent element is the interests of the parties (which may include, by proxy, the interests of other persons, such as children, for whom they have responsibility). Crudely, it would normally comprise receiving more rather than less of the material resources available to both parties, and either having care of the child or having more rather than less contact with the child. But of course the concept is more complex than that, for matters other than the material interests of the parties are at stake. Nevertheless, with due acknowledgement of that fact, one might reasonably see the parties' interests as largely revolving around such material considerations. The law also provides norms, albeit of a rather general character, according to which these interests are reconstituted within an agreement. These norms therefore confer entitlements, and these entitlements are not necessarily identical with the parties' interests (as conceived above). It is these entitlements of their clients which solicitors have a primary duty to safeguard.

Yet lawyers are often perceived to aggravate conflict by identifying themselves too closely with their clients' interests. Richard Tur, for example, writes: "In the ordinary run of cases, where lawyers zealously pursue the conflicting interests of their clients, very considerable costs may be run up without either lawyer deserving reproof. Indeed, each lawyer could point to a professional ethical duty zealously to pursue the interests of each client".[3] At the same time, lawyers are said to be too detached from their clients; that they take over the negotiations and

---

[3] "Family Lawyering and Legal Ethics" in Stephen Parker and Charles Sampford (eds), *Legal Ethics and Legal Practice: Contemporary Issues* (Clarendon Press, Oxford, 1995), p. 150.

produce "their" solution rather than that of the clients. Davis et al.[4] write that "... we observed legal representatives in alliance, not *against* their clients but rather in seeking a solution to various problems presented *by* their clients", and Ingleby[5] refers to the "notion", which he dubs a "myth", that "solicitors sell out their clients and force them to accept solutions against their interests in an effort to maintain their relationships with their colleagues and the courts". There is clearly a contradiction between these two representations of characteristic lawyer behaviour, and, though we cannot account for the behaviour of all lawyers, our data supports the view that the position eventually adopted is the outcome of a complex process of negotiation between solicitor and client. There are three key elements to this negotiation: the lawyer's perception of the client's interests, the normative standards set by the law (and also perceived ethical behaviour) and the expression of client autonomy as revealed in the client's instructions.

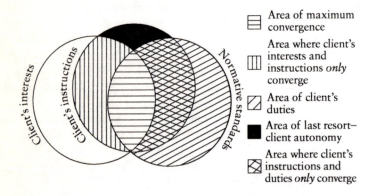

Area of maximum convergence

Area where client's interests and instructions *only* converge

Area of client's duties

Area of last resort– client autonomy

Area where client's instructions and duties *only* converge

Figure 5.1 The Decisional Matrix

Figure 5.1 shows how the client's interests, normative standards and the client's instructions may diverge and converge in the decisional matrix. In the complex fact situations of actual cases, we see lawyers paying attention to all three factors. The ideal negotiating strategy

[4] Gwynn Davis, Stephen Cretney and Jean Collins, *Simple Quarrels: Negotiating Money and Property Disputes on Divorce* (Clarendon Press, Oxford, 1994), p. 216.

[5] Richard Ingleby, *Solicitors and Divorce* (Clarendon Press, Oxford, 1992), p. 11.

seeks the convergence of all three of them, so the outcome corresponds to the "area of maximum convergence" indicated in the figure. There is also an area where the normative standards are at variance with the client's interests (the "area of the client's duties"), and we will see that in those cases the solicitors endeavour to align this as far as possible with their client's instructions. Situations also arise, however, where instructions coincide neither with the normative standards nor with the client's interests. In this "area of last resort", solicitors reluctantly accept that the client's instructions must ultimately prevail. The analysis which follows explains the working of this model.

The client's interests

On the whole, in the case of women clients, their interests and legal entitlements coincided. This was because they were generally in the position of claimants, seeking resources from their former husbands, and the law supported those claims. The difficulty for the solicitors tended to arise with regard to the third factor: the client's instructions. Did the women really want these claims to be pursued? One solicitor summed it up graphically:

> "I had to work very hard to persuade her to instruct me to pursue her interests at all". (306)

We will return to the issue of client autonomy later, for the first issue was sometimes to get wives to understand what their interests were. So, in one case where a husband had made an initial offer after mediation:

> "she came back thinking it was a good idea because she had no idea about finances – I said, no way: I certainly wouldn't be advising her to do it". "I had to sit her down and explain what she was going to do with the money. Within a year the £14,000 would go and she needed to be staying in the house". "She was so concerned to have the children she was looking to accept whatever he was offering". "So she went away and found out that there was no way she could survive on just taking £14,000 . . . so she understood at that stage why I was saying this isn't reasonable". [she eventually got the house with a 30 per cent charge back]. (302)

Another solicitor said:

> "Initially, all the client knew was that she wanted to stay in the matrimonial home with the children. But when the husband started pressuring the wife into agreeing that the matrimonial home be sold, and the proceeds split 50:50, she agreed to his proposals, despite my advice that they should aim to secure the matrimonial home for her and transfer the property to her sole name. I . . . pointed out the unfairness of the husband's proposals, the likelihood that she would not be able to buy somewhere decent with her share of the equity, the need to provide a secure base for her sons until they were ready to leave home and so on." [After the solicitor had asked her to reflect on these matters (and on hearing news the husband had moved in with his new girlfriend) she accepted the advice to reject the husband's proposals, and re-stating clearly in correspondence to the solicitor that the matrimonial home "was not just 'bricks and mortar' but a 'home' to her and the boys and she wanted to stay there": [this was achieved eventually in a Consent Order]. (317)

It should not be thought, however, that it was always wives who appeared to fail to perceive their interests in the early stages after separation. In one case a wife had demanded all the proceeds from the sale of the house. The solicitor commented that he told the husband it was

> "daylight robbery, but it's up to him". "He wasn't sure, because at that point he was still feeling terribly guilty, and when they're feeling guilty they'll agree to things they wouldn't agree to four months hence. But the guilt factor doesn't last very long – that's reality" [they ultimately agreed a 75/25 split] (311).[6]

Sometimes, of course, the clients' failure to appreciate their interests followed from lack of legal expertise. So in one case a husband, without legal advice, had given the wife £12,000. The solicitor drew up a document stating this was to be in full and final settlement, and had this incorporated in a Consent Order (Case 314). But while it is true that some clients did not fully appreciate what was in their interests, it was more usual for them to fail to appreciate their legal entitlements.

The clients' entitlements and duties (normative standards)

We would say that the theme of failure of clients to appreciate their entitlements arose so frequently that it was a pervasive feature of our

---

[6] Another solicitor remarked on the "guilt" factor in respect to men: (110).

case study data. Usually it involved the solicitors giving assurance to women that there was a good chance that they would be able to remain living in the home. This was also a feature of our observational data. Ignorance of entitlements, coupled sometimes with powerful (inaccurate) representations by husbands, was perhaps most striking in cases involving individuals who had recently immigrated to this country who had not assimilated the apparently more egalitarian gender norms prevailing here, but could occur in any context:

> At this early stage, the solicitor advised the wife that she was entitled to more than she was proposing to claim and advised she could include assets accumulated pre-marriage during cohabitation. "She did well. She got £37,000 more than her first plan". (106)
> The wife had thought the husband's representation of his entitlements was correct. "This worried her; we could reassure her on this; the family should remain intact in that home". (108)
> "(The husband) had expressed that he was keen to sell the marital home, and the client wanted reassurance on this". (109)
> [The husband had demanded £9,000 to leave home]: "I made it clear to her that she did not have to pay him for him to go" [the husband subsequently left under threat of an exclusion order; now he had gone, things improved and they were more likely to sort it out themselves]. (113)
> [The solicitor summarised her role]: "Trying to get her to realise what she could claim for . . . making her realise that she wouldn't agree to anything without coming back to me. Making it clear that actually she had a very good claim. . .". (205)
> "She wanted to settle, she wanted him out of the house, and she just wanted it all sorted. She seemed to think she would only get what the husband would give her. I was saying: 'that's not actually how it works' ". (306)

In the case of male clients, the task of bringing their interests into closer alignment with legal norms usually involved lowering their expectations so as to try to acquire instructions which coincided with the result. This sometimes worked:

> "I was saying to him, really throughout, given the level of equity in the property and other assets, £60,000 might have been a little high at the outset, but as other bits of information came through, £50–60,000 wasn't going to be a bad settlement". "I remember time and time again saying to him, I know how you feel about her being the one that's in the wrong, but it's going to make absolutely no difference whatsoever, and you are going to have to raise capital to pay her off". (301)
> "The husband's initial position was: 'she left me and the kids – how dare she

come back and ask for money'. But I talked him out of that one". "There was a slight degree of arm-twisting". (308)

"I think that sometimes they come with this view that they're joint owners – they're going to get 50% of the house. That's often how men think. So you have to break the news to them, early on, that it's not going to be that way". "He wanted to stop paying money to the house altogether. I advised him that would be a daft thing to do because the first thing she'd do is charge to court and get a maintenance order". (311)

The solicitor advised compromise and the husband agreed to accept £4,000 plus the car rather than the £10,000 plus the car, which he had wanted. (315)

"He wasn't being realistic . . . I said that at the end of the day, it's going to be an off-setting arrangement; you're either going to have more of this, or less of this. If you want to keep your pension, you're going to have to give her more of a lump sum in compensation for that . . . he didn't like it at first, but he's gradually coming round to the fact that you've got to be realistic. . . . You cannot possibly expect to run off with the equity in the house, and keep your pension (9/10 year marriage)". (322)

Yet solicitors had to manoeuvre the advice in such a way that it aligned with the requirement of client autonomy. We have already noted the solicitor who commented that he had to "work very hard to get her to instruct me to pursue her interests at all" (Case 306), suggesting the presence of a good deal of pressure being exerted on the client. Others seemed equally robust. In one case the wife brought a draft separation deed which the husband had asked the wife to sign:

"surprise, surprise, [it] was very weighted in his favour . . . she brought it along to me and I said – bin it, we can't have this. It's patently unfair". (319)

But, as we have also seen (Case 317), the solicitor, after explaining the situation, may ask the wife to go away and reflect on the advice. On other occasions, the wife might push the solicitor hard before accepting the advice:

"She wouldn't accept advice lying down – she was not the sort of client where you could say – 'Do this, and it will be alright'. She would ask questions. She was never reluctant to accept advice, but wanted it confirmed and would speak at length". (320)

There were other cases where the solicitor took the back seat. The parties essentially dealt with the matter themselves, and the solicitor provided *ex post* oversight:

The solicitor initially thought she was being rather generous giving him half the house as, on the face of it, it had been a gift from her parents; but once the wife had explained the financial history, the proposed arrangement did seem fair and so he did not advise against it. (303)

The solicitor didn't push her into anything she didn't want to do. For example, she estimated half the equity in the house was £20,000 and this was what she was asking for. The solicitor mentioned the endowment policy and his pension, but she stuck to £20,000 and he didn't push her. His feeling was it was better to stick to an offer which was something the husband might agree to, rather than asking for more and having to go to court; even if they won, the legal costs/statutory charge may reduce the wife's overall result to less than £20,000". (304)

The solicitor warned the husband that as he didn't give her full disclosure she couldn't advise whether his offer to the wife was equitable as far as he was concerned, but she felt it was, and did not advise against it. (310)

The client's instructions: client autonomy in the decisional matrix

But in other cases, the client ignored the solicitor's advice. Mostly this was because the client was prepared to accept an outcome less than their entitlements would indicate; this might nevertheless be in the client's interests (the "area where instructions and interests only coincide" in Figure 5.1), but might even be outside the client's apparent interests (the "area of last resort in Figure 5.1). The category into which a given outcome falls depends of course on how the clients' interests are determined. In any event, the client's decision will prevail.

One might have thought that men are more prone to resist solicitors' advice than women, and our data supports this. Of the thirty-one cases involving female clients, eight (25.8 per cent) gave clear examples of such resistance whereas half of the twelve cases involving men furnished such examples. The reasons for women ignoring advice tended to be that they wished to bring the matter to a close:

"Maybe she could have done better if we had gone for more information on his Form E. She didn't want to . . . because she didn't want to prolong it .. she wanted to be settled . . . and because her priority was having a place to live in the short term while she was studying. She was happy with an order which gave her the house". (205: legally aided client)

The wife quite often disregarded advice – e.g. paying mortgage when he defaulted, and paying the husband. £2,000; "He's about 6 foot 4 and she's about 5 foot nothing. She gets quite emotional; it doesn't take much before he bullies her. So I don't think she necessarily does it to go against my advice, but just because she wants a quiet life and to get rid of him". (307: legally aided client)

"I would have applied for a Prohibited Steps Order earlier. But she was reluctant to do so. She was reluctant to be involved in court proceedings, until she felt much more frightened after she was actually divorced" [the fear was that the husband would abduct the child]. (313: legally aided client)

The solicitor advised the wife to delay application for decree absolute until the finances had been agreed. "However, she wanted to do so and we did". (317: legally aided client)

Husbands, however, tended to disregard advice that they should settle, or at least adopt postures which might make settlement easier:

"At the end of the day he ended up having to pay more and her costs, which was a shame because if he'd taken our advice, we would probably have settled it because we'd got to the stage where we were talking £50–55,000 on the pre-trial review . . . but the client was saying: 'No, I'm not prepared to go that high'. . .". "I very rarely go for pre-trial reviews, but I did in this case because he wasn't listening to me". "I tend to find that a lot of male clients are very much like that. You're banging your head against a brick wall because you know they're going to have to pay. And they won't hear it from you. So you end up saying 'Well, let's try and get round it this way, and try to persuade them that you should offer half of what I think you should, which is still more than you want to offer . . . Then you end up putting in a low proposal – what can you do, really?". (301: private client)

"The without prejudice offer made before the FDR was against my advice. It was far too low in my opinion. And I told him that, but he said 'well, let's have a go' . . . we were pissing in the wind. It was just bollocks. It was against my advice, but there you go. There's nothing you can do about that. He said, put it in and I put it in". (308: legally aided client)

The solicitor's advice was throughout: "Is it worth the cost of this to recover £10,000?." His answer was "I feel very peeved about it and want it back". The solicitor talked about principles being very expensive, "but he was adamant he wanted it back". (315: private client)

"The suggestion was that we offer £15,000. The client was not prepared to pay more than £5,000. Unfortunately, despite our efforts, he refused to let any letters go out saying we'll give you £15,000 . . . so to some extent, whenever we were trying to negotiate with the other side, we did have one hand tied behind our back": "we thought he was being quite unreasonable in the way that he was conducting himself, but we had to follow his instructions" [they eventually settled at £11,000 plus increased child support]. (318: private client)

In one case the husband's attitude seemed to work directly against his interests:

"He's got a real thing about getting his golf clubs back, because he's going on a golfing holiday. He's asking me to write to the wife saying I want them back, and then in the same letter saying we cannot afford to keep the children in school, and all the rest of it. So of course the other side write back and say, if your client can afford a golfing holiday, he can afford to keep the children in school. So it kind of weakens our position, but those are my instructions and if he wants me to ask those, then he's entitled to". (322: private client)

But lest one becomes tempted into constructing stereotypes, two wives showed greater appetite for combat than their solicitors, in each case resulting in higher awards for themselves:

The client resisted signing a Consent Order, against advice, although she had already agreed its terms. In the end she renegotiated a better deal. (316: legally aided client).

After the district judge had indicated that the wife should accept the husband's disclosure as full and frank, the solicitor advised the wife to go away and consider three options: (i) to settle on this basis, (ii) to try to get more disclosure, or (iii) to go "hell for leather" and get third parties to probe the assets. The solicitor warned of the danger of fighting further – "the issue of legal costs, and the risk you run if the court finds against you . . . one must endeavour as far as possible to achieve a balance between the need to ensure that one has obtained full disclosure on the one hand, and the legal costs and the risks of litigation on the other. It is for you to make the decision how far we go". Here the wife, having spoken to her mother, opted to "fight all the way" [settlement was eventually reached just before hearing, with substantially increased benefit to wife; it had nearly collapsed because the wife insisted that her solicitor should do the conveyancing of the home, contrary to the husband's wishes; the solicitor suggested a third party should do it, but eventually the husband "caved in"]. (319: private client)

In another case, the husband, who wanted to have the house sold, resisted advice to put pressure on the wife because he thought this would disturb the children, who were taking examinations:

Letting proceedings drift "was against advice in as much as I was telling him how he could bring it to a head. And I think he was more generous than perhaps he needed to be in one sense, but on the other hand, if you look at it through his eyes, he had a different agenda which was he wanted his children to do well, and he didn't want to make life difficult. And that's perfectly valid. It's not for me to say how he should weigh up these things. All I was telling him throughout was 'If you want to bring it to a head, you've got to be hard and firm and we've actually got to be a bit more, not aggressive, but we've actually for to do something' " (e.g. applying for some directions in the Ancillary Relief proceedings, or petition for divorce). (314: private client)

What this analysis shows is that lawyers rapidly seek to align their client's expectations and perceptions of their interests with what the lawyer believes to be their entitlement, in terms either of legal doctrine or what they believe a court would decide, with the object of obtaining instructions which were consistent with these. One lawyer put it like this:

"You don't say – we're going to do it this way. It's up to them to give you instructions. You give them the information and hope they understand it". (311: private client)

Something of the flavour of the "private client" cases which we described in the previous chapter comes across in those quotations: where the private client in fact dictates the course of action to be followed. However, the case studies show that in legally aided cases as well, clients could sometimes have the same effect. Case 316 is a good example. In this case the husband's bankruptcy greatly complicated the issue. But when the wife came to see the solicitor, "she was fairly clear about what she wanted to achieve; and wanted advice about how to achieve it. She wanted the boys living with her and she wanted to stay in the house". The deal however involved sale of the house, and the wife agreed to a 82 per cent share in the proceeds of an immediate sale, which was incorporated in a draft Consent Order. But then she found that would not be sufficient to finance a satisfactory alternative home, and she refused to sign the order. Although the solicitor told her it was too late to renege, the wife was adamant and won an important delay in the sale. However, it may be relevant that she was dealing with the husband's trustee-in-bankruptcy rather than the husband himself. In general, legally aided clients seemed more inclined to go for settlement against the better judgment of their solicitors than private ones, at least in the sample above, which may reflect the fact that many of them were women clients who perceived their interests more broadly than in material terms This contradicts perceptions that legally aided clients might be more inclined than private clients to spin things out since they lack financial incentives to settle. Indeed Davis et al, who noted that legally aided cases were less likely to settle than private client cases, do not offer the "incentive" reason for their result, but suggest it arose from the nature of legal aid cases. We will return to the issue later (p. 169).

But while the case studies provided some support for the deduction from our observational data that private clients are more likely to control, or attempt to control, the agenda than legally aided clients, ultimately in all cases the solicitor can only act as the agent of the client. The solicitor's task then becomes one of bringing the element representing the client's autonomy into line with the other two elements. Solicitors often achieve this; but where they do not, the client's decision will prevail. This is inherent in the solicitor-client relationship, though it can, as we have described, lead to considerable frustration for the lawyers, though, as we also saw, on occasion the client's determination led to a more favourable establishment of the client's entitlements than the solicitor had envisaged. In a society which values individual autonomy, this must remain the client's prerogative.

It will be observed that we have expressed the normative standards in terms of entitlements rather than duties or responsibilities, although normative standards clearly include both rights and duties. This is clear from Figure 5.1 which shows that the applicable normative standards do not always coincide with the client's interests. In such a case, the client is under certain duties (the "area of client's duties" in Figure 5.1). It will be the lawyer's task to align the client's instructions as far as possible with those duties. Yet the lawyers' language did seem to employ a rhetoric which was cast in terms of the client's entitlements rather than their duties. This might be partly because, as stated earlier, they were more commonly engaged in raising the expectations of female clients than in lowering the expectations of husbands. Yet even when they were curbing some of the hopes of the husbands, they did this more on the basis that these hopes were unrealistic rather than by emphasising the legal duties the men owed to their families. It was more a question of "you won't get away with this", rather than, "you ought to do that". This must at least partly be because clients would feel that they are not paying a solicitor to be preached at about their duties, but also may have something to do with the fact that the solicitor initially focuses on the client's interests (as defined above) and these may frequently diverge sharply from (his) duties. The result is to try to find out how far the client can "get away with" minimising his duties.

One possible explanation for this approach could be that it is a result of the traditional structure of English family law, which (in contrast to civilian systems) has been reluctant to spell out familial duties in general terms, preferring instead to create procedures for the making of claims. The concept of parental responsibility introduced in the Children Act 1989 was thought to be a significant departure from this, but that concept is highly complex, and in any case is rarely relevant in matters of finance and property. The new child support legislation is also heavily weighted by the language of duty. But child support seems rarely to be an issue with the solicitors in divorce cases, either because it is not contested, or because it is left to the Child Support Agency. If it was clearer what the objectives of the "ancillary" jurisdiction were, it might become more natural for lawyers to cast their advice more in terms of their client's duties, and when the issue of occupation of the matrimonial home by the children is in issue we imagine that solicitors must sometimes put it to their clients that it is really their duty to ensure that their children, and their carer, has a home. However, we saw little evidence of it. We did find one example where a solicitor did something like that. The husband was seeking a clean break after the end of a fifteen year marriage with children aged thirteen and eleven. At one point the husband's solicitor considered "loading the maintenance on to the children" as a way of reconciling the wife's claim with the husband's wishes (Case 103).

Nevertheless, we would argue that the emphasis which lawyers place on their clients' interests and entitlements is inherent in the solicitor-client relationship. Solicitors do not see their task as being to teach their clients how to behave. That forms no part of the negotiation between them. Rather, the negotiation is over the best way to secure the client's interests given the parameters set by the decisional matrix described above. This marks the role of solicitors as being very different from that envisaged by the Government for the information meetings under the Family Law Act 1996. The goals of these meetings have been stated as being to concentrate on "information which would help parties to consider whether their marriage is really finally over"; "marriage support services available to help"; "help for the survivors of, or those fearful of, domestic violence"; "the decisions which have to be made, the consequences which have to be faced, and the impact of divorce on families, especially children, if the decision to divorce is finally taken". They would also encourage couples to meet a marriage counsellor, and "explain the helpfulness of mediation".[7] The general ethos of the information meeting is to make intending divorcees "face

---

[7] *Supporting Families* (1998), paras. 4.31–33.

up" to the consequences of such an action, especially on the children. The emphasis is therefore placed on responsibilities, not rights. That the orientation of the lawyer-client relationship is different is, we would argue, nothing less than what should be. It would be a disaster for civil liberties in general if lawyers were to become agents for transmitting to the clients the Government's view of what was "right" or "responsible" behaviour. Indeed, it is arguable that it is objectionable that governments should use the legal process at all in an attempt to instil one particular vision of what amounts to "responsible" family behaviour.

The primacy of the client's wishes thus circumscribes the ambit of the role of the lawyer. It also provides a condition precedent to effective representation at all. For while a lawyer can at any time provide legal advice, there are grave difficulties in representing a client unless that client gives some indication in which direction he or she wishes to go. Some clients have expressed frustration that the lawyer doesn't tell them what to do.[8] On the other hand, a lawyer will find it difficult to know what to do with an indecisive client. There were two such cases in our sample. In one, the parties had been separated for two years after a twenty-one-year marriage. The wife had moved out and was living rent-free in a house her parents bought for her. The complaint of the solicitor was that the wife didn't know what she wanted . . . "either in the financial settlement or in the rest of her life". The solicitor kept asking "we can do a number of things for you. But it would be really helpful to know what you want to do, what your medium and longer-term plans are, because unless I know I can't gear things to suit you. The wife just shrugs her shoulders and says 'I don't know what I want to do' " (Case 312). In the second case (Case 314) the client (the husband), wanted to have the house, occupied by him and wife, sold. However, he was unwilling to take the steps the solicitor considered were necessary to bring matters to a head because he thought this would disturb the children, who were taking examinations. Of course many would sympathise with the husband's position, as did the solicitor, but it did raise serious obstacles to the lawyer's role. In such situations the inevitable conflicts must be resolved by the clients, as, indeed, they were.

---

[8] See G. Douglas, M. Murch, A. Perry, K. Bader and M.Borkowski, *How parents cope financially on marriage breakdown*, Report to the Joseph Rowntree Foundation, November 1999, p. 40.

Children issues

The above analysis has centred on financial and property issues. King[9] has raised similar questions in relation to issues concerning the children. His suggestion is that in these cases solicitors reconcile their role as acting as representatives for the client with the predominance given to the welfare of the child in the modern law, especially after the Children Act 1989, by assuming an expertise in child welfare, or, at least, by using the rhetoric of child welfare, and in this way attempting to divert clients away from pursuing their self-interest and towards compromise. "Close observation of solicitors at work would be able we suggest, to unmask this feat of conjuring by catching sight of the almost imperceptible switching from one discourse or system of communication to another". This strategy might be somewhat different from the one described above where compromise over financial matters was represented as being in the *client's* interests, and solicitors did not appear to use the language of duty towards the other side as a means of aligning the client's wishes with the prevalent normative standards.

Our case studies certainly produced examples of solicitors wanting the parties to sort out contact issues themselves. We suggest later some reasons why they felt this was more appropriately done directly than through solicitors (below p. 112). No doubt solicitors would have said to their clients that it would be better for the children if court proceedings were avoided, in words such as: "I emphasise how much it is in the child's interests to deal with it (contact) between themselves" (Case 319), but they tended to use more inclusive language to us:

> "[I said] For God's sake sort it out without bringing it to court because it's so much better for everyone". (308)
>
> [The solicitor advised] it was better "for all concerned" to avoid court proceedings. (321)

In this way the lawyers could align the welfare of the child with the client's interests. In Case 321, where the wife was denying contact where the husband wanted it, but he was worried about the effects of his insistence of contact on the children, the solicitor actually went further in support of the (husband) client's position, saying he should not let the matter rest and should put his position in writing to his wife. He added

---

[9]   Michael King, " 'Being Sensible': Images and Practices of the New Family Lawyers" (1999) 28 *Journal of Social Policy* 249.

that "the children aren't necessarily the best judges of when they should be seeing you". But where they wanted the client to reduce his or her expectations, they sometimes referred to the likely attitude of the court:

> "He has a tendency to act on emotion rather than taking a step back and look at the situation, so I have to try and steer him in the right direction. He will say, for example, 'why should I take them and deliver them home?' And I will say, 'Look, at the end of the day, if we're in court, what do you think the judge would say – one parent take, one parent take back. Then he'll say, 'O yeah fine – we'll do it like that' ". (322)

> In a case where the wife wanted residence, but the divorce court welfare officer found against her, the solicitor discouraged a contest on the ground judges almost always follow the welfare officer, but counsel advised her to contest residence as a way of maximising contact. Something close to shared residence was agreed at door of court. (316)

Alternatively, the solicitor may appeal to the likely effect on the other party:

> [In discouraging the husband from going to the school to see the children]: 'well legally you can, but contact me and I'll make the necessary arrangements. Because common sense dictates it's going to cause problems'. (322)

Or the solicitor might refer to the fact that the children were old enough that it was not worth imposing the client's will on them.

> The solicitor advised that with children 11 and 14, "the kids are old enough for contact to be child driven" (308).

So while we do not say that solicitors do not appeal to their own, or to current notions of, the welfare of children, in advising client's on child-related matters, our sample tended to frame their advice in language which recognised the client's interests as well.

C SUPPORT IN ACTION

In order to demonstrate more vividly the way in which solicitors are able to offer support to their clients while they move them forward through a period of crisis in their lives, it would be helpful to give complete accounts of some cases. We have chosen two out of many which could illustrate this feature of the work of family law solicitors. We have chosen them because they illustrate how, in different ways, the solicitor is able to use the relationship for the benefit of the client in more ways than simply settling a dispute with the other party.

Case 1 The depressed wife (Case 111)

The case concerned began when Emily came to see our interviewee, Harry, in June, accompanied by her maternal aunt, saying she could no longer bear living with her husband (George) as he constantly taxed her about an earlier relationship of hers. She needed to be apart from him, but she had a child of two (William) and was pregnant with their second child. Harry was able to assert that, although there was a young child, it was unlikely that George would be ordered out of the house. He gave advice on benefits, the possibility and procedures of divorce, and financial matters. It was decided that she should move into her aunt's house, which was standing empty. Emily felt unable to communicate with George, and insisted that Harry write to him, saying that she felt the separation was permanent, and wanted to make arrangements for him to visit William. In addition, Harry raised the question of maintenance, and asked for various pieces of financial information from him, such as details of his current salary, benefits in kind, properties and charges on them, savings and so on. He also suggested that he should see a solicitor. George however had been taken completely by surprise, not realising the state the marriage was in. He wanted reconciliation and made contact with a counselling agency. The couple were now communicating only through Harry, who passed on the information about George's wish for reconciliation. Emily however now decided she wanted divorce. All this had happened within a fortnight from the first meeting between Emily and Harry. Within a further week contact had been sorted out, and Emily instructed Harry to prepare a divorce petition. She had now moved in with her parents, and was drawing income support. Harry observed that Emily's depression seemed now to have lifted; she was more positive. Moving away from George and asserting herself had apparently done her good. Harry therefore pressed on. The petition was issued in September. George had now availed himself of the suggestion that he should obtain legal advice, but had produced no documents of his financial position. He was in a small family business, and there were some investment properties. Harry felt the only way he could move forward was by issuing for ancillary relief, so he applied for legal aid. The position which Harry had negotiated with Emily was that, essentially, she wanted a home for herself and the children. But the financial waters were muddied by the fact that George's uncle had been assisting the couple in the payment of their (jointly-owned) house and George claimed this constituted a debt to his uncle. Harry was able to assure Emily that a court would put the housing needs of her and the children above any possible debt to the uncle, and that in any case the payments would probably be construed as a gift.

By September Harry still did not feel he had received sufficient information to conclude negotiations, and that only a court direction would lead to resolution. But now Emily was having doubts about whether to proceed; so Harry said: "no problem, put everything on hold". He even suggested withdrawing the petition from the special procedure list, but Emily said: "no". The decree nisi came through the next day! However, the couple were not speaking, and Emily was complaining that George was not seeing William. Harry advised that this was not a reason not to press on with the proceedings. Emily was finding it difficult living with her parents , and so they issued for ancillary relief proceedings. This was now October. They considered trying to remove George from the home by an exclusion order, but Emily's baby was now nearly due, so they held off this challenge as Harry thought that a court action would be too stressful for Emily at this stage. In the meantime Emily needed advice on a tax demand for investment income she had not received. In December an assessment for child support was completed, and the couple discussed a possible settlement, but the uncle was still demanding a share in the proceeds of sale of the house, which would have left too little for Emily to house herself. Harry insisted that they should disregard this alleged "debt", and they made a *Calderbank* offer accordingly, but when this did not receive a response, they sought directions for a hearing. It was now January and Emily, who now had had her new baby, wanted George to take more interest in the child and was becoming very anxious to sort things out. Harry was pressing for an early ancillary relief hearing, which he considered a better way of securing the house for Emily than an exclusion order. Under this pressure George came round to Emily's parents' house in early March and gave her the keys to the house. He was moving out. With Emily back in the house, negotiations for a final settlement continued, and by June they had reached an agreement acceptable to Emily and Harry. No sooner had this been attained when Harry received a telephone call from Emily's father who had gone round to Emily's house: "She's gone; he's done her in!". Harry suggested he go round to where George was living. There Emily opened the door. The couple were back together.

This case is not one in which it is easy to point to concrete "gains" by the solicitor's client. Indeed, no property was recovered, so there would be nothing from which the legal aid moneys to meet Harry's bill of £2,000 could be recovered. It might even be argued that this case should have been settled through counselling or mediation without ever involving lawyers. Harry, we would note, was not a member of the SFLA, though he did specialise in family law cases. But there is an alternative reading. The support of the solicitor, backed by the norms of family law, allowed Emily to withdraw from a position which she had found increasingly unsustainable, with some confidence that, in the long run, her own position and that of her young children could be protected. The case also illustrates a major difference between family law cases and most other legal work. Characteristically, people come to lawyers after an event has occurred; an accident, breach of contract or other occurrence which Genn describes as a "justiciable" event.[10] In family law cases, however, the lawyer is usually introduced at one point in an unfolding series of events, sometimes of quite dramatic character. In Case 111, as it turned out, the lawyer provided advice and assurance during a rapidly changing period in the relationship between Emily and George, when Emily was suffering the strains of looking after a two-year-old while pregnant with her next baby, exacerbated by conflicts involving the wider family. It is arguable that Harry should not have initiated divorce, or ancillary relief, proceedings quite so quickly when George was seeking a reconciliation. However, in view of Emily's clear attitude at that time that she wanted the divorce proceed, and was not even willing to talk to George, it is questionable whether counselling or mediation would have succeeded at that point. What Emily needed was, in the rather hackneyed current jargon, "empowerment" through the legal system. The solicitor provided this by keeping Emily's interests sharply in focus as he responded to the changing circumstances of this turbulent year. This gave a client who, in the solicitor's view, was basically quite capable but temporarily overborne by her circumstances, the confidence to assert these interests not only against George, but also against his uncle.

Case 2 Working with a psychiatric patient (Case 104)

The solicitor in this case, Janet, was a large, warm, motherly woman, working in a five partner firm spending all her time on family work of which two-thirds was legally aided. Her specialism was helping patients at the local psychiatric hospital. The client in this case, Mary, was in her mid forties with a history of depressive illness, who was then

[10] Genn, above p. 5

in hospital following a suicide attempt on learning of her husband's longstanding affair. Janet had first seen Mary in the hospital in September 1997. She wanted a divorce because of the deceit. Janet at this stage gave reassurance, "a lot empathising" but could not get financial details. Later she learned that the husband (Jack) earned £23,000 and had a surprisingly good company pension. Mary had not worked for a long time because of her illness. She had met a new "gentleman friend" in the hospital. The family home had negative equity. There was one adult daughter. Her family were pressing her to take the £2,000 the husband was offering as a clean break. Janet thought she should have ongoing maintenance because of her illness, the long marriage and the difference between the couple's earnings. We will recount the case largely in Janet's own words.

"The husband went to the daughter to put pressure on her... she was alcoholic, so a £2,000 lump sum would not help her. The husband now lives in the family home with his new partner and is in a hurry to divorce. There is no hurry for my client. Decree nisi is due 28 October 1998, but we needed a short hearing because he was refusing to pay the costs of the divorce, which were only £136. The client now lives in a rented flat, and he provided the deposit because we said if he did not she would have to move back to the family home. She is on housing benefit and has just got disablement living allowance at the third application. I have spoken to her key worker. We applied for interim maintenance. It was defended but the judge ordered £15 per week. He argued she was cohabiting . . . the stress for my client and her friend who is also ill was considerable. It didn't seem fair on them being cross-examined . . . the motivation was to put pressure on her to accept . . . it's a shame. Hopefully she will get what she deserves in the end". "She changes her mind . . . at one time I wrote to her saying this is my advice but if you want to accept the £2,000 do so . . . she didn't. Contents is a sticky issue. I tend not to get involved with it . . . that picture of Auntie Ethel . . . things just get silly . . . but I hope to get a few more bits for her flat. I hope it will settle. I'm having to question in my mind the advice he is being given. At the interim hearing the district judge herself said the offer was not realistic. I think that if she had about £6,000 or £7,000 and ongoing maintenance of £35 per week . . . like that, not extravagant . . . His pension . . . transfer value is £17,000, he has admitted to a lump sum of £37,000 plus £13,000 per year . . . and that is only half of it. When I get the information (I had to apply for a penal notice to the questions raised last August) I will see counsel about earmarking. I thought I was being thick about pensions, then I went on a course and found a lot of solicitors are unsure what they can and cannot do . . . I can't be a financial adviser, but I need that kind of knowledge. Pensions are difficult. Until I get used to it I don't want to be negligent, clients these days are very litigious. Her bill so far is £1,500, may go up to £2,000 if there is a full hearing. There may be a statutory charge if she receives capital". "I suggested mediation at the beginning as I do for everyone . . . but in this case I would have been anxious that there would have been unevenness in the discussion, she could lose her temper but she couldn't discuss or vocalise her needs as well as he could. I keep in touch with her GP and consultant. All this could have been stopped a long time ago. Clients ask me how much it will cost. I say it depends how silly everyone is".

Once again we see a solicitor assessing the essential needs of a client who is in a disadvantaged position, and who is under pressure not only from her estranged husband, but also from other family members, to settle on terms which, in her solicitor's view, do not adequately cater for her interests. The case is more complex than the previous one since the client has suffered clinical mental illness, and this necessitated the solicitor communicating with a wider network of persons who were bound up with Mary's care, and also with third parties on her behalf. Although refreshingly candid about her uncertainties over dealing with pensions, Janet remained committed to the client's cause, but still hoped it would "settle". The case had not yet concluded.

6

The "Other Side": Achieving Settlement

W E NOW TURN to the way the solicitors in our case studies dealt with "the other side". In this chapter we look at our case studies primarily with a view to understanding how the solicitors who described their cases to us approached the task of resolving conflicts between their client and that client's partner, or former partner. Once again, the overwhelming push towards settlement comes across, to the extent that there were only two cases (Cases 202 and 301: 5 per cent) where a solution regarding property or finances had to be imposed after a full hearing, one regarding protection against violence (Case 112) and one regarding residence and prohibited steps orders (Case 313). However, the court was frequently used as an aid to the settlement process. Indeed, in nineteen (nearly one-half) the court played an important part, either through some kind of preliminary procedure or by being imminent in door-of-the-court settlements. We will examine the role of the court in this process in detail below. We start, however, by considering other matters which were important in dealings with "the other side".

A THE SIGNIFICANCE OF LEGAL REPRESENTATION

Usually, the other side was represented by a lawyer, but not necessarily. In five of our forty cases (nearly 12 per cent) the other party was unrepresented, at least for most of the time. It was clear that the solicitors felt that considerable difficulties, involving delay and possible extra expense, could be attributed to the absence of legal representation by the other side. So solicitors would say things like:

"[this case was] so easy to deal with as both took legal advice immediately". (103)
[The fact the other side had no solicitor] "turned out to be one of the problems; she appeared to be reluctant to take advice: probably for financial

reasons . . . she seemed to think that everything could be sorted out by agreement but it was a rather one-sided approach . . ."
"because she wouldn't go to see the solicitor therefore I don't think she could
really understand what the point of it was: she thought she had an agreement, but the fact that there had to be divorce proceedings in order to have
the sort of financial orders made didn't seem to register with her". (201)
"the husband never instructed solicitors.. he acted in person throughout . . .
which made things quite difficult . . . it usually leads in many cases to the proceedings being prolonged . . . because we did make offers to settle earlier but
he wouldn't accept them and it was only after a court made an order that he
came back to us". (202)
". . . that's a feature in lots of these cases; I've got a few where there's a
respondent in person and they drive you mad". (205)
". . . the lady (solicitor) on the other side deals with nothing but family law
as well. That always helps because everyone has a much better idea of what
you're likely to get if you can't agree and you go to court . .. so there was an
early exchange of information". [In this case the solicitor thought the parties
would not have been suited to mediation because "every time they met they
had an argument and it became a matter of principle about teddy bears"].
(311)
There was a long delay because the wife was unrepresented. (314)

There seemed little doubt that, from the lawyer's perspective, matters are made considerably easier if they can deal with another lawyer,
at least if that lawyer is considered competent. So difficulties could
arise if the other side's lawyer was not a family law specialist:

The client (the husband) had come from another solicitor, who had not
known much about family law "which is always a bad thing" (e.g. he had
pleaded the petition like an affidavit). (315)
"I've a feeling that the husband had instructed his entertainment lawyer who
knew absolutely nothing about family law . . . which was another reason to go
to court; it's not for me to tell him how to do his job, but the court won't let him
muck it up . . . there were some very odd things". (204)

On some occasions, the solicitor felt the opposing lawyer had not
maintained a helpful attitude:

"all too many go to the conveyancing shop . . . the client says I want you to
write a snotty letter and they do . . . it's not how I see my job; I wouldn't do
it; it's short sighted". (108)
"He's less antagonistic than his solicitors. It was interesting to see once they
split how much of the acrimony was coming from them, not him". (316)
"The husband's solicitor was sadly exceptionally aggressive. I firmly believe
that we needn't have gone to trial – exceptionally aggressive and caused a lot

of real distress to my client, some of the things that were written in letters about her – disrespectful comments that I would never write. . . . she said she was a family specialist and a member of the SFLA, which I was shocked to hear. There were periods when she and I weren't talking; and that's never happened to me before in any case . . . The contents of some of her correspondence were so hurtful and distressing – total disrespect for my client – no doubt based on her instructions, but then she could have acted as a better sieve. That wasn't just my view – my counsel was shocked when he saw it". (319)

"You can't talk sensibly to this solicitor; you get some solicitors with whom you can have an off the record chat, and try to get an understanding of the whole thing. With this particular gentleman, he's very unable to maintain an objective view". (322)

Legal representation begins to lose its purpose if the representative fails to achieve an acceptable working relationship with the representative of the other party. Isolated though these cases may perhaps be, it behoves all practitioners to interrogate their practice to see whether they are not falling short in this regard. Not surprisingly, the solicitors were more ready to see faults in others than in themselves, though one was quite open and unrepentant about his reputation:

"There are solicitors here who won't even talk to me, but there are others with whom I have a good relationship". (317)

While this solicitor justified his approach on the basis that it was designed to achieve more rapid settlement, it was not clear to us that solicitors were more likely to settle when they perceived aggression on the other side. Indeed, aggression from the other side was seen to create obstacles to settlement.

One reason why lawyers felt that they might achieve greater success in negotiating between themselves than where clients were left alone was in their insistence on keeping financial issues separate from issues concerning residence and contact. We will present evidence in the next chapter which gives some support to this view. Clients often found it difficult to keep these matters apart:

"We managed to separate the two". (107)
"If you have got to resolve the financial issues and you make a contact order or something like that, the temperature goes shooting up and it becomes very much harder to solve some of the other issues". (201)
The wife had written directly to the husband, mixing contact with finances.

"She hasn't appreciated this is a separate issue and should not be part of the financial package". (201)

". . . if you start getting involved in contact issues as well as ancillaries, you know, it just hikes the bill up enormously". (319)

This is not to say that the solicitors thought that everything is best dealt with through lawyers. They themselves had clear ideas that there were matters which were best left for the parties to sort out between themselves. Dividing the contents of the home was one such issue:

"I tend not to get involved . . .cost and fuss, emotions, that picture of aunty Ethel; things just get silly". (104)

Another was over details of contact arrangements and sometimes child support:

"*She told me* they had arranged contact one day and staying over at week-end". (111)
The solicitor encouraged couple to sort out child support themselves. (303)
"My general advice was, for God's sake, sort it (contact) out without bringing it to court, because it's so much better for everybody". (308)
The solicitor suggested they sort it [contact] out themselves. (310)
"So I always say – Do try to sort out contact with your husband. Here are the legal principles, write to him, try and reach an agreement. If you can't reach agreement, come back to me and I'll deal with it'. But I emphasise how much it is in the child's interests to deal with it between themselves . . .". (319)

Why do the solicitors prefer to leave such matters to the parties, which could be said to raise issues of entitlement as much as the normal topics of ancillary relief? One reason has already been mentioned: it could be unwise to link contact issues with financial ones. Another might be because the details of any arrangement lie so peculiarly within the parties' own knowledge and experience (the value, sentimental or monetary, of household goods; the convenience of times for exercising contact) that the parties' representatives are ill-placed to make evaluations about them. Which is not to say that a solicitor would not give general advice on such issues:

"We weren't saying the eight year old can do what she wants, but she has got a mind of her own and father needs to get her back on side, allow time and space for that to happen". (107)
The solicitor advised that the girl was of an age (fourteen) that she could decide. (301)

"My advice about contact was that for children of that age (eleven and fourteen) effectively they're going to vote with their feet, particularly the fourteen year old, that obviously you should encourage contact, but it needed to be child-driven". (308)

"When we were discussing the question of increasing the times for weekend contact, my advice was that the father should have contact for the day". (309)

The solicitor advised of what usual contact arrangements were: "I gave him an idea of what the court will order. . ." [In fact all was amicably settled]. (310)

"I advised him about parental responsibility and legal rights for his daughter aged seventeen but then said frankly a girl of that age would make up her own mind about most things anyway". (311)

Where the wife wanted to formalise contact, the solicitor suggested she write to the husband with her proposals, but should consult child (eight) about them. (319)

The solicitor advised the husband the he should consult the wife over schooling, as the wife has joint parental responsibility. After contact had been stopped in the wake of sexual assault allegations – subsequently withdrawn, the solicitor advised the husband "to consider writing (the wife) a letter, or having us write to her through her solicitors, to raise the possibility of contact, or say, I'm here, I'd like contact . . .".(321)

"(The husband) has a tendency to act on emotion rather than taking a step back and look at the situation, so I have to try and steer him in the right direction. He will say, for example, 'why should I take them and deliver home'; And will say, 'look, at the end of the day, if we're in court, what do you think the judge would say . . . one parent take, one parent take back?' Then he'll say, 'O yeah fine, we'll do it like that' ". (322)

We do not therefore find an excessive, or even noticeable, zeal among lawyers to meddle in the conflict between the parties, despite this perception of lawyer activity by some of its critics (see above, p. 6). Many indeed stated either that they had suggested mediation or that mediation had occurred and failed, or that it would clearly have been no use trying:

One mediation session was held, and failed. Both parties "preferred to work through solicitors". (106)

Mediation [over child issues] was suggested, agreed, and a mediator seen more than once: it didn't work. (107)

There was no point in mediation: "she actually was quite frightened of her husband and, having met him myself in court in person he was a domineering character . . . he didn't believe she was ever entitled to any money. . .". (202)

"I'm a great fan of mediation; I think it's ideal when it's conducted by solicitors even if it is only done by adopting a common sense approach . . . there's no point at all in developing acrimony . . .". (203)

"I've just qualified as a mediator, so I'm very keen on mediation . . . but in a case like this . . . it would have needed mediators who were very good at power imbalances: one of the tragic features was . . . when we went to court two times, when she saw him she just ran over to him . . . she was still in love with him. (204)

"The first time everyone got around a table it was all sorted out . . . I believe in mediation . . . I think if clients get together they are able to achieve an awful lot more than letters via solicitors, but you have to have the basic facts in front of you . . . unless you mediate when you've got disclosure, it's extremely difficult, especially when you've got a wife who's in a disadvantageous position". (205)

Mediation was suggested re residence of the daughter, but not followed through as the wife withdrew her objections. (301)

Two mediation sessions re contact were unsuccessful. (302)

"We talked about reconciliation and marriage guidance, but she'd tried all of those things; she'd tried her best but she'd decided that she wanted a divorce" [in this case the parties were still living in the same house]. (302)

"When we wrote to the court asking for a date, I'd said that this case would most appropriately be listed for a conciliation appointment as contact was not opposed in principle . . .".(305)

"I asked him if he wanted to go to mediation – I nearly always ask that. The husband wasn't interested – he said he couldn't talk to her". (311)

Mediation was suggested re residence conflict; it failed. (316)

"(The wife) had not discussed divorce with her husband – she did not want to talk to him about anything direct". The solicitor at early stage suggested mediation, which the wife rejected. (317)

In a contact dispute, "counselling or conciliation was suggested" but not accepted by the husband. (321)

B SOME NEGOTIATING STRATEGIES

We have stressed that it is not the solicitor's sole task in divorce cases to negotiate resolutions to disputes. Nevertheless, it remains an important part of their work, and we consider here some of the ways in which they endeavour to secure agreement between the parties.

Bargaining

A good deal of what has been said about decision-making is relevant to negotiating. As we stated, the decisions to which we referred earlier referred to how the solicitors brought clients to adopt a position, whether it be over what proposals to make about the final settlement, or how to respond to actions or proposals from the other party. The position would, ideally, reflect the maximum convergence of the client's interests and the applicable normative standards underwritten by the client's instructions. This in itself could be said to be a preparation for the negotiation process, for the tempering of unreasonable demands by a client will enhance the prospects of successful negotiations, while the raising of a client's expectations sets a benchmark for that client which it is hoped will be maintained during the negotiation process.

Much of the negotiation process had the features of straightforward "horse-trading", for example, over the amount of a lump sum to be paid. But often the bargain would revolve around a fixed element, which one party was not prepared to forsake. This would frequently be occupation of the house, though it might also involve maintenance. In such a case this element might have to be traded off against others, and the discussions involved these trade-offs:

"I said, put maintenance for the children up, and down for her: the result would be the same". (103)

He eventually accepted that she had a claim over the house . . . which initially he was not accepting . . . But in the end he agreed to transfer the house into joint names on the basis that they each paid half the mortgage. (205)

"My advice was that you can't settle on not having any maintenance because you won't be able to make payments on the house and it will be repossessed . . . so we went before the district judge – he indicated that maintenance should be paid . . . at court the husband said he would consider accepting a charge back of 22.5 per cent so he went down on what he was asking, but still would not budge on maintenance" [eventually maintenance was agreed at the door of the court, with a 30 per cent charge back]. (302)

"Then we quite happily fax and say we can now give you £10,000. They come back and say, we'll take £13,000. We finally settle on £11,000, but only on the basis that we increase maintenance payments for the children. From the outset, he had always said to us that he never had any problem paying money for the children". (318)

If the "other side" was not prepared to negotiate on other matters (for example, a sum which would buy out a husband's interest in the home), then negotiations could stall and might not be resolved (Cases 304 and 307). We were interested in techniques lawyers might use to enhance the prospects of agreement. We consider three such strategies below: *Calderbank* offers, pressurising tactics and use of the court.

Calderbank offers

One strategy, sanctioned by judicial authority and rules of court, is to make a *Calderbank* offer (also referred to as a *Calderbank* letter: among family practitioners, the noun has now become a verb). This is a proposal in which the offeror indicates that, if it is not accepted, that party will request the court to take note of the offer if the decision is less generous to the offeree than the offer, and to reflect this in the order for costs.[1] The purpose of course, is to put pressure on the offeree to accept. *Calderbank* letters were referred to in six of our cases, 111, 201, 204, 301, 308 and 315. They seemed, however, not to have the desired effect, and negotiations generally continued without abatement after the letter had been sent. There seems little point in making such an offer which is much lower than the solicitor believes should be offered, as occurred in Case 301. There may also be little point in sending it very early in the process, as in Case 315, where it was sent a few days after the first appointment with the client because many things remained to be sorted out anyway at that stage. Even an "extremely generous" *Calderbank* letter failed to ward off an application being made for a directions hearing (Case 111) and a letter containing proposals which the solicitor believed incorporated what the other party was asking for had no effect (Case 201), and elicited a counter-letter much later in the proceedings. In two cases (Cases 204 and 308) a *Calderbank* letter led to settlement, but in each case it had been delivered only after the first FDR appointment (see below p. 119) and was the outcome of a long negotiation process:

"we were advised we weren't going to do better, so we accepted it". (204)
"I think Mum was pretty fed up with it by this time as well. By the end of January, we were at idem". (308)

---

[1] Although common in family practice, the strategy is not confined to it. See the discussion by the Court of Appeal in *Butcher* v. *Wolfe and Wolfe* [1999] 1 FLR 334.

Pressurising tactics

However, there were cases where it seemed that the pressures of the negotiating process were exploited by the one of the parties. For example, in one case (Case 308), the wife's solicitor presented the husband's solicitor with a questionnaire which they said they intended to serve if there was no agreement reached. The husband, whose business activities were questionable, was anxious to avoid detailed investigations of this kind. The tactic did not, however, succeed. The same solicitors tried something similar before the final hearing. They delayed drafting the final consent order, then,

> "two days before the final hearing I got a letter from the other side saying: 'O, by the way, there are all these repairs that need to be done to the property . . . and can we both agree that out of the money in . . . we'll take £3000 to cover this'. I went ballistic. I said: 'You must be kidding. We have a concluded agreement. It is appalling for you to make this proposal at this late stage". [This caused severe friction between the solicitors, and was eventually effectively withdrawn]. (308)

Such last-minute amendments are unlikely to be supported by the courts. In *Xydhias* v. *Xydhias*[2] the Court of Appeal held that, while agreements reached in the course of negotiation prior to incorporation in a court order were not to be treated as binding legal contracts, such agreements were nevertheless intended to "reduce the length and expense of the process by which the court carries out its functions" and the court could therefore hold the parties to its essential provisions. We have seen that in one of the cases, where the client (wife) sought to re-negotiate the agreement, the solicitor strongly advised against it on the ground that the agreement should be respected; nevertheless, the client insisted and successfully re-negotiated the deal (Case 316).

But solicitors can use the pre-agreement stage to pressurise their opponent either into reaching agreement or accepting terms more favourable to their client. This might take the form of resisting a request for disclosure until the other side makes disclosure first (Case 307) or serving questionnaires on the other party with extensive requests for information.

> "I know he's running up costs and getting a bit sticky, probably asking his solicitor what's going to happen . . . concerned about his future". So the

[2] [1999] 2 All ER 386.

solicitor tried to put as much pressure on the other side as possible by serving a questionnaire on the husband. He described the questionnaire as "simple, only five pages". (Researcher's note: I think he was being sarcastic at this
point] . . . the solicitor explained that some questions he asked were unreasonable – he flicked through the questionnaire proudly to show me his most
unreasonable question. The solicitor was concerned "to make him run as
much as I can". (317)

This solicitor (who was a member of the SFLA) went to some lengths to
justify what might be regarded as aggressive tactics against the other
party. He said he would go to "inordinate lengths" to prevent his opponent from finding out what he was doing, as this led to a better chance
of a good settlement. He felt that if he pestered the other side enough, by
threatening affidavits and issuing applications, "they'll just want to get
rid of me" and settle. He was the solicitor referred to earlier in this chapter who admitted that "there are solicitors here who won't even talk to
me, but there are others with whom I have a good relationship". The
approach did not achieve rapid settlement in the case he discussed with
us, because, although it resulted in a consent order, this followed a directions hearing; and the solicitor had threatened further legal proceedings
when the other party delayed implementing the order. One solicitor
engaged in very questionable tactics, suggested by counsel. One issue
was whether the client (the wife) was able to obtain employment:

"The client agreed to apply for jobs left, right and centre, to throw her hat in
the ring so that she could build up a file of job applications and letters of
rejection etc. We said 'Look, if you get an interview or they offer you the job
and you don't want it, just bin it. We only need to disclose things we want to
disclose' ". (319)

It is difficult to see how this differs from concealing material assets.

Use of the court

The most common method of seeking to resolve negotiations which
had become intractable was to issue proceedings. In our sample, in the
London area, this would involve using the ancillary relief pilot project,
which was very popular with solicitors. We examine this process in
some detail in Chapter 8. But it was striking how far the courts were
involved, in one sense or another, in the settlement process. In financial
cases, we can characterise the court as being involved where the court

imposed a solution after a full hearing (three Cases: 202, 301, 316), or where the settlement was reached under the imminent threat of proceedings (either at the court's door or very shortly before then) (three Cases: 111, 318, 321) and many more where the parties only reached agreement after an initial appointment or hearing had taken place and further proceedings were a possibility (eleven Cases: 105, 106, 108, 201, 204, 205, 302, 304, 308, 315, 319). Thus the courts were involved in seventeen such cases. Other court involvement included an order for interim maintenance (Case 104); a directions hearing to have the husband answer a questionnaire (Case 317); injunctions and undertakings against violent molestation (Case 112); directions regarding residence order applications (Case 302) and hearings regarding residence and prohibited steps orders (Cases 107, 305, 313). It would thus appear that on our data only around half of financial cases were settled without the "aid" of the courts (although of course in most of these cases a Consent Order would eventually be made).

We were concerned to see whether there were any particular features which might have predisposed a case against settling without judicial involvement. Of the seventeen cases on financial issues where the court imposed a solution or where the parties reached a settlement under pressure from the court, one or both of the parties were legally aided in thirteen (76 per cent) of them. This is more than the proportion of the whole sample where one or both parties received public funding (54 per cent), giving some support to the view that legally aided cases may be more likely to take longer to resolve, a question which we consider in Chapter 8, and to require the assistance of a court. On the other hand, we cannot support the assertion of Davis et al[3] that legally aided cases *always* involve an application to the court. There was no court involvement in six of the cases where one or both cases was legally aided (that is, 27 per cent of such cases). There did not seem to be any feature associated with the presence of legal aid *in itself* which predisposed a case to become difficult to settle. There seemed a slightly stronger association with *lack* of legal representation: three of the five cases in which the other party was not, or only irregularly, represented by a solicitor required assistance of a court.

However, we needed to look more deeply to see if we could discover whether there were some characteristic features of the cases where resort was made to a court to achieve settlement. In a number, one of

---

[3] *Simple Quarrels*, above p. 53, note 32.

the parties appeared to be either relatively indifferent to whether the divorce went through (or even wanted reconciliation) or was content to allow the situation to drift. Hence, in Case 105 the wife, who was not "desperate" for divorce, was unwilling to prejudice her potential widow's pension benefits. An important reason why a party was content to leave things as they were was where the husband was still in the house, either alone or with the wife. So, in Case 111 the parties were living together when the wife approached the solicitor; the husband did not wish to leave the house and wanted reconciliation. He therefore made no response to requests for information, so the solicitor said: "I felt the only way we would get anywhere was with a court order". Similarly, in Case 205, the parties were living together, neither being in a hurry to separate; the husband just wanted to sit tight. The parties were living together also in Case 302. The husband simply wanted to stay in the house, and refused to contemplate paying maintenance. In Case 301, where the parties were again living together when the husband came to the solicitor, the husband did not want a divorce (unknown to him, the wife had another partner) and basically refused to co-operate with the wife's wish to negotiate: "Getting information from him was like getting blood out of a stone, I have to say", said his solicitor, adding: "I very rarely use counsel for pre-trial reviews, but I did in this case because he wasn't listening to my advice". In Case 304, where the wife had left the husband in the home with the children, the husband wanted reconciliation, despite perpetrating various acts of violence, and simply ignored all requests for information, resulting in a contempt hearing. The husband was also in the home in Case 318, and he resisted the wife's attempts to re-open the informal arrangements made when she had left, despite all attempts by his solicitor and counsel to persuade him otherwise:

> "We'd dealt with this guy before – once he'd set himself in a particular way, there was no way you were going to get him to budge, come hell or high water".

So a major reason why some cases are propelled towards judicial involvement is that one party *lacks incentive* to agree a solution. They are not particularly anxious for a divorce, or are even opposed to it, and are content (or at least not desperately unhappy) with the situation they are in. Where a husband is living in the house, and is not anxious to move out (for example, to set up another home), his interests all lie in staying where he is. He is unlikely to be seeking anything from the wife. It is different if the wife is in occupation, for then the husband may want the house sold, or at least payment of compensation for loss of his interest in it. In such cases the opposing solicitor will become frustrated with the lack of progress, and may wish to bring the matter to a head by launching ancillary relief proceedings. In one case the fact that the husband's solicitor failed to respond to a request for information for three months was cited as the reason for issuing an ancillary relief application (Case 319). In most cases, as we have seen, these will bring about a settlement. Similarly, where one party appears indecisive as to what they really want, a solicitor may take the view that the only way to resolve the issue is with judicial assistance (see Case 201, and the quote associated with Case 314, p. 98, where proceedings were not in fact initiated).

The lack of incentive to negotiate can lead to extreme obduracy by one of the parties. Cases 301, 302, 304 and 318 referred to above, were such cases. But obduracy can arise for other reasons. In Case 308 the husband was desperate to avoid revealing too much of his financial circumstances because of possible criminal dealings (drug trafficking). In Case 315 the husband was greatly upset by the wife's refusal to return £20,000 which he had given to her in an earlier attempt at reconciliation. A matter which should have been resolved without judicial intervention settled only after an initial appointment, at which she returned to him his golf clubs. In Case 202 the solicitor commented:

"They were both [south European] clients, and although I tried to explain to him [the husband acted in person] what the law was and what my client was entitled to . . . he made it very clear very early on that he didn't think she was entitled to anything".

That husband even refused to obey the court order, and enforcement proceedings were initiated.

Sometimes progress towards agreement appeared to be upset by intervening events. In Case 106 the initially amicable atmosphere became conflictual as a result of a contact dispute. But there were occasions when it seemed that the solicitors were ready to use the court procedure almost as a matter of course:

"I haven't had a case go beyond FDR yet, so there doesn't seem to be any advantage to go on and on negotiating; the court helps that process now and also everything you're going to get in terms of disclosure. Instead of arguing you can do it on Form E which asks most of the questions you would want and then clarify and identify things which aren't disclosed . . .so unless it is

very clear that things are going to settle very easily I would always issue it
(an ancillary relief application). (204)

"I like the pilot scheme that the principal registry run, I think it's good, apart
from the delays in giving you court dates . . . I like the Form E and I like getting to court at the first appointment, I have had several cases that have settled at the first appointment . . . going to the first appointment with a
properly completed Form E seems to cut a lot of nonsense away where there
was no court imposed timetable". (205)

It may be therefore that the very success of the pilot project procedure
can reduce incentives for solicitors to reach settlement without involving the courts. It must be said that the pro-active attitudes of the judiciary accounts for much of this involvement. The obvious danger is
that solicitors may be tempted to bring in the courts unnecessarily
early, when a negotiated settlement was achievable, and the scheme
may become a victim of its own success. Already there were some
remarks about the in-built delays: in one case, six months between the
application and the first appointment (Case 205). If it becomes widely
accepted that solicitors cannot negotiate without having resort to judicial assistance, there must be a danger of excessive reliance on court
machinery. The solution must lie in giving parties who presently have
no incentive to settle some such incentive. Courts are willing to draw
adverse inferences about a party's means if they unreasonably resist
disclosure,[4] and could lead to penalties over costs. Courts can also take
"financial (mis)conduct" into account in making their final orders. But
prevention is better than penalty and we wonder whether solicitors
might make constructive use of these possibilities in negotiation, by,
for example, constructing proposals based on such inferences, rather
than waiting until the disclosure occurs, or indicating that their claim
might increase to reflect "financial misconduct". It is important to
remember that while one party is resisting disclosure, the other might
be incurring expenses which should be met by the other, or is being
deprived of benefits to which they are entitled. It takes experience and
decisiveness to know when is the best moment to make a proposal and
at what level it should be pitched. But well-timed proposals create an
incentive for the other party to produce counter-proposals, supported
by the desired disclosure.

[4] *T v. T* [1994] 2 FLR 1083.

C NEGOTIATION: CONCLUSIONS

Strategies

In a guide to English lawyers on negotiating strategies,[5] Ann Halpern, drawing on a well-known American book,[6] distinguishes three types of negotiating strategy:

1. The competitive, positional or win/lose. This assumes the parties' interests are diametrically opposed; that there is no room for compromise, and the "other side" is not to be trusted. The style favours an aggressive approach and the use of threats or bluff. It is felt to be useful where there is an imbalance of power between the parties.

2. The constructive, co-operative, collaborative or win/win. This is useful if the parties have an ongoing relationship. The case of disputes between divorcing parties about children is given as an example where the style would be appropriate. It involves a willingness to initiate offers and make compromises However, it could put the negotiator at a disadvantage against one adopting the competitive model.

3. The principled, problem-solving or win/win. This differs from the second model in that it focuses on the problem in issue in abstraction from the parties' subjective wishes. It proposes some objective or fair outcome which both parties work together to achieve. In this model, negotiators try to reduce the emotional heat of the dispute in order to concentrate better on the objective standards which should be reflected in the outcome. It is also necessary for each side to know the needs of one another and to make their own circumstances fully known.

Reviewing our data, it appears that elements from all three paradigms play a part in the way solicitors seek to resolve family disputes. Interestingly, the evidence for this comes as much from the way solicitors "negotiate" with their own clients as from the way they deal with "the other side". The desire to adopt a "collaborative" approach is evident in the data presented in the previous chapter in the way solicitors

---

[5] Ann Halpern, *Negotiating Skills* (Blackstone Press, 1992).
[6] Roger Fisher and William Ury, *Getting to Yes: Negotiating Agreement without Giving In* (Business Books, 1989). For a similar discussion, and review of the theoretical literature, see Andrew Boon and Jennifer Levin, *The Ethics and Conduct of Lawyers in England and Wales* (Hart Publishing, Oxford, 1999), pp. 327–39.

tried to persuade their clients, especially men, to avoid inflexible and unreasonable positions. But it is also apparent in the account of the bargaining process with the other side, and in the solicitors' preference for the parties to sort out child-related problems between themselves. Yet Halpern's account points to the advantages of the competitive approach where there is disparity between the parties' strengths, and the evidence about the way solicitors frequently sought to raise the expectations of women clients might suggest that they were following that model. It is certainly true that one solicitor openly proclaimed such a stance. However, we think it would be more consistent with the solicitors' accounts to identify their approach more closely to the third paradigm. We have observed that they seek to align their client's expectations with the normative, objective, standards which they believe operate through the law, and also reduce the emotional tension which might be generated by intermingling "children" issues with financial ones. This is consistent with the third model. There were indeed occasions when a solicitor, operating on a client's instructions, pushed for an outcome which seemed to be outside the scope of those standards, and sometimes even at odds with the client's own interests. We also saw that, where a client wished to pursue, or defend, his interests in a way which was at odds with his duties, solicitors did not appear to preach the language of duty to try to bring the client into compliance with those duties. Rather, they would point to the futility, and unnecessary cost, of such behaviour. Nevertheless, when acting under instruction, they would make proposals of which they disapproved. In such cases one might expect the lawyer to adopt a more "competitive" negotiating stance, and it is possible that this lay behind some of the problems concerning disclosure. We look at the problem of disclosure separately later (see p. 162–6). Here we would point out that, while in some cases resistance against disclosing information was employed as a tactic to further a client's interests, our later analysis shows that this was usually because the client nursed some special grievance, and the resistance was more a result of that grievance than a tactical decision by the solicitor to adopt a competitive negotiating strategy. Indeed, the solicitor might find it as hard to obtain the information from his own client as from the other side. But we also observed possibly inappropriate *demands* for disclosure. This could result, however, from a genuine espousal of the third, "principled", negotiating strategy identified by Halpern. This is because, as she notes, the quest to reach a solution best in line with some objective standard assumes that each party is fully informed of each party's circumstances. So a solicitor would feel reluctant to advise a client without full knowledge of the circumstances of both the client and the other party. But the search for such information could be expensive and time-consuming, and might have little impact when discovered. We return to this point later (p. 166).

We therefore find that the model which corresponds most closely to the way the solicitors in our sample approached negotiation was that presented as the "principled" one. The lawyers had some idea in their heads at the outset of what a reasonable outcome would look like, and they generally tried to steer their clients towards this. Their strong urge towards settlement meant that they understood the likely need for compromise, though where such compromise might result in surrender of what was perceived to be (especially) the weaker party's entitlements, statements more akin to the competitive model would emerge. This could also arise in the furtherance of a principled solution when the solicitor believed that he or she lacked information from the other side which would allow such a solution to be reached. However, here too it may sometimes be necessary to sacrifice full adherence to the principled model in favour of a compromise solution which will actually work.

The normative aspect

We referred in the preceding chapter to the importance of the normative standards in which the solicitors operate when "negotiating" with their clients. It is also very important in dealing with the "other side". Of course, anyone involved in assisting parties to reach settlement in financial matters in divorce will be aware that failure to reach agreement may have the consequence of contested proceedings. Mediators may hold out this prospect as an incentive to the parties to reach agreement. This prospect is also used by lawyers in encouraging parties to settle. However, it also appears that solicitors use the norms of the law at an earlier stage, and in a different way. This is because they bring with them to the case an understanding of the expectations which the legal norms applicable in the context create. The result is that they do not *simply* set the client on a path which is most likely to result in agreement. They *do* set out on this path, for, as we have seen, eventual agreement is the strongly desired goal. But they do so with some notion of what they think that settlement should look like from the point of view of the client.[7]

The evidence allows us to throw some light on what normative standards are employed by solicitors in these contexts. The matter is important because it can sometimes appear that the jurisdiction exercised by the courts is so discretionary that any normative standards are either nonexistent or barely visible. This view has been encouraged by many judicial statements, of which the following is only one: "The function of the Family Division judge is not so much to state principles as to reflect the relevant circumstances of the particular case in the discretionary conclusion".[8] It is indeed the case that the governing statute[9] simply sets out a variety of matters to be taken into consideration, but does not itself indicate (at least, not expressly) the ultimate direction towards which the decision-maker should be aiming. Yet the courts have devised some principles, although they are reluctant to describe them as such, perhaps because they fear (mistakenly) that to do so would restrict the flexibility of the decision-making process. The approach is well described by Lord Hoffmann as follows:

> Thirdly, the exercise of the discretion under s 24 in accordance with s 25 requires the court to weigh p a large number of different considerations. The Act does not . . . lay down any hierarchy. It is one of the functions of the Court of Appeal, in appropriate cases, to lay down general guidelines on the relative weights to be given to various factors in different circumstances . . . These guidelines, not expressly stated by Parliament, are derived by the courts from values about family life which it (sic) considers would be widely accepted in the community.[10]

It is widely accepted that one such guideline is that a home for the children and their caregiver should be secured if possible, preferably by avoiding moving from the present matrimonial home.[11] We have seen that the solicitors follow this strongly. However, in cases where this can be achieved (usually by securing continued occupation by the wife) and further matrimonial assets (usually owned by the husband) remain, it is unclear from the case law on what basis such assets are to be redistributed (if at all). A number of matters are relevant to a

---

[7] This was explained in Chapter 5 when reference was made to the Normative Standards which affected a solicitor's negotiations with the client.

[8] *Atkinson* v. *Atkinson* [1995] 2 FLR 356, *per* Thorpe J.

[9] Matrimonial Causes Act 1973, ss. 24 and 25.

[10] *Piglowska* v. *Piglowaski* [1999] 3 All ER 632 at 644.

[11] Jackson et al, above p. 28, note 97. John Eekelaar, *Regulating Divorce* (1991), p. 71.

decision on the matter. For example, the wife's "reasonable requirements" might be such that they can be met only by a share in those
additional assets;[12] or her contributions, either to the acquisition of the
assets, or to the welfare of the family, may be such that she has
"earned" a share in them.[13] But these "guidelines", if they are such, are
insecure and their application uncertain. We wondered whether our
cases could throw any light on the way they might be applied by solicitors in practice.

We might acquire some indication of this by looking at those cases
where a wife's claim to accommodation was satisfied, but further assets
were available for a potential additional claim. It emerges that the
solicitors certainly did view the wives as having such a claim, but the
bases for the claims varied. In Case 319, for example, the solicitor
thought the wife should settle for more than a half share of the proceeds of the home, when it was eventually sold, because the wife felt
that they had not received full disclosure. Settlement was however only
achieved at the door of the court. In Case 107 the wife had originally
seemed content with sharing the proceeds of sale, but the solicitor
thought she was "entitled" to an equal share in the accumulated assets.
The wife only pressed for this after contact became disputed. In neither
of these cases did the basis for the claim seem clearly articulated, and
they may not have been pressed had there not been alternative grounds
for friction (non-disclosure in one; contact in the other). This point is
underlined in Case 304, which was a seventeen year marriage, and the
solicitor considered that the wife was entitled to more than just half of
the equity in the home. But the wife did not wish to claim it, and the
solicitor did not push it because of the risk of aggravating the situation
and raising legal costs (it was a legally-aided case). These solicitors
were therefore aware of what they consider a wife's "entitlements",
especially after a long marriage. This is most evident in their concern
about pensions. In Case 104 (another long marriage case) the solicitor
was unhappy about the wife's position having become aware that the
husband had four pension policies, so there was reason for having a
"substantial lump sum", and this issue, as well as ongoing maintenance, was holding up settlement. In Case 204 the existence of the husband's very substantial pension fund was the occasion for settling for
the outright transfer of a high-value matrimonial home. When eventually the wife sold it, she would have enough to rehouse herself and a

[12] *Dart* v. *Dart* [1997] 1 FLR 21.
[13] *Conran* v. *Conran* [1997] 2 FLR 615.

substantial lump sum. The concerns which an opponent wife's solicitors raised (late in the day) about a possible share in the client husband's pension rights was also a reason for protracting the dispute in
Case 201. It seems clear, therefore, at least on our evidence, that solicitors acting for wives believe that clients have an entitlement to a share
in assets remaining over after the accommodation issue has been disposed of, at least in the case of long marriages. The exact amount will
be subject to negotiation, and this might be influenced by externalities,
such as how far the client believes the other side is revealing about
assets, or even other points of conflict. The Government's suggestion,
therefore, that, after matters concerning housing are settled, there
should be a division of surplus[14] would seem to reflect perceptions and
strategies of solicitors in current practice, but the suggestion that the
division should be equal does not necessarily reflect current norms.

[14] *Supporting Families*, para. 4.49.

7

Outcomes:
Are Solicitors Cost-effective?

WE HAVE DESCRIBED what we observed solicitors doing for divorce clients, commented on technical and practical assistance offered in guiding divorcing parties from A to B and explained how they reach outcomes. But were the clients receiving good value for money? This is of course a very difficult question to answer. It is very easy to complain about the costs of legal services. But then people complain about the cost of plumbers, garages, private medicine, rail fares: just about everything. So how do you measure value for money in the case of legal advice? One way to try to do this is to compare the final bill against the value of assets that are *at stake* in the case. Technically, in divorce cases, the entirety of the assets of both of the parties are subject to discretionary disposal by the court, and, for this reason, are therefore potentially subject to negotiation. It could therefore be said to be financially worthwhile for a client to commit a sum equivalent to a certain proportion of the totality of these assets to protect the client's interests in these assets. The larger the assets, the greater the responsibility of the lawyer. Hence, fixed-cost schemes, like that in Germany, relate the fee claimable by the lawyer to the total value of the assets at stake.[1] This process would also allow comparisons to be made between costs of the clients in our study with analogous professional work which fix their charges by reference to the value of assets dealt with on a commission basis. For example, we might make a comparison with the commission charged by estate agents in securing property for a client. Although this is inevitably only a rough comparison, it does provide some marker against which to assess the value provided for clients by their lawyers.

---

[1] See Barbara Willenbacher, "The Changing Role of Professionals in Divorce in Germany" (1996) 10 *International Journal of Law, Policy and the Family* 159.

We are able to make such calculations in many of our cases. However, such information does not indicate by how much a client is better off in financial terms after seeing the lawyer. It might be thought better to try to calculate that sum, and to set it against the legal bill. We are also able to make this calculation. We can in most cases see how much the client was left with after the case concluded. Of course this does not prove that the client would not have ended up equally better off without seeing the lawyer. Some people can save a great deal of money through do-it-yourself, but the hazards of this are also manifest. They might achieve similar results through the services of some other professional, but to date there is no significant competing profession to assist clients in the area we are considering. We have noted above the reluctance of people to settle financial and property issues through mediators, so we cannot tell how "well" clients would do if they used their services rather than those of lawyers. No doubt information allowing such comparisons will be obtained at some time in the future. In the meantime we think it will be useful to attempt an assessment of what clients can achieve by using lawyers.

In setting the outcomes for the clients against the bill that has to be met, either by the client or by the legal aid system, we have to note that this is only a crude, materialist, measure. As one of our solicitors heatedly observed, being secured the home is worth far more to the client than the straight market, or equity, value of the house. Such an outcome keeps intact the fabric of the social life of the client and, usually the children. "A house is not just bricks and mortar". But we cannot put a monetary value on such social capital. Nor are we able to put a money value on the effect of the kinds of support and reassurance which solicitors provide clients described in Chapter 5. These are all substantial shortcomings in our evaluation of outcomes and our account of the cost-effectiveness of solicitors. However, in making our materialistic evaluations, we meet those who would judge the value of such services solely on a materialistic basis on their own terms.

B THE COSTS AND BENEFITS

The cases will be examined according to whether the client is the husband or wife, and by whether they are responsible for their expenses or legally aided. In calculating the value of the assets, we include the equity value of the matrimonial home and add on other clearly defined assets (such as endowment policies) which were in issue in the discussions.

The private-client husbands (11)

We have information about eleven men who were private clients. We will set aside one case (Case 315) which we might term an outlier, in that the dispute was limited to the return of golf clubs, some cash and an expensive car, and where the bill came to £3,000. The client got his clubs and £4,000 rather than the £10,000 he wanted, but at quite a high price. It was, however, a case where the client was noticeably obdurate in resisting legal advice. Of the remaining ten private cases where the client was the husband we have information about the assets which formed part of the negotiation. We would not have been told about undisclosed assets or about the transfer value of a pension which did not form part of the negotiations. Also we were often told "there were some small policies . . . the value was not clear . . ." and sometimes there were rather shadowy debts to family members (often a father-in-law who was in the building trade and had worked on the family home, or loans from family members to help with house purchase where the repayment obligations had not been formalised).

With these caveats, we look first at the range of equity values of the *homes* which were at stake in the negotiations. These lay between £336,000 and £7,000 for this group of men, and the average amount available for distribution was £14,100. The final bills which they paid (including VAT and disbursements) ranged between £460 for the man whose equity was £12,000, to £10,000 for the man whose equity was only £57,000. The legal bill for arranging the distribution of the equity of £336,000 was only £2,500. The average bill, if we include the high costs case, was £2,442. But if we exclude the two bills of over £5,000 and the case where the bill had not yet been finalised, the average bill paid by the male private clients was £1,325. Note, however, that four of these men were respondents not petitioners and we expect the petitioner's lawyer to be the active participant and thus to charge for doing more of the associated work. If we add in major available assets, such as pension transfer values, and discount acknowledged debts, Table 7.1 shows the value of the "pot" to be divided, and the final bill incurred.

In these cases the median percentage of the bill in relation to the assets is 2.6. There is no direct relationship between the total value of

Table 7.1 *Lawyers' bills as percentage of value of assets at stake: private clients (men)*

Case No.	Assets £	Bill £	Bill as % of assets %
101	17,500	460	2.6
102	396,000	1,300	0.3
103	440,000	2,500	0.6
201	147,000	10,000	6.8
301	145,000	6,000	4.0
310	7,000	640	9.0
311	70,000	1,200	1.7
314	177,000	1,000	0.6
318	140,000	3,500	2.5
322	550,000	not finalised	n/a

the assets and the size of the bill, which is to be expected, for the bill reflects work done, not the property at risk. Nevertheless, when these bills are seen as percentages of the total value of the assets, they compare favourably with the charges levied by an estate agent for assisting in the sale of real estate, which varies between 1.5 per cent and 3.0 per cent. In Germany the legal charges are limited to 6 per cent of the value of the assets.[2] The two cases where the bill was a higher proportion were very different. In one (Case 310), the assets available were so limited that even a modest bill took almost a tenth part of the assets. In the second (Case 201), the costs had risen because, although the wife had produced a "home made" plan for a clean break, she was reluctant to petition for divorce, not apparently realising that a divorce decree was a pre-condition for achieving a clean break. She had sought legal advice intermittently, so the full nature and implications of the clean break seemed only to be appreciated by her in stages, causing additional delay, uncertainty and almost certainly extra legal cost.

If we consider what these husbands acquired in return for their money we find that three of the ten clients definitely emerged with more of what they wanted from the settlement than their lawyers initially expected. The first two (Cases 102 and 103) sought a clean break, and in both cases, despite factors which could make this difficult, i.e., the

---

[2] Personal communication from Professor Dagmar Coester-Waltjen, University of Munich.

presence of young children (aged eleven in one case and eight and thirteen in the other), health problems of the wife (in one case), and great disparity in earning capacity in both cases, the lawyers were able to achieve this. In both cases there were sufficient resources to offer flexibility (assets of over £300,000) and in both cases the costs were relatively low (£1,300 and £2,500). Both cases took just over a year to settle and both avoided court, though in the second case there were frequent meetings between the lawyers involving tough negotiation. In the first of these two cases the lawyer interviewed expressed surprise that the other side had accepted the clean break so quickly, and thought that court would not have done so. In the second case the lawyer was a highly experienced family lawyer, a mature lady of great determination, who went back again and again fine tuning her offers until the other side accepted one from her menu of three choices. There were no problems around contact or residence. A third case (Case 101) also yielded a better than expected result for the husband. The lawyer had advised that a court might award all the available capital to the wife plus child support of £800 a month, but was able to negotiate that the first £15,000 from the sale of the house should go to the wife and the next £5,000 to the client. He attributed the effectiveness of the negotiation and the speed of settlement (six months from first interview to decree absolute) to having a "good" i.e., experienced solicitor on the other side. Again there were no child related issues. In one case (Case 310) the client came out with exactly what he had asked for. This was a straightforward matter where the husband was willing to transfer the house to his wife, and this was done quickly and cheaply. The major input from the solicitor was to explain the endowment policies to his client. (Bill of £640, equity at stake £7,000, duration ten months).

In two cases the client got the result that he wanted but in one it took longer than expected and in the other the cost was far higher than anticipated. In Case 314 the husband got what he wanted, which was the sale of the family home, but slowly. The speed of the process was determined by the client who was adamant about not pushing too fast in order to avoid upset for his teenage children who were taking important examinations, but the bill was low (estimated as around £1,000 over a period of several years). Delay, as we will demonstrate further (see Chapter 8), does not add to costs where no action is being undertaken. In Case 201, mentioned earlier, the husband gave the house to his wife as he had expected to do, but the bill reached £10,000. We will refer to this case again in Chapter 8.

In the remaining four cases the husbands went away with less than they had expected. In Case 311 the client had indicated that he wanted half the proceeds of sale from the house, but his lawyer had to make it clear early that while he might be able to achieve that "at a push", it would require waiting until the child had left home, and he was likely to have to pay maintenance for the wife. Some bickering developed over contents which was firmly stopped by both solicitors working together. The final agreement was for a 75–25 clean break. The other two cases in which the client did not get what he sought involved men who were in a particularly volatile emotional state. In Case 318 the couple had had a judicial separation and financial agreement in 1993, but the husband's business had developed since then and the wife was now coming back seeking a divorce and full financial settlement. The husband was understandably confused and angry about this, and the solicitor had difficulty in convincing him that a court would be likely to award a further sum to his wife. The case was settled after a directions hearing, and the husband was required to increase the child support and pay an additional £11,000. He was described as "domineering". In Case 301 the husband had not wanted divorce and was very angry about his wife's new relationship. He thought the breakdown of the marriage was all her fault. He adamantly refused to accept the solicitor's (and later counsel's) advice:

". . . right up until we went to court, I was saying to him, and then counsel said exactly the same thing: 'Offer £50,000, offer £60,000, and that will be fine'. At the end of the day, he ended up having to pay more and her costs, which was a shame because if he'd taken our advice, we would probably have settled it because we'd got to the stage where we were talking £50–55,000 on the pre-trial review . . . But the client was saying, 'No, I'm not prepared to go that high'. He was saying: 'Offer £30,000'. Which was nowhere near".

The final case (Case 322) involved an element of violence, and there had been a non molestation order against the client. But this case, which was unfinished at the time of interview, was the only one which had given rise to serious difficulties related to the children. The solicitors in other cases had described occasional "hiccups" over contact, but nothing to warrant legal intervention and the lawyers clearly referred any such problem back to the couple to deal with by themselves. But in this case, where the husband did not want divorce and sought reconciliation, financial matters were not even being addressed though substantial resources were at stake (equity of over £300,000 in the family home) and he seemed to be seeking to prevent the marriage from ending by trying to hang on to the children. The case was still ongoing and we do not have a final bill.

Thus it appears that where the client was reasonable, though not clearly in the best legal position, the solicitor was able to negotiate and reach the desired outcome, even though this sometimes took longer and cost more than was expected. The cases where the solicitor was not able to deliver what the client wanted were cases where the client was angry, upset, and unwilling to accept legal advice.

The legally-aided husbands (2)

The activity and outcomes achieved for husbands under legal aid were very different in character from those which were privately funded, as these legally aided cases were predominantly concerned with children issues. These issues were noticeably missing from the legal interventions for private client husbands for whom the lawyers were concerned with working out financial settlements. The first (Case 308) concerned a husband whose wife had gone to the former holiday home in Spain with a new partner, and the was now in financial difficulty and therefore seeking a divorce settlement. The children were living with their father. The final bill was £4,000, but the matter was complex, and the father ended up keeping his home and sharing the remaining assets in a way that was acceptable to him, a satisfactory outcome for the client. The second case (Case 321) was only concerned with the children, since there was no property or income. The father had been having regular staying contact with the children, but was suddenly accused of sexually abusing the twelve year old girl, though no attempt was made to end contact with the other child. The charges were dropped, and the lawyer clearly felt that he had supported this man through a very difficult time, and secured for him continuing contact with both children. This case had not yet concluded.

The private-client wives (8)

All the wives were petitioners and we may therefore expect to see their lawyers being more active than those representing the husbands, who were largely respondents. The focus of their work was financial. There were no established cases of domestic violence, though in Cases 109 and 113 the solicitor referred to the presence of "hassle". In both of these cases the couple were still sharing the family home, and were highly stressed and conflicted. There was little serious difficulty about arrangements for children. In Case 303 the lawyer mentioned "the usual friction" about contact, and there were difficult episodes, such as in Case 109 where the husband ran off to his mother's home with the youngest child after discovering his wife's long-standing affair. But the solicitors on both sides worked to calm this down and were able to help the couple to do so. Another wife (Case 107) was anxious about her five-year-old staying over with the father who had a new partner, and a court welfare officer's report was required after he issued proceedings, but this too calmed down as the solicitor assured the wife that a court would accept his request for this form of contact and there was little point in arguing the case.

In considering the cost-effectiveness of the process for these wives, we asked the following questions. What assets were available for distribution? What costs did the wives incur, and how did the outcome relate to the wives' interests? Had these women worked out what they wanted from the settlement when they approached the lawyer? If so did they achieve what they wanted?

Looking at only the equity in the matrimonial home, the final bill as a percentage of the value of this equity for the private-client wives did not exceed 4 per cent. But if we add in the value of other assets explicitly included in the negotiation by the solicitor, the results are shown in Table 7.2. These costs as a percentage of the totality of assets at stake

Table 7.2 *Lawyers' bills as percentage of value of assets at stake: private clients (women)*

Case No.	Assets £	Bill £	Bill as % of assets %
105	210,000	6,700	3.1
107	240,000	5,000	2.0
109	85,000	not final	n/a
113	62,000	810	1.3
303	200,000	700	0.3
308	divorce only	230	n/a
319	645,000	16,000	2.5
320	120,000	1,000	0.8

are lower than those paid by the husbands who were private clients, despite the fact that all the wives were petitioners. Perhaps this was because all of these cases settled. The costs were higher where proceedings had been initiated. Case 319 (£16,000 costs) came under the pilot procedure, and a date was set but the case settled at the door of the court. Case 105 (£6,700 costs) had a date for an interim maintenance application hearing but settled before trial, and in Case 107 (£5,000 costs) the husband had issued proceedings about contact, but after a court welfare officer's report the court declined to intervene as the question was only whether or not the child should stay over, not whether or not there should be contact.

In one of the cases (Case 308) the wife, who was Spanish, only sought advice concerning the technical legal aspects of her divorce from her Muslim husband. There were no children, and the financial aspects of the separation were not discussed with the English lawyer. The cost was £230. In all of the remaining cases there were financial arrangements to be made and all of these women (four of whom were working and had savings and pensions of their own) had a clear idea of what they wanted. Five of the seven wanted to stay in the matrimonial home, and four of these women had children living with them, though some were over the age of eighteen. Those with younger children also sought child support, but no-one sought spousal support except the childless wife. Hers had been a second marriage to an older man, and her business had recently got into difficulty.

Three women achieved their goal of staying in the family home. In Case 109 there was little room for manoeuvre, but by selling all the small policies and with the help of the wife's annual income of £16,000, it was just possible for her to afford the outgoings on the house with child support of £75 for each child. The solicitor was pleased to have achieved transfer of the house from the husband in return for some capital to help him finance his own house move. The solicitor had also acted as financial adviser, making the tightly stretched resources achieve what the wife sought, and worked with the husband's solicitor to keep things from escalating when the husband discovered his wife's long-standing affair and threatened to contest residence of the youngest child. In this case the equity was only £85,000, but the wife's earning capacity made the outcome possible. In the second (Case 113) the wife was also working and able to pay the outgoings on the house. In this case the contribution of the solicitor was to persuade the husband to leave the family home without the £9,000 he had demanded, to transfer the house to the wife and pay £350 a month child support. In the last case where the wife stayed in the house (Case 320), there were adult children in residence and it had been a twenty-six year marriage. The husband had wanted to sell and share, but eventually agreed that the wife should stay with a lump sum of £3,000.

Two women who had wanted to stay were unable to do so, but left with financial settlements which were far higher than the original offers made by their husbands. The first case (Case 319) concerned a long marriage where the wife did not work and there was an eight-year-old son with learning difficulties. The husband had first offered less than 50 per cent of the equity in the family home, and £300 a month child support. The wife had been unclear about what to do, and was firmly advised by her lawyer that this was not good enough. After some arguments over contact the wife felt more aggressive and decided to "fight", supported financially by her own parents. She failed to stay in the house, but she received 75 per cent of the proceeds of sale, i.e., an additional £107,000, and £400 a month for her son. The case was settled at the door of the court and cost £16,000. The second wife (Case 105) who was unable to stay in the home had only low intermittent earnings as a home hairdresser, but felt that she had provided the bulk of the capital for the house. (It was her husband's second marriage, and he had already made one divorce settlement. Her father had carried out the improvements on the property). The role of the solicitor was to persuade her that, as she could not afford the upkeep of the house, she must agree the sale. She did so, and instead of the 50 per cent her husband had offered, her lawyer was able to negotiate 65 per cent , which was an additional £28,000, as well as interim maintenance. The bill was £6,700.

Two women sold and shared as they had expected to do (Cases 303 and 107). In the first case the lawyer was initially surprised that the wife, his client, was content with only an equal division, as she thought that with a six-year-old child and a part-time job, the wife should seek more. But on learning the history of the case and that the husband was unemployed, the lawyer agreed with her client that a 50–50 split was the proper outcome. In the second of these cases the solicitor also thought that the wife was not seeking all that she was entitled to. The couple were both earning, had a six-year-old child, and had agreed between themselves to sell the house and share equally, each party keeping their own savings. But the solicitor for the wife thought that her client's savings were less than those of her husband as result of being a mother, and that all the savings should therefore be pooled and shared equally. The wife was not interested in this argument until matters became more hostile after disagreements about contact. After this falling out she agreed to ask for more, and received £176,000 instead of £95,000, with child support of £75 a week.

So *all* these women did well, and their financial settlements were enhanced in every case (except the Spanish wife, who did not seek it) by legal intervention.

The legally-aided wives (20)

Twenty wives were funded from public sources. Of these, in four the initial contact was about children issues. In all but one case there were financial issues and in five cases domestic violence was mentioned, including two of the cases primarily concerned with children. All the legally-aided wives were either mothers of dependent children or were leaving marriages of over twenty years' duration.

As might be expected, the assets available for distribution for this group were lower, ranging from nothing at all to £170,000. The average figure was £65,000. A third of the cases were without significant property to divide. Two were in rented property, one family home had negative equity, in a fourth case the husband was a bankrupt, and in two other cases the equity in the family home was under £10,000. The bills incurred ranged from £400 to £14,000. This is shown in Table 7.3. The median percentage of the bills in relation to assets was 5.0. This compares with a median percentage for the private client wives of between 1.3 and 2.0. Does this mean that legal aid clients pay more than private clients? The answer is no. The percentage is higher because the values of the assets at stake where the wives were legally aided were much lower than where they were not. The median value of the assets for the legally-aided wives was £42,000, whereas for the private-client wives it was £240,000. In fact, there was not much difference in the total bills charged between the two groups. The median for the private-paying wives was £1,000; for the legally-aided wives it was £1,500. Our sample size was such that we cannot draw any conclusions from those figures, except to comment that the total value of the assets did not seem to have much effect on the eventual bill, suggesting that as much work may be often be done on low-asset cases as on those involving property with higher values. We return to the distinction

Table 7.3 *Lawyers' bills as percentage of value of assets at stake: legally-aided clients (women)*

Case No.	Assets £	Bill £	Bill as % of assets %
104	37,000	1,500	4.0
106	5,500	1,000	18.0
110	170,000	580	0.3
111	81,000	2,000	2.4
112	34,000	2,000	5.8
202	60,000	8,000	13.3
203	unknown	1,000	n/a
204	400,000	4,000	1.0
205	15,000	1,250	8.0
302	42,000	4,000	9.5
304	40,000	2,000	5.0
305	none	1,750	n/a
307	52,000	not known	n/a
309	8,000	not known	n/a
312	88,000	1,500	1.7
313	none	400	n/a
316	70,000	14,000	20.0
317	50,000	2,500	5.0

between legal aid costs and private costs in Chapter 8 (see p. 177). Of course it could be argued that the legally-aided wives received less *value* than privately-paying wives, if you look only at the material value of the totality of their assets. However, as the account of their cases which follows shows, what these women sought, and acquired, cannot be measured solely in such terms.

What, then, did the lawyer do to move these women along the path away from a problem and towards a solution? These were divorce clients, but it would be misleading to describe divorce as their only objective. According to their lawyers, these women often wanted "to stay in the house" and to "sort the money out". By and large they accepted that their children should stay in contact with their fathers but they needed help with the difficulties which arose in organising this especially when the couple were in conflict. It is worth noting that we also had cases of former wives asking for legal help to make their former partners see *more* of the children.

The solicitors' work ranged from helping the woman to clarify her objectives within the range of the possible (both legally and financially) and then putting into effect action to secure as much of the desired objectives as possible, to simply ratifying and helping to put into effect a plan already made by the client. The clarity reached and the degree of information prepared and precision of plans envisaged ranged from general aspirations to detailed plans which were ready for action.

Three of the wives arrived for their first appointment with clear instructions and the necessary information (Cases 110, 202 and 304). All three got what they came for, though one paid a heavy price and one according to her lawyer could have asked for more. In Case 110 there were no new partners involved. The wife was quite clear that she wanted a divorce and she knew that the equity in the family home was £170,000. She wanted to buy a house with three bedrooms within reach of the children's schools and she knew that this would cost £115,000. She wanted this clear of a mortgage and otherwise sought only child support. The solicitor thought that this was tight but could just about be done. The wife negotiated with her husband directly and all was done for £581. The second client with a clear plan was less fortunate (Case 202). She had left a domineering husband, and the children had stayed with their father. She was working, and wanted half the equity from the family home in order to house herself. Unfortunately the husband was very hostile, and was not represented. The solicitor had a difficult time trying to persuade him that he must disclose his financial position and that he must share the marital property. The husband came from a southern European country and believed that he had no further responsibilities towards a wife who had left him and the children. He totally refused to co-operate with the legal process. Two orders were required for disclosure, there were two hearings and an enforcement hearing after the court had ordered him to pay her £23,000 out of the equity of £60,000. The wife's bill came to £8,000, but the legal aid fund did not suffer as the wife had to repay the fund from her lump sum, so she would not be able to rehouse herself from that sum. The solicitor thought the bill would have been around £5,000 if enforcement proceedings had not been necessary. In the third case (Case 304) the wife had moved in with her new partner and sought only £20,000 from the equity in the family home of £40,000, but there were other assets. The solicitor originally advised her to ask for more, and a contested hearing was set down in order to achieve disclosure. But the client was clear that she did not seek more, and she went away with £20,000 after the FDR hearing with a final bill of £2,000.

Continuing to look at the clients' priority at first contact, in four cases the issue was related to children rather than property, and involved fear of violence. In two of these cases (Cases 305 and 313) property never became an issue; the parties were in rented housing and the wives were on income support. In the first case, a couple from Africa, the wife approached the solicitor for help with contact as she was afraid of her husband's violence towards her and the children, and that he might leave the country taking them with him. The solicitor was able to explain the kinds of protection offered by the British system, and gradually contact was established under a court order. The lawyer said of his client "she was timid at first but gradually found what she wanted". The bill was £1,750. In Case 313 the wife was described by her lawyer as "not very assertive". She had moved into local authority housing to get away from her husband's violence, but wanted him to have contact with their three-year-old child provided it could be supervised, as she was afraid he would take the child away. An order was made, and the final bill was £500.

In two other cases children and violence issues were the primary reason for contacting a lawyer, but in these cases (Cases 106 and 112) financial issues were also sorted out. In both cases the lawyer dealt with injunctions and reassured the women. In Case 106 the eight-year-old daughter was unwilling to stay overnight with her father and his new partner as she was afraid of being punished by the new partner. The solicitor calmed the mother, saying that the court would require this kind of contact eventually and helping her to persuade her husband to work towards being patient with the little girl, and to rebuild his relationship with her rather than try to coerce her into staying over. Matters calmed down and were resolved without court intervention. The violence between husband and wife in this case seemed to be related to the separation period and was not long term. The solicitor was also able to help her to stay in the house where the equity was £2,500. She was on income support, and the final bill was £1,000. In Case 112 both parties were in a highly emotional state, with the wife being asked to stay away from her husband's place of work and the husband being asked to stay away from the family home. In this case the solicitor encouraged the couple to go to mediation concerning the children, but this failed and injunctions were needed. The lawyer expected to be able to keep her in the house, as she wanted, partly because the husband's new partner had a good job. The equity in the house was £30,000 and the final bill £2,000.

Of the remaining thirteen cases, the initial concern of the wives was with money matters (though a residence dispute flared up briefly in Case 302 and a full scale dispute developed in Case 316 where the mother lost residence). Of these women, all except the three who had already moved out wished to stay in the family home, but had not made the detailed plans to do so which characterised the cases discussed above. (Thirteen of the total twenty wished to stay). We will therefore look more closely at these cases to examine how feasible the solicitor thought that might be and what steps were taken to achieve it or to persuade the wife to accept an alternative outcome.

In three cases the wife had already moved out (Cases 312, 104 and 316). The wife in Case 312 was already living in a house bought by her parents with her children aged seventeen and twenty-one, and was awaiting disclosure in order to make a financial settlement. In Case 104, discussed in Chapter 5, the wife had recently been discharged from a psychiatric ward into sheltered housing, and her solicitor was struggling to get a small maintenance order for her to top up her income from benefit. She had attempted suicide after discovering her husband's long-standing affair. He had offered her £2,000 which she was willing to take, but her solicitor thought this to be quite unfair, especially as the husband had a pension with a transfer value of £40,000. She was unsure, however, how far to push the matter on the wife's behalf. In Case 316 the wife had left and had lost residence of the children by a court order but had been awarded 80 per cent of the equity (her husband was a bankrupt and willing to let go his assets). The first two women were rather sad cases, whom the lawyers described as not having ideas about what they wanted but needing support and encouragement from their lawyers, while the last was a strong young woman branching out on her own though surprised and distressed at losing residence of the children to her husband. This case incurred high costs, but it seems that the husband was not concerned about this since conserving costs would protect only his creditors.

Of the four women in the cases which were directed mainly at child-related issues, three (Cases 305, 106 and 112) wanted to stay in the family home, while one (Case 313) had already left. Of the three with clear plans, all had achieved what they wanted. This did not include staying in the family home. Thus we heard about ten women who had a wish to stay in their home after the break-up of their marriage, but had not made detailed plans before consulting a solicitor. In three cases the wives had been told by their husbands that the house must be sold and the proceeds shared. (Cases 108, 317 and 111). In the first case there were children of one and seven, the wife was not working and the husband had left suddenly with a new partner. The wife was shocked and depressed and had no idea that she could stay. The solicitor told her that this was possible, and made it happen. A clean break was offered as a bargaining tool, as spousal support was unlikely to be available after child support of £650 a month had been agreed. The house together with income support for the time being was a better option. In this case there was a directions hearing followed by settlement. The equity at stake was £19,000 and the final bill £1,500 (Case 108). The wife in Case 317 had agreed informally with her husband that they were going to sell the house and divide the proceeds equally. She was then told by her lawyer that this was not fair, after a seventeen year marriage, with children of fourteen and seventeen. She was "weak", with "no clue about money" and "would agree to anything", saying, according to her lawyer: 'All I need is a little flat for myself'. The solicitor asked her 'what about when the boys come to stay? With that share of the equity, you'll only be able to buy a tiny one-bedroom flat. The boys might not leave home at seventeen, and they will need to be in a house with 3 bedrooms until they are in a position to move out' ". Eventually the property was transferred to her sole name (equity of £47,000). The bill was between £2,000 and £2,500. In the third such case (Case 111, referred to in Chapter 5) the wife was on benefit, had a child of two and was pregnant. The husband was insisting that they must sell the house and he must repay a loan of £30,000 to his uncle before they shared out what remained. Her solicitor told her that it should be possible for her to stay in the house as a court would regard her need for housing as more important than the repayment of a debt. The equity at stake was £14,000 on the family home but the total assets amounted to £74,000, including a number of other properties. The couple finally reconciled.

Of the six remaining cases where the wife wished to stay (Cases 306, 205, 307, 203, 302 and 204) the first involved a twenty-seven year marriage in which the husband appeared to have spent all his spare time bird-watching. The wife, who was suffering depression, asked for nothing more than a roof over her head, but the solicitor thought that at the very least she should have an unencumbered property, and achieved this. Case 205 involved an eastern European couple who did not understand the English system, but were satisfied with the lawyer's suggestion of a Mesher order enabling the wife to stay in the home with the children for the time being. The wife in Case 307 had left the home with her child as a result of violence and wanted to move back. The solicitor managed to negotiate this, after dealing with lesser problems such as the car. Case 203 was unfinished, but the husband had agreed that the wife should stay in the house for the time being. In Case 302 the lawyer had to persuade her client not to accept an offer of £14,000 but to hold out for a transfer of the family home (equity £36,000) with a charge to the husband, and spousal and child support. And in the last case (Case 204), where the former husband was a wealthy former pop star, the house was transferred without difficulty to a very diffident and "other-worldly" client whose main concern was to persuade the father to see more of the children, now aged ten and twelve.

The cases are varied and complex. The lawyers often seemed to be supporting women who had little knowledge of their entitlements, and little stomach for a struggle to realise them except on behalf of their children. The central issue was to secure a roof over their heads, and here the solicitors played an important technical role in explaining the right to occupy, in putting forward proposals to try to meet the needs of the wives and children for housing without depriving the husband of the ability to house himself. They were also very aware of the capital value of the home, and anxious to ensure that this value could, where possible, also be used to contribute to safeguarding the wives' accommodation needs. The work required experience, technical expertise and skill in handling people through tense and irreversible decision-making about their property. And the smaller the amount of property at stake, the less the room for flexibility.

Spousal maintenance played only a minor part in these cases. Seven of the women are known to have been working, and eight were on income support at some stage during the case. There was little prospect of spousal maintenance, though in one case the husband was paying the mortgage, and the solicitor for the psychiatric patient was trying to get an order. In all of the cases where the wife was caring for dependent children a child support amount was recorded, but we do not have reliable information about compliance. Pensions were rarely mentioned (again the psychiatric case is the exception as the husband had worked for a firm with a generous scheme for many years and though he never disclosed the full value it was thought to exceed £40,000). There were cars, small amounts in building societies and small policies, to take into account. There were also rather unclear financial arrangements within families, including queries about the value of work done by a family member in the building trade on a house and whether this was to be paid for. The house was always the main asset, and often of more value as a roof than as a realisable amount of equity. In the private cases where the realisable equity would be sufficient to underpin a new purchase and the question at issue was finding the income for the ex-wife to maintain the associated expenses, there was more flexibility in negotiation than in this group. In the legally-aided group, selling the house would often not provide enough capital to underpin a new purchase, but leaving the wife in the house would enable her to live on benefit. Selling the house would mean paying the statutory charge and being unable to remain in the owner-occupied sector.

If we summarise these outcomes, we can see that the three "planners" achieved what they wanted, at bills of £500 and £1,500, but with outlier bill of £8,000 as a result of the unrepresented husband's refusal to co-operate with the legal process in any way. In the four primarily children cases, two contact disputes involving violence were resolved at a cost of £500 and £750. Two cases involving financial matters as well as contact were resolved at a cost of £1,000 and £2,000. Three women had moved, two successfully for £1,500, but the third had incurred a bill of £14,000 because of contested residence which she had lost. Of the remaining ten cases, three were enabled to stay in their homes who had not previously realised that this might be possible. Their bills were £1,500, £2,500 and £2,000 and the equity involved was £19,000, £47,000 and £14,000. Of the remaining seven cases, two were unfinished and without a final bill. Of the others, five had secured advantage from the legal involvement beyond purely management, such as the eastern Europeans who were told of the possibility of a Mesher order (bill £1,250), the depressed woman who was enabled to have her flat free of a mortgage (bill £1,000), and the three other women who were able to stay in their homes with similar bills, one of whom was persuaded by her solicitor to reject an initial lump sum. Though her bill reached £4,000 she benefited to the extent of retaining a house with equity of £36,000 and a 30 per cent charge over it, plus maintenance.

C IN CONCLUSION

It might be argued that, given our evidence that solicitors produced material advantages for their clients, the other side was doing badly by legal advice (assuming there was such). That might be the case, but there is a different possibility. We did not think that the solicitors who made gains for their clients operated outside the normative standards which we have discussed in the previous two chapters. If that is so, then the opposing solicitors could still be said to have achieved an outcome for their clients which was within the bounds of those standards. Indeed, as we have also seen, they may have worked hard to persuade their clients to accept those standards.

The purpose of this chapter has been avowedly pragmatic. It sought to demonstrate the kinds of financial values which are at stake in property negotiation on divorce. The sums are seldom trivial, and the practical value of the properties to clients is often extremely important. The evidence suggests that, when we look at the final outcomes, the way the legal process handles these matters is broadly satisfactory from the point of view of the clients. The costs seem to be, on the whole, well related to the value of a service provided by a professional person. This does not demonstrate that other processes may not achieve satisfactory outcomes as well. However, our data provide some kind of benchmark against which further investigations can be measured.

8

Process Issues: Duration and Cost

THE EXAMINATION IN the previous chapter of the end results achieved by the involvement of lawyers with divorcing clients enables us now to re-examine some details of the process with a broad understanding of what it aims to achieve, and what it does achieve. No one, least of all ourselves, would wish to claim that the process is perfect, even making allowances for discrepancies in the ability, commitment and organisational capacities of lawyers. The purpose of this chapter, therefore, is to consider two features which are often associated with this process: delay and cost. We have, we hope, already disposed of the oft-made contention that it is characteristic behaviour of lawyers to aggravate conflict, whether intentionally or otherwise. The previous chapter also sought to put the issue of costs into a broader context of the issues at stake and the achievements attained. Nevertheless, variations in costs do occur, the matter does raise special public concern, and it does therefore warrant further consideration. The same can be said of delay; or, as we would prefer to put it (because the word "delay" implies some untoward action, or inaction), duration.

In examining the course of events from initial contact between client and solicitor to the latest stage of the case, we need both to separate out certain specific issues and also to acquire some sense of how they all come together. The reason for separating out some discrete elements is to enable us to focus our analysis more sharply and to determine the role these features of the process play. We will therefore be examining the following matters in turn:

Obtaining the divorce decree
The Ancillary Relief pilot project
Financial disclosure
"Constructive delay"
Structural reasons for delay
The relevance of legal aid

Intrusions of extraneous matters
Obstructiveness of the parties
Efforts to speed up the process
Solicitor-induced delays

We will then conclude by making some observations on the relationship between duration and cost, and offering some suggestions about the direction the process might take in the future.

A OBTAINING THE DIVORCE DECREE

In examining these issues, we start by looking at the process of obtaining the divorce itself. This is, it must be said, a subsidiary matter to the larger question of bringing closure to the whole legal process of settling the "ancillary" issues. Yet it is of special interest in the context of the proposed new divorce scheme under the Family Law Act 1996 (see p. 1 above) under which, no less than three months after the initiating party has attended an information meeting, a compulsory period of reflection and consideration, initiated by giving notice of breakdown of marriage, and lasting at least nine months, or fifteen if there are children or one party so requests, must run before the divorce is finalised. Thus the total period could be as many as eighteen months from its initiation by attendance at an information meeting. That scheme would reverse the present position, under which the process of *divorce* is, as it were, a process within the process of financial settlement, to one in which the process of *financial settlement* would be conducted within the divorce process. To that end the new scheme would change the present requirement that no court order disposing of financial and property matters can be made until the divorce decree is made to one which, in principle, would require such matters to be disposed of, whether by order or agreement, before the divorce itself is finalised.

In our case study, two clients had already issued divorce petitions before contacting the solicitor. However, the median duration between first contact with the solicitor and issuing the petition was three months, the minimum time (ten cases) being within a month. Lest one may think that this represented a rush to divorce egged on by solicitors, we should point out that the median period from the couple's separation to the issue of the divorce petition was five months. In most cases (three-quarters) the parties had already separated when first contact was made with the solicitor. In nine cases, however, the couple were still living together at the time of contact, and indeed when the petition was issued. In several cases (not always those where the parties were still living together) the client was uncertain at the time of the first visit to the solicitor whether or not he or she wanted a divorce, and desired simply to know how divorce might affect their financial situation or their relationship with their children. The solicitors actively encouraged such clients to go away and reflect on the information they had provided:

"We left it at the end of the meeting that she needed to go away: have a think about it and make sure this was definitely what she wanted to do; and then for her to come back to me and discuss how we move forward". (302)
"But at that stage we didn't issue proceedings immediately. I asked her to go away and think about it, so she could consider her position as to whether she wanted to take that sort of action". (309)

When there were such uncertainties the divorce petition was rarely launched rapidly. There were seven such cases:

Case 107: petition four months after initial contact; parties had separated for one month at time of initial contact.
Case 109: petition four months after initial contact; parties still living together.
Case 304: petition six months after initial contact; the wife had then left home, but there had been a brief reconciliation during this period, but thereafter the wife decided to go for divorce.
Case 305: petition at least eighteen months after first contact. This made it one of the longest cases in our sample from initial contact to final resolution. The wife was very uncertain about divorce, but also very apprehensive about the husband's behaviour and initially hoped that "the mere act of coming to a solicitor would make the husband realise how seriously she viewed the situation". The solicitor had written to the husband immediately about his behaviour, and a year passed before the wife returned, now seeking divorce.
Case 309: petition two months after first contact; but the parties had been separated already for one month, and the wife had been physically assaulted by the husband, occasioning police intervention. Although husband wanted reconciliation, the wife did not. The solicitor had initially asked her not to petition immediately but to think about it.
Case 314: petition some five years after first contact; this was a protracted case, commencing some five years previously with the wife's petition for judicial separation.

In Case 302, the petition was launched in about one month from initial contact, but only after the solicitor had counselled reflection, as the citation above shows. Case 111 might, however, be an exception. This case has already been discussed at length (see Chapter 5, pp. 104–106) where it was remarked that, while a case can be made that more vigorous pursuit of counselling or mediation may have averted fairly protracted legal efforts, including launching a divorce petition which eventually turned out to be redundant, it is by no means clear that they would have succeeded, and in any event the support given by the legal system, through the solicitor, to the wife's interests, may have been particularly beneficial to her at that point in her marriage, and may even have contributed to the eventual reconciliation. And of course the fact that a decree nisi had been granted did not prevent the couple from resuming cohabitation.

We had not expected to discover that holding back on serving a divorce petition, or on applying for a decree nisi, was sometimes used as a tactical device. In two cases, the wife was unwilling to launch proceedings because she felt this was what the husband was hoping for. One solicitor said this was fairly common:

> "It would be playing into his hands – a common reaction. He can wait; he wants the divorce, not me". (107)

Sometimes wives delayed launching proceedings because they were not in immediate need of financial provision. If the husband was still paying the bills, there seemed no need to rush into a procedure which required service of a possibly hostile-looking document on the other party. The solicitors advised: "Let the dust settle" (Case 108). A wife might even go as far as to hold back from serving a petition until the husband had agreed a suitable settlement:

> "If he was keen to have a divorce then tactically that was something she could offer him in return for get the finances sorted out". (320).

This tactic would of course only work if the husband was unable to serve a petition himself, which might be the case if he could not readily find any grounds on which to base the petition.

The point at which the divorce petition was served in these cases would be replaced under the new procedure either by a visit to an information meeting (if this had not already occurred) or the lodging of notice of breakdown of marriage. In the types of circumstances mentioned above, attending the information meeting at the equivalent moment could be seen to be largely redundant, since the solicitor had already conveyed not only relevant information, but also given advice. If the client had attended the meeting earlier (either before seeing the solicitor or very shortly after the first meeting with the solicitor) this would largely reduplicate part of the function of the solicitor, although of course one of the intentions is that it might divert the client from seeing the solicitor at all. This seems to be an unlikely outcome for most potentially divorcing parties, who need advice as well as information (as the research mentioned in Chapter 3 indicates)[1] and in many cases could be damaging to the person concerned by depriving them of the kinds of support which we have observed solicitors giving. It might also "play into the other party's hands", at least if it became known to that party, and to avoid this some people might delay attendance, which would have the effect of pushing back the ultimate dissolution of the marriage much further. On the other hand in a case like Case 111, the strong emphasis expected to be given by the information meetings on the value of counselling might have produced a reconciliation in a way which the solicitor was not able to achieve. In this case the solicitor appeared to do little more than act as go-between between the parties and pass on information about the husband's counselling. Yet we have seen that solicitors are not desperate to push parties into divorce, and the objectives of this aspect of information meetings might be equally well attainable by placing on solicitors duties to provide information to clients about counselling services, which could be monitored through the franchising process.[2]

Of greater significance, perhaps, is the period from petition to grant of decree nisi. The median period here was four months. Since the processing of divorce petitions under the special procedure[3] is essentially an administrative matter for the courts, the length of this period is a function of the court process, not of the behaviour of the solicitors, or of the parties. In all, the median period from first contact

---

[1] See pp. 48–9.

[2] At present there is a statutory requirement for a solicitor to certify in the divorce application *whether or not* the possibility of reconciliation has been discussed between solicitor and client and given the names and addresses of persons who can help in that process: Matrimonial Causes Act 1973, s. 6(1). This weak provision could be replaced by a positive duty to raise the issue. However, Article 11 of the SFLA's Code of Practice states that "you should make sure that your client knows about other available services such as mediation and counselling) which may bring about a settlement, help your client and other family members, or both".

[3] This is explained below, p. 155.

with the solicitor to decree nisi was six months. On this basis, of course, the proposed divorce procedure under the Family Law Act 1996 would be much slower at reaching the stage when an application could be made for an order for divorce, and thus the marriage be brought to an end. However, one feature reduces the contrast. A marriage is not terminated by decree nisi. It is necessary first for the decree to be made absolute. The petitioner must wait six weeks after decree nisi before making the requisite application. If this is not done within three months from decree nisi, the other party may apply for the decree to be made absolute. The original purpose for the delay was to allow the Queen's Proctor to investigate whether there had been any improper collusion over the divorce process, but since divorces are now invariably consensual (or at least not defended) this device seems archaic. However, it seems to be common practice for solicitors to delay application for decree absolute while financial matters remain unresolved, for they wish to retain the applicant's status as a spouse for succession or pension purposes (or sometimes to keep alive matrimonial home rights). The median time therefore between petition and decree absolute was 7.5 months (almost double that between petition and decree nisi); and between first contact with the solicitor and decree absolute it was eleven months. This brings these periods closer to those set out in the Family Law Act 1996, but there would still be a significant difference between the two processes if a client, under the new scheme, has not attended an information meeting before seeing the solicitor, and has children. In such a case, the divorce could not be applied for before eighteen months from attendance at the information meeting. It is true that the proposed compulsory attendance by legal aid clients of a meeting with a mediator would probably spin the process of reaching financial settlement still further, but even so it would seem that in the standard type of case the ancillary issues are likely to be disposed of some six months before the divorce can be finalised. Whether this makes any sense at all we very much doubt. The fear that a visit to a solicitor to obtain advice on divorce matters leads to precipitate action is not borne out by our data. Indeed, the solicitors actively encouraged "reflection and consideration", though, unlike under the proposed scheme, clients could take as long, or as short, a time over this as they wished.

But the structure of the present divorce law did cause difficulties. As the law now stands, the party seeking divorce must allege one of five "facts" in the petition. These are:

(a) that the respondent has committed adultery and the petitioner finds it intolerable to live with him;

(b) that the respondent has behaved in such a way that the petitioner cannot reasonably be expected to live with him;

(c) that the respondent has deserted the petitioner for a continuous period of at least two years;

(d) that the spouses have lived apart for a continuous period of at least two years and that the respondent consents to the decree being granted;

(e) that the spouses have lived apart for a continuous period of at least five years immediately preceding the presentation of the petition.[4]

The first two "facts" are by far the most commonly used because they do not require long periods of time to pass before the petition can be launched.[5] In theory the petition may be opposed by the other party, but this is usually futile because this will only delay the inevitable outcome and incur unnecessary costs. The result is that most petitions are processed without any defence through a "fast track" process known as the "special procedure" which simply involves the judge reading the papers and, if satisfied that the allegations satisfy the statutory requirements set out above, pronounces decree nisi. The fact that the petition makes allegations against the respondent (concerning adultery or other forms of "unreasonable behaviour") has no practical effect on the situation, and will not influence the outcome of any financial dispute, should there be any. It has been reduced merely to a formulaic incantation. Nevertheless, in six of our cases dispute arose as to which party should lodge the petition and what the grounds should be (Cases 107, 113, 310, 311, 317, and 321). For instance, in Case 311 the husband had drafted his petition based on unreasonable behaviour and was ready to file it at court when the wife decided that she would rather petition on his adultery. In Case 321 there were protracted arguments for nine months about who would petition. The husband petitioned on the basis of the wife's adultery, which was the only ground that was acceptable to him within his religion, and the wife petitioned on the basis of his unreasonable behaviour. A contested divorce hearing loomed until the solicitors brokered a solution. In another case (Case 201), where the wife was reluctant to initiate proceedings, the husband felt forced into setting the process in motion by constructing a petition based on unreasonable behaviour. The solicitor commented:

[4] Matrimonial Causes Act 1973, s. 1(2).
[5] See Chapter 1, p. 1.

"It is very often the case that if you start a petition it means the other party at least has to react; so I said to him, 'you'd better start proceedings against her on the basis of unreasonable behaviour . . . she would deny it and with a bit of luck she'd cross-petition'; so we issue our petition and serve it, so they reject it . . . if the clients had carried out their supposed intentions at the out-set we wouldn't have been in this situation . . . proceedings would have started straight off . . . and we're into a potentially contested divorce (reads letter): 'in the circumstances our client sees no point in defending . . . and will allow them to proceed undefended, but reserves her right to dispute the allegations': all highly artificial. . .". (201)

The divorce procedure produced still further complications. In about a third of the cases some delay occurred between the issue of the petition and acknowledgment of service. In the majority of these cases, the delay was caused by the respondent's reluctance to co-operate with the divorce proceedings. In three cases (Cases 202, 203, and 312) the petitioner's solicitor had to organise bailiff service of the papers, in one case (Case 305) the papers were re-served care of the respondent's solic-itors and in another (Case 314) the petitioner obtained a court order to proceed without acknowledgment. We should add that problems with the courts sometimes caused delay. In Cases 303, 314 and 321 the long gap between petition and acknowledgment was due to the time taken by the court to process the papers. In two the respondent's solicitor was the cause of the delay; in one (Case 102) by mislaying the documents; in the other, as a non-family specialist, not being aware of the procedures.

The new divorce scheme, if introduced, ought to reduce, if not elim-inate, some of these difficulties, and it may very well be that the new procedure, which establishes irretrievable breakdown of marriage solely on the basis of lapse of time between lodging notice of break-down and application for divorce, without the opportunity of making allegations, will be an improvement on the old in this respect. However, the sheer length of time which must elapse before divorce can be finalised under the proposed procedure might work against these advantages.

B   THE ANCILLARY RELIEF PILOT PROJECT

This project has been described in Chapter 1, and eight of our cases (Cases 201, 204, 205, 304, 308, 315, 319, and 322) had encountered its operation. In one other (Case 312), the solicitor was intending to suggest that the client should use it. The solicitors generally expressed very favourable views about the scheme. It was thought to impose a discipline on the process, and to speed it up:

"I think it's marvellous because it stops lawyers taking the piss because the procedure's so straightforward. They've taken the procedures and taken all the dodginess and all the things that the old hacks could do about delaying things . . . they've taken all that out. The court really takes a tight hold". (308)
"It brings things along very quickly". (315)

Some solicitors commented that matters could even be settled as a result of the First Appointment:

"I have had ones . . . where the judge has given, even at the [first appointment] a view as to how this probably should settle, and has been quite directive". (308)
"I like getting into court at the first appointment. I have had several cases that settled at first appointment and . . . you know . . . going to the first appointment with hopefully a properly completed Form E seems to cut a lot of nonsense away where there was no court imposed timetable." "Why I like the pilot scheme, the judges are prepared to give an indication of what they think the level of settlement is going to be, based on Form E and it's sometimes very useful for someone to hear from the judge how a court would approach the division of assets. They wouldn't accept it from the wife's solicitors, sometimes they won't accept it from their own solicitors, but if they hear it from the judge . . . this is how it's going to go . . . it concentrates the mind". (205)

Form E was felt to be an improvement on the use of affidavits:

" . . . on an affidavit people just waffle on about anything, including behaviour – you know: 'She left me and that's why I want more money' etc. And with Form E, you're dissuaded from doing that. It's very much about hard facts. And having been to a few final hearings recently, the courts are just interested in – How big is the pie and how are we going to divide it". (312)
"[With Form E] there's no fuzziness as there was with affidavits". (319)
"The advantage of the pilot scheme is that the main bit of the work comes when you do the Form E, and there isn't this free for all that you get with the other schemes. With those, all you get is a pile of bank statements and you think: 'What on earth is the use of these?' There was no structure to it, and the judge at the final hearing looks at it all and says, 'Is all of this necessary?' The thing with the pilot scheme is that the judge has to approve the questions that you're asking: so you don't have a fishing expedition". (322)

"She was asking for disclosure, so I felt – if we are going to have to provide disclosure, it's got to be reasonably detailed if she's not going to go along with the basic agreement – to avoid duplicating a lot of effort, let's put our information in form of a formal Form E statement". (201)

The general point was that the structure and the timetabling focuses attention:

"It gets the adrenalin going if there's a court hearing. Often with files nothing happens until – ooh, there's a court hearing. Rush, rush, rush . . . psychologically not only for the clients but also for the solicitors, you think: 'Right, I've got to have my house in order by that date, not just to make sure that I've given full disclosure for my client but to make sure that I've analysed husband's material so that I know what the issues are'". (319)

There were criticisms, but these seemed to be the result of singular bad experiences:

"I came out thinking – Oh, I don't like the pilot scheme any more, but I think that was very much a one-off – where I think the district judge erred . . . she'd had a quick look at the documents and drew too many conclusions too fast – she didn't let things open up a little bit . . . at FDRs in the pilot scheme, the judges are entitled to comment on the likely view the court will take, and she was just with a wave of her hand saying, 'Well, of course husband has probably made full disclosure' – it was a load of rubbish". (319)

The solicitor claimed this had a devastating effect on the client. Another solicitor recounted a bad experience:

" . . . the problem we're having, and it's a problem I think all practitioners are having, is that certain DJs – you get in front of deputies on a FDR and they are just fantastic. And, interestingly, I've had two or three in front of deputies, which is the best of all because they're still practitioners and they really kick arse. They do what the FDR is meant to do. . . . this one was in front of [] . . . the concept to him of having some kind of negotiated conciliatory FDR, I mean he was just disgusted by even being in the room! . . . he hates solicitors and he loves barristers, and there was very posh counsel from King's Bench Walk on the other side who treated it as a hearing . . . he effectively made submissions for half an hour. So I was sitting there thinking, 'I'm sure this isn't the way this is supposed to go', and my client was there saying, 'I thought you said this was a discussion – what's happening?' So he heard submissions, nodding sagely at every point . . . and then he turned to me and stared right down his nose and said, 'Yes?' . . . So they need some education, but otherwise the pilot project is marvellous". (308)

Even Form E was subject to some criticism:

> "I like the pilot scheme, but the forms are dreadful to complete, especially when you've got assets all over the place". (319)

All in all, however, solicitors welcomed a machinery which appeared to move the process along. How far it actually did so, however, is harder to measure. In seven of the eight cases which used this procedure, the application for a first appointment was issued within five months of the divorce petition. The reason for the time lapse was, of course, usually because the solicitor was establishing information and exploring possibilities of settlement without going to court. One of the cases had to wait a further six months before first appointment, two a further five months, three waited four months and the remaining two only three months. The median (four months) is slightly longer than the KPMG research found (where the median was eighty-seven days), but we read nothing into this. This means that in the standard case, if there is such a thing, which used the pilot project procedure, some seven to eight months will have passed since the divorce petition was filed before the first appointment occurs. In only one case (Case 205) was agreement actually reached at the first appointment. The gap between the first appointment and the Financial Dispute Resolution (FDR) hearing tended to be short: one month in two cases and two in three; but in one it was five months. In one case (Case 201) the FDR hearing was aborted, and the case only settled seven months after it would have taken place. In two (Cases 304 and 315) settlement was reached before the FDR hearing and this also happened in Case 204, but under pressure of the imminence of the hearing. For the two cases (Cases 308 and 319) which went on to a full hearing after the FDR, the hearings were fixed for five and seven months' time respectively. One settled at the door of the court and one during the hearing.

It is not easy to establish very clearly how far the pilot project cases were processed faster than the others. If we take the median time from applications for ancillary relief hearings (excluding consent applications) to disposal in our cases it was eight months for the pilot project cases and seven months for the rest. KPMG found the median number of days from application to conclusion to be 183 (just under six months) for pilot project cases and 236 (seven and a half months) for control cases. In all our cases, the median time from *petition* to disposal (by consent or otherwise) for the pilot project cases was thirteen

Table 8.1 *Duration of cases, from petition to disposal, comparing pilot project and other cases showing major stages in process*

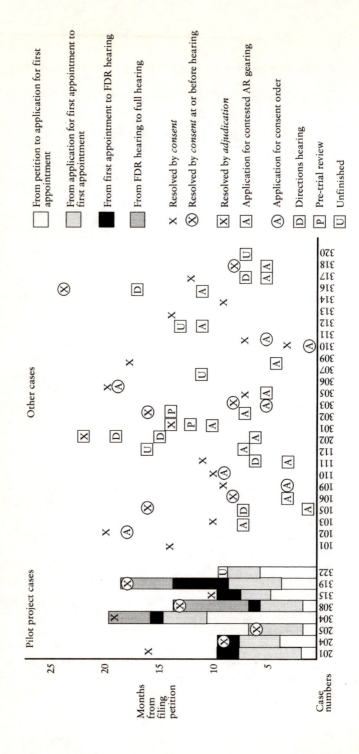

months compared with between eleven and twelve months for *all* the others, however disposed of. Although our sample size precludes us making a valid statistical comparison with the KPMG figures, it is still disappointing that in our set of cases the pilot project did not seem to bring matters to a quicker conclusion than when other procedures were used, though none of them went on for quite as long as the longest "non-pilot project" cases (Table 8.1). This seems to be true even though, in our cases, lawyers brought the matter to the courts more quickly when the pilot project was available. This may be because, if it is not available, lawyers spend more time trying to negotiate a deal without resort to the court. This occurred in Cases 102 (settlement reached eighteen months from petition), 110 (settlement reached nine months from petition) and 303 (settlement reached five months from petition). Contrast the pilot project cases, where seven out of the eight saw applications made to the court within five months from filing the petition. But we should perhaps not only refer to the consent applications here, but also to applications for contested proceedings which were afterwards settled without any court activity: these were Cases 103 (application made seven months from petition), 305 (application made five months from petition) and 309 (application made four months from petition). Had the pilot project been operating, it is possible that all these cases might have activated the court machinery under the scheme. They may have settled more quickly as a result (median time of settlement was at ten months from petition, compared with the median of nine months for our pilot project cases) and the two "outlying" cases were longer than the longest two of the pilot project cases, but whether money would have been saved is doubtful.

This information gives some support to the view that the presence of the pilot project might draw cases into the court process which might otherwise not have gone there. Some solicitors interviewed by KPMG suggested that the scheme might encourage early applications, but the KPMG report felt unable to express a concluded view on this, although it admitted it might have a considerable bearing on the overall cost of the scheme.[6] Our data does not settle the matter conclusively either way, though it keeps open the possibility that the scheme might encourage solicitors to use the courts when the case might have settled anyway, given more time spent in negotiation. One solicitor thought that the assistance of the court would save costs:

[6] KPMG Report, paras. 6.1.2; 7.8.5.

". . . unless things are going to settle very easily I would always use it . . . if we can afford it, you are more likely to get a speedy result now with the pilot procedure, certainly not under the old system. I think it's cheaper . . . if you've been negotiating for a year . . . if you cost it, it's actually more expensive, firing off letters and doing everything .. sort of being drip fed, rather than a great pack of disclosure. I actually think it's cheaper". (204)

But the solicitor obviously had not worked out how much judicial time costs, and seemed willing to use up that time in all but what seemed to be very easy cases. Another solicitor indicated that the procedure might be quite expensive for the parties:

"This is one of the problems of the pilot scheme even in some of the really potentially very straightforward cases, you have to involve counsel if you're going to be sensible about it . . . if you're a solicitor protecting your own back as well . . . so that the barrister has to have some input". (201)

We will return to the question of costs in relation to the pilot project later (p. 178).

C   FINANCIAL DISCLOSURE

Problems over obtaining disclosure of information from a party were a major reason for adding to the duration of a case. Sometimes the reasons were straightforward. Delays were caused by waiting for third parties to produce necessary information. A self-employed man may be reluctant (for a variety of reasons) for information about his income to be known. Sometimes delays were caused by waiting for third parties to produce necessary information.

Sometimes the parties' circumstances accounted for the difficulty: for example, in Case 307, the husband was a long-distance lorry driver, difficult to get hold of (the case remained unresolved eleven months after petition), and, in the same case, the solicitor said of the wife:

"(She is) a bit vague and works at her own pace. So you ask her, and after a few chases, she then rings you up out of the blue and provides the information. That's because she just lives in her dream world. Gets on and does her work, and then when she thinks about it, she gets back to me".

In other cases, the problem seemed to lie in the parties' attitudes. In Case 319 the husband's circumstances had improved since separation, and he was unwilling to reveal the extent of this. This was a pilot project case, and it took eighteen months to resolve from time of petition. Indeed, one of the purposes of the pilot project is to assist this process, for each party is supposed to make disclosure in terms of Form E thirty-five days before the first appointment. Seven days before the appointment they must file with the court, and on each other, a questionnaire seeking what further information they want, and at the hearing the district judge will decide how far the questionnaires need to be answered. In four cases (Cases 104, 202, 304 and 317), penal notices had been served on non-disclosing parties, one leading to committal for contempt; one of these was a pilot project case (Case 304). One of the non-pilot cases (Case 202) took longer than the pilot case, but the others were shorter. It would not therefore seem that the pilot project necessarily produces quicker results where a high degree of coercion is required.

But why was information so difficult to obtain? In one of those four cases (Case 317), it was forthcoming anyway, and the issuing of the penal notice was a tactic used to speed things along by perhaps the most aggressive solicitor in our sample. But in the other three, the husbands were simply being obstructive. It is difficult to know why. In Case 202, he simply refused to regard himself under any obligation to the wife; in Case 304 the husband refused to play any part in negotiation, and indeed resorted to violence. In Case 104, the obstructiveness may have been encouraged by the fact that the husband had at one time thought the wife had accepted an informal offer, which, after consideration by the lawyer, had subsequently been rejected. Such an occurrence also lay behind three other cases where disclosure was a problem (Cases 102, 201 and 318). In those cases the issue came to the solicitor after some informal agreement had already been reached between the parties. In one case this had happened several years earlier. Now that matters were being finalised through formal divorce, solicitors often raised questions (such as over pensions) which the parties may not have considered, and required further disclosure in order to give appropriate advice. The other party, who had thought the matter settled, tended to resist providing this information.

This evidence might support the perception (see p. 6) that lawyers "re-open settled agreements". But were they right to do so? In all cases the lawyers had given the client the chance to reflect on what to do, after having discussed the matter with them. In Case102, which lasted some two years, the wife's solicitors (who were the "other side") had tried to obtain additional information from the husband. He felt aggrieved by this, but set about providing it. Eventually the wife changed her solicitors, and the Consent Order followed the original agreement. The efforts by the wife's solicitors here prolonged the case by about a year, for no appreciable gain by her. On the other hand, the husband's solicitor did feel he had got "a better deal than a court would have awarded", so it may be that the wife's original solicitors had good grounds for believing that their client could reasonably hope to do better than she had done in the agreement. Case 201 went on for some thirty months, and resulted in a settlement not very different from the one originally contemplated by the parties. There were a variety of reasons for this, one of which was the requirement of disclosure about the husband's pension position, which was activated when the husband's solicitor (our interviewee) insisted (reasonably) that the Consent Order should contain an order waiving any future claims against his pension. Part of the problem in this case appeared to be lack of proper legal advice in the early stages. The wife had wanted a clean break, but had not seemed to realise what needed to be done to achieve such a result. Had she been properly advised about this when they reached their original outline agreement, and dealt with it then, the matter could have been disposed of. There was the further difficulty that the wife did not seem to realise that finality could only be achieved within the context of a divorce. Case 318 was unusual in that the parties had informally separated some five years earlier, splitting the equity of the house more or less equally. Now that the wife sought divorce, she wanted a lump sum. The husband resisted disclosure, but after an application was made for an ancillary relief hearing, the parties settled (eight months after the petition), the wife obtaining an extra £11,000.

So in two of those cases the husband's resistance to further disclosure may have been avoided, or lessened, had the issues been fully settled earlier on. Of course, that cannot be certain. There are clearly many cases where the parties make their own arrangements without involving lawyers and no problems subsequently arise; formal legal involvement might prolong matters at that stage. It would be particularly unfortunate if parties had been through mediation and reached settlement only to have matters re-opened when the agreement was examined later by a lawyer. This is not to suggest that the lawyer would be wrong to raise matters at that stage if it appears that the agreement does not adequately protect the client's interests. Rather, it suggests the importance of having those interests understood and represented from the beginning. This is becoming more important to the extent that legislation grants additional rights to divorcing parties, as in the case of legislation on pensions. If mediation is to become widely used, especially in financial matters, it is important that it should mesh in with appropriate and timely legal advice.

Nevertheless, it remains a difficult question of judgment whether a client should be advised to settle when all the facts may not be known. We have already mentioned one way in which an obdurate opponent might be encouraged to make disclosure, which is by putting forward concrete proposals based on inferences about the opponent's financial position, since this is what a court may do if not satisfied about disclosure (above p. 122). That might be accompanied by further requests for disclosure, but it also needs to be decided whether pressing for disclosure is always going to improve the client's case. One solicitor expressed the decision as being whether doing so was cost-effective:

> "You have to decide whether it's worth digging any deeper – it's not cost effective". (105)

Perhaps the criterion of cost-effectiveness is too loose. In Case 201, although the opposing solicitor may have felt that it was worth delving further into the husband's pension position, in view of his general income position (which was known) and the offer on the table, it was unlikely that further information from the husband on the matter would have altered matters much, and indeed it did not. The requests simply held up progress. This seemed also to have been true for Case 102. On the other hand, insisting on further disclosure sometimes seemed necessary, as in Case 301, when more information was sought by the client husband when his wife moved in with another man; and indeed the husband himself had not been fully frank with his solicitor (our interviewee) when disclosure was sought from them:

> "We then started to find out that not only had he got a plot of land, but he also had a garage which he hadn't mentioned . . . things like that tended to crop up". (301)

The solicitor found out about them from letters from the other side; when confronted, the husband would confirm it. Nevertheless, we think that solicitors can sometimes be too insistent in seeking information. The SFLA's Good Practice Committee has issued a Guide to Good Practice in Family Law on Disclosure. This however concentrates almost entirely on the duty to *make* disclosure and issues such as entrapment and when self-help is permissible. While these are no doubt important, our evidence suggested that guidance about the extent to which parties might be pressed *for* disclosure might be given some attention. The Pre-Application Protocol issued on 25 May 2000 (see below p. 178), while stressing the importance of avoiding friction and unnecessary costs, does not address this issue. Nor should it be necessary for the court to be enlisted to impose this kind of discipline. We think that the criterion to be applied for persisting in seeking disclosure should be whether there are strong grounds for believing that the further information will significantly improve the client's position.

D "CONSTRUCTIVE DELAY"

There are a variety of reasons why a solicitor might think that delay could be helpful to the client. We have already noted (above p. 153) that there were seven cases where the solicitor allowed time to elapse before issuing the divorce petition because it was felt that clients should not be rushed into a divorce when they were uncertain whether they really wanted it. In two cases (112, 304) proceedings were held up because of reconciliation between the parties.

Other "constructive" grounds were more matters of tactics. It was sometimes thought that a "softly, softly" approach was more likely to avoid aggravation and lead to agreement, as the solicitor put it in Case 111. Similarly, in Case 108, where the wife, whose husband had just walked out on her and the children, was said to be "shell shocked and not seeking reconciliation", the solicitor advised that she took her time:

"If the bills are paid and there is no world war 3, let it simmer". (108)

It was often thought it was desirable to settle various matters consecutively, because to try to deal with too many issues simultaneously can confuse and aggravate the issues. This was particularly so with respect to issues concerning the children and financial matters. So in Case 106, where the wife wished to bring the contact issue to resolution, the solicitor considered it best to resolve this issue first, since the husband was continuing to pay the mortgage. In Case 316 likewise, the solicitor thought it best to stall on the husband's financial offers while the outcome of proceedings regarding the residence of the children were awaited. The solicitor explained:

"My experience is it's a disadvantage when you've got a Children Act dispute, quite apart from the fact that you can't decide the finances before you decide the children, it tends to focus attention elsewhere. So in theory there's no reason you couldn't issue your Ancillary Relief applications and have it running in tandem; in practice it's not that common". (316)

Similarly, in Case 203, the solicitor remarked:

"The first hurdle to be overcome was to get to the stage of decree nisi, and when it was clear the divorce was going to proceed without difficulty, it was time to consider finances. The wife was residing in the house with one child of the family, so her position wasn't unduly prejudiced in the intervening period; what I wanted to do was to get the divorce progressed to the point of decree nisi or close thereto". (203)

The problem with this approach, though, is that "constructive" delay might become obstructive, for where a party (such as a husband who is living in the home) has no incentive to settle, it might take coercive action or its threat to kick start the negotiation process. We have observed (above pp. 120–1) that this appears to be one of the main reasons why the aid of the courts is enlisted when we considered the problem that lack of incentives to negotiate can create.

Another reason for holding back arose in connection with application for decree absolute. It was quite common for solicitors to wish to wait until financial matters were finally settled before applying for a decree nisi to be made absolute. In this way, the wife's inheritance, pension and matrimonial home rights would be preserved intact until the finances are secured. (Cases 103, 110, 202, 317 and 318). In one case the solicitor said he would not apply for decree absolute until his bill was paid (Case 308). If it was known the "other side" was anxious for something which was within the solicitor's control, it seemed quite reasonable to use this as a bargaining counter. So in a case where the husband was keen for the divorce to come through, but the wife was not, the solicitor advised delaying the petition in order to put pressure on the husband to provide information about his pension (Case 104).

E   STRUCTURAL REASONS FOR DELAY

In seven cases, reference was made to delays originating from the processing of legal aid applications. In one case (Case 321) the solicitor appealed an initial rejection of legal aid. In Case 307 the Board error had led to an initial refusal, a revised offer and finally an appropriate certificate six months after application. In Case 312 the Board has mislaid papers sent by the client, and the certificate took some three months to arrive (similarly in Case 110). Other matters also took time, especially obtaining valuations of property and other assets.

> "You write to someone about a pension . . . it takes its normal course . . . a few months". (107)

Dealings with the courts were frequent causes of delay, a point which might cause some apprehension in view of the likely increased involvement of courts when the "pilot project" is made general. The worst cases were:

> 205: four month delay in obtaining first appointment under "pilot project";
> 301: local court two months behind on divorce petitions;
> 302: court flooded; two month delay;
> 312: court lost documents, accusing solicitor of not sending them, then finding them;
> 314: four month delay in court sending out judicial separation papers; further delay in consent order as court insisted on hearing as wife was unrepresented;
> 316: four month gap before final contested hearing because of court unavailability;
> 322: solicitor had to chase up decree nisi.

Solicitors often cited as a reason for delay the fact that the other party was either unrepresented by a solicitor, or was only represented for intermittent periods. This clearly made dealing with them very difficult. Thus in Case 102, the solicitor found it difficult to deal with the wife (the "other side") who chopped and changed between solicitors, and sometimes acted on her own. This was also a serious problem in Case 201. In Case 113 the husband, who was ensconced in the matrimonial home, refused either to go to mediation or to see a solicitor. Eventually he made an offer which left no room for negotiation; the matter was finally resolved after the solicitor wrote to him and threatened injunction proceedings.

F THE RELEVANCE OF LEGAL AID

In *Simple Quarrels*[7] Davis and his colleagues suggested that the fact that a case was legally aided meant that it took longer to work through the system than if it had been privately funded. Our own data support this, but only very weakly. Table 8.2 shows the length of time (in months) from first contact between client and solicitor and resolution of the issue in cases involving money or property. The median period for cases where both clients were paying for themselves was twelve to thirteen months. Where it was known that at least one of the parties was legally aided, the period was fourteen to fifteen months. This compares with a figure of an *average* period of 16.8 months for the period from first contact to "settlement" for legally aided cases revealed by the Legal Aid Board Research Unit.[8] The LABRU figures show a lower average of 7.36 months for children only cases, but we cannot make any comparisons from our data with that figure because we have insufficient data. However, our figure for financial and property cases is close to that of the LABRU data and is only slightly higher than that for privately funded cases in our study. Indeed, the difference may be accounted for simply by the time taken to acquire a legal aid certificate, which we have already seen can be a cause of delay. We do not therefore find any evidence that, apart from the time taken to process the legal aid application, the fact that one or both of the parties to a case is legally aided was *itself* a reason for the case taking longer to reach resolution. This finding differs from that made in *Simple Quarrels*.[9] One reason for the difference may lie in the nature of the sample: we were looking at a wider range of activity than in that study. However, it is also possible that the effects of franchising have played a part in reducing the phenomenon of "drift" which the earlier study found to be present in some legal aid cases.

We will consider the connection between legal aid and cost later (p. 177).

---

[7] Above p. 53, note 32, pp. 139–49; 263.

[8] Sarah Maclean, *Report of the Case Profiling Study: Legal Aid and the Family Justice System*, Legal Aid Board Research Unit, 1998, p. 44, Fig. 4.12.

[9] *Simple Quarrels*, at p. 263, above p. 53.

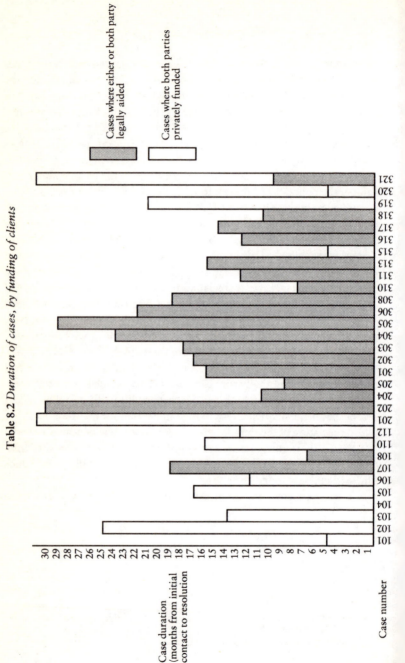

Table 8.2 *Duration of cases, by funding of clients*

G INTRUSION OF EXTRANEOUS MATTERS

It was remarked above that solicitors usually tried to dispose of discrete matters separately, so that for example, they were unwilling to have problems regarding contact to become entangled with financial negotiation. Of course it was not always possible (or desirable) to deal with children and financial issues consecutively, and when they were dealt with concurrently, solicitors tried hard to prevent one issue obstructing progress on the other. This was successfully achieved in Case 107, where the solicitor was proud to have prevented such entanglements. But where they failed to keep such matters apart, delays could occur. So, in Case 102, just when financial matters were almost agreed, the wife suddenly said she would only provide sought-for information if the husband agreed several changes to the contact arrangements, causing some delay. In Case 106, the parties appeared to be proceeding to an amicable settlement, when a contact dispute flared and the wife sought more than she originally asked, eventually doing better by some £37,000 after a directions hearing. Even more striking was Case 109 where, after the draft Consent Order had been submitted to the court, the husband discovered that the wife had been having an affair. He wanted to withdraw the agreement, and raised matters of residence and contact that had not been in issue before. Both solicitors here believed that they should avoid exacerbating the situation, since they believed that in time the husband would "calm down". A similar event occurred in Case 301, when the husband withdrew his offer after discovering his wife's affair. Other externalities were less dramatic, as where the wife had a new baby, or where the sale of the house fell through (Cases 112 and 311), but some were even more disturbing, as when one of the parties became subject to drug trafficking investigations, another was subject to bankruptcy proceedings and a third prosecuted (unsuccessfully) for sexual abuse (Cases 308, 316 and 321).

H OBSTRUCTIVENESS OF THE PARTIES

Considering all the factors mentioned above, it can be well understood why cases can take a longer time to conclude than at first sight would seem reasonable. But on top of those matters, we must add perhaps the most common reason for holding up progress, which was the general acrimony between the parties. Arguments could arise on almost every conceivable issue. Here are a few matters about which parties became deeply conflicted:

- Who should pay the costs of the divorce (Cases 101, 102, 105).
- Items of furniture (Case 103: "suddenly he starts talking of clocks after he gets the clean break").
- Who should petition (Cases 102, 105, 112, 201, 321).
- Grounds for divorce (Cases 107).
- Family debts (Case 111).

Extreme obduracy could lead to very prolonged procedures, such as where the husband refused to recognise he was under any obligation whatever, and ignored even court orders (Case 202). In other cases, the "other side" either ignored communications or responded very reluctantly (Cases 203 and 305). We have already discussed resistance to disclosure of information (p. 162–3).

I EFFORTS TO SPEED UP THE PROCESS

We discussed in Chapter 6 the occasions when solicitors had resort to the courts, or threat of it, to bring about resolution to the problem (p. 118). Although court applications might take time, solicitors often thought that this would bring about a quicker resolution than prolonging fruitless negotiation. We will not repeat these cases here, though we would note that a wish to speed things along was as pervasive a motivation as the wish to resolve the problem itself. But solicitors would also urge the parties to avoid argument as far as possible, knowing that such disputes only prolonged matters. This wish lay behind the common advice to the parties not to complicate matters by introducing extraneous matters, such as who should petition, or matters about the children, into the financial negotiation. But besides such persuasion, some solicitors urged a meeting with counsel as a way to move things along. In Cases 308 and 312, for example, the solicitor called a meeting with counsel in an attempt to have their clients take a more realistic view of their situation. In Case 103 a round-table meeting between the two solicitors was held in the first month to speed things through; when matters subsequently became difficult again, another meeting was held. The second meeting was described as "constructive", though it did not lead to an immediate resolution of the negotiation.

Solicitors attributed a variety of reasons why some cases proceeded more quickly than others. They felt that intelligent clients who had some idea of finances were more likely to move matters forward faster, and it was also important that the other side should take legal advice. There were a variety of comments suggesting that it was helpful if the other solicitor was a family law specialist, and even more helpful if the solicitor was known to them.

J SOLICITOR-INDUCED DELAYS

We must not be thought to suggest that shortcomings of solicitors themselves played no part in slowing down the process. Sometimes the reasons were innocent enough; in four cases matters were held up while either or both of the solicitors were on holiday. But in eight cases progress was impeded by mistakes made by one of the solicitors. Sometimes these were of a relatively minor nature, as where Consent Orders were returned because of errors (Cases 102, 109, 110 [order returned twice], 201 and 311), or where the same happened regarding the divorce petition (Case 304) or acknowledgement of service (Case 315). On a couple of occasions the error was more serious. In Case 102 the other side's solicitor claimed to have sent an acknowledgement of service of the petition, but months later found it in the office. In Case 306 both solicitors made errors; the other one, not a family specialist, kept sending the wrong forms, and the interviewed solicitor himself forgot to apply for decree absolute, being reminded to do so by the interview!

K CONCLUSIONS: DURATION AND COST

The above analysis shows that there is a variety of reasons, some good and some bad, why resolution of the issues might take longer in some cases than in others. But the easy and almost automatic inference that the longer a case takes, the higher the costs, which has informed so much official (and popular) criticism of the divorce process needs to be questioned. For example, one might criticise the relaxed attitude of the solicitor who seemed undisturbed by the fact that it might take two months to receive an answer to a question about a party's pension position, but at a time when it was known that pension companies were finding it difficult to deal with the volume of such inquiries, it would have raised costs had the lawyer written fruitless letters seeking to prompt more rapid action. So it does not follow that the passage of time necessarily runs up legal costs. Of course, while issues remain unresolved one or possibly even both parties may be incurring unwarranted expenses, and it is possible, as one of our solicitors suggested, that further complications may arise while a case is becalmed, but it is also possible that various issues may resolve themselves during such periods. In any event, an analysis of the costs to the client in relation to the length of time from initial contact with the solicitor to resolution of the issues, demonstrates that there is no necessary connection between the two. We set this out in Table 8.3 for the cases in which we had sufficient information to do this. The median cost does rise from just under £1,000 for cases disposed of within nine months to £2,500 for those resolved between ten and eighteen months, but *falls back* again to £2,000 for cases lasting between nineteen months and two years.

As we have already observed, the size of our sample is too small for confident generalisations to be made. However, our cases certainly show that many cases of longer duration can cost less than shorter duration cases. The connection, insofar as there is any, between cost and duration, may be indirect, since various other features which push costs up may also extend duration. To try to detect what these may be, we examine closely those cases in our sample where the costs to the client were £5,000 or higher. These were Cases 204, 106, 316, 105, 301, 319, 202 and 201. We also include case 321, for which the solicitor was unable to give a precise figure for costs, but estimated that it would run to "several thousands".

Case 204: The client (the wife) was legally aided. This was fairly straightforward, the only complication being working out the husband's extensive pension assets. But there was no disclosure problem. The solicitor, who was very enthusiastic about the "pilot project", made an early application under the scheme, and the matter was settled at the FDR hearing. Although the use of the pilot project brought about relatively rapid resolution, the factor which raised the costs here was the use of counsel which increased them by £1,000.

Case 106: The wife was a private client. Here the case had started relatively calmly, but became conflicted as a result of a contact dispute. A

Table 8.3 *Cost of case to client by length of process*

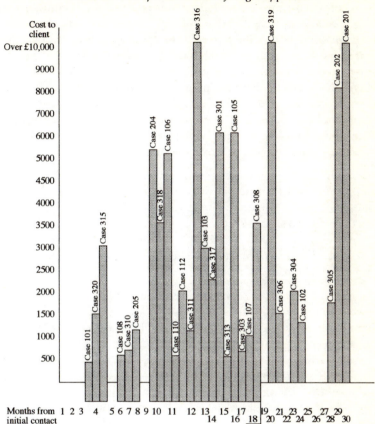

mediation session was held, but failed. The contact issue went as far as a directions hearing, and the dispute exacerbated the financial resolution, which occurred eventually by consent.

Case 316: The wife was legally aided. The case was greatly complicated by two factors. First, the husband was bankrupt, so the wife needed to establish a beneficial interest in the matrimonial home under the law of trusts in order to preserve it for her from the trustee-in-bankruptcy. Proceedings were issued to determine this point. There was also a conflict over the residence of the child, which was settled at the door of the court after mediation had failed.

Case 105: The wife was a private client. The case was relatively straightforward, mostly revolving around how the modest equity in the home should be shared. Yet negotiations failed and settlement was achieved only during the hearing. The solicitors considered that the case was not helped by the husband being represented by "out-of-town" solicitors, but that the main reason for failure of the negotiations lay in the fact that both parties were "very entrenched. [It was] very acrimonious from the outset . . . [their] positions remained the same until the hearing date". One reason for this was that the husband was disappointed by a failed attempt at reconciliation, and feelings were aggravated by conflict over an informal debt to the wife's family.

Case 301: The husband was a private client, and the parties were living together at initial contact. He became extremely upset when his wife moved out and he discovered she had a lover. He withdrew his previous offers and resisted all attempts by the solicitor to make a more realistic offer. The husband eventually lost the contested hearing, the court ordering him to pay an amount close to that which the solicitor had advised him to make all along.

Case 319: The wife was a private client. The parties had long been separated at the time of initial contact, and had agreed to an informal arrangement without advice. She now sought to renegotiate the whole arrangement, which the husband resisted. Whether the wife was making sufficient efforts to support herself became a major issue, and the husband's dissatisfaction on that score caused him to resist disclosure. After a FDR hearing under the pilot project had been unfavourable to the wife, the solicitor urged her to think very carefully about prolonging the dispute, but the wife decided to press on, and eventually secured a much better deal at the day of the hearing.

Case 202: The wife was legally aided. The case was complicated by the fact that the husband, from a southern European country, refused to accept that the wife was entitled to anything, and refused to make any response to her claims. The matter eventually went to a full hearing. The husband failed to comply with the order and a judgment summons was issued.

Case 201: The husband was a private client. Here the parties had made an initial agreement, without advice. The wife sought a clean break, but was unwilling to initiate divorce proceedings which were necessary to secure that objective. When she sought legal advice, her solicitors raised issues over the husband's pension, and were not satisfied with his offer. The matter was resolved at first appointment under the pilot project. The issues were relatively straightforward (apart from the divorce wrangle), and the costs were pushed up by the employment of counsel.

Case 321: The husband was legally aided. This case was complicated both by a dispute over who should petition for divorce (there were religious complications) and a serious contact dispute which arose after there had been an unsuccessful criminal prosecution against the husband for sexual abuse of the child. There was no real dispute over finances, which issues were resolved nine months after initial contact.

A significant cause for costs to rise appears to be where the financial issues are combined with other conflicts (such as contact or residence) or other legal problems (as in the case involving trusts). These additional conflicts not only generate costs in themselves, but are also capable of making resolution of financial issues more difficult. The solicitors are clearly right in wanting to keep these matters distinct. This is consistent with the apparent willingness of solicitors to refer child-related matters to mediation, while retaining control over the settlement of financial issues. This gives us a further ground for concern over the new procedures introduced for legally aided clients by section 29 of the Family Law Act 1996 (discussed above p. 24) under which "all issues" should in principle be referred to mediation prior to consideration of an application for legal aid.

Although there appeared to be no necessary connection between the duration of a case and its costs, and no apparent relationship between its duration and whether the case was legally aided or privately funded and its duration, it may still have been the case that the costs of legally aided and privately funded cases were different as a result of some other factors. However, as Table 8.4 shows, we did not find an obvious difference. The median cost in the privately funded cases in our sample was between £2,000 and £2,700; for the legally aided cases it was £2,000 . This compares with the *average* cost of legally aided financial and property cases of £1,400 described in the LABRU report.[10] But that is an average figure, and excludes expensive outlying cases where costs were above £5,000. Were we to exclude similar "outliers" in our sample, the median would reduce to £1,500 for the legally aided cases and £1,200 for those which were privately funded. So, while private clients

[10] Sarah Maclean, above p. 169, note 8.

seem to spend more if "non-standard" cases are included, for the "standard" case the difference was so small that we must conclude that, in our sample, legal aid had no significant impact on costs.

The most significant reason why some cases appeared to be more costly than others seemed to lie in the attitudes of the parties themselves. This might indeed have been present in the cases where a variety of matters become conflicted, but it could also have driven up costs where money and property alone were in issue. Sometimes the basis for the bitterness might have lain in the fact that the parties had reached an informal agreement, without legal advice, at an earlier stage, and one of them now sought to depart from the arrangement (Cases 201 and 319). In other cases (Cases 105, 301, 319 and 202) the hostility, whatever its origin, caused one party either to cling doggedly to a set position, whatever legal advice might have been given, or to refuse to recognise any claims made against him at all. There seems little that can be done in these cases other than to deploy the legal process in favour of the claimant. Mediation is unlikely to resolve these cases.

We note with some concern that three of these nine expensive cases fell under the Ancillary Relief Pilot procedure. Perhaps they would have incurred similar costs under the old procedure, though there seems to be some reason to believe that Case 204 might well have been settled without the use of that procedure, and the employment of counsel significantly increased overall costs. This might also have been true for Case 201. In fact, the median cost to the client of the pilot project cases in our sample was £3,500. In comparison, the median cost to clients in the other cases in the sample *where a contested application for ancillary relief was issued* was between £3,500 and £5,000. If these figures have any suggestive value, it is that the pilot project cases are not necessarily cheaper where the parties are conflicted. The major issue is whether the new procedure will draw in cases which otherwise would have settled, for if we include the costs of cases settled after a *consent* application among all our cases (other than those under the pilot project), the median drops to just over £2,000. It is therefore clear that it generally remains cheaper to settle a matter through negotiation than through the pilot procedure, even if it might take a little longer (for the question of duration of pilot procedure cases, see p. 159).

But negotiation processes could be improved, and the evidence given above suggests some areas where improvement could be made. A Pre-Application Protocol was issued in May 2000[11] which urges restraint,

[11] *Practice Direction* [2000] 3 All ER 379.

Table 8.4 *Cost of case to client by funding of clients*

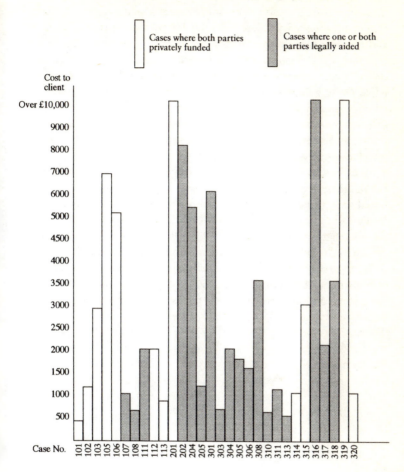

openness and a sense of proportionality in negotiations conducted prior to making any ancillary relief application. But it warns solicitors against trying to reach settlement *without* using the new procedure unless settlement is reasonably likely, thus encouraging early court applications under the scheme. We think that the use of round-table meetings between the parties' lawyers could be helpful. Halpern comments that face-to-face negotiation is much better than writing letters "if you want to keep control and avoid delays" and that it builds up better relationships.[12] Although this was used only once in our sample, and did not in fact lead to an immediate settlement, we would observe that one reason why settlement at the door of the court occurs so often is that this is usually the first time the opposing lawyers actually meet one another. Of course, the imminence of going before the judge is a strong incentive to reach agreement, but we should not overlook the gains to be achieved by close physical proximity in the bargaining process. Indeed, it may be that many of the results achieved by discussion at a first appointment or pre-trial review could be reached without the judge being present at all. This is suggested by two cases, one of which overran when the case listed prior to the hearing overran, giving the parties' lawyers unexpected time to work out an agreement before the judge became available. Conversely, in another case, the solicitor noted that, as the case came on quickly, the parties had insufficient time (forty-eight minutes) to settle it. We would therefore suggest that when it seems that extensive negotiations are likely to take place, the parties' solicitors should agree a schedule under which they would pencil in a date for a round-table meeting, and that such a meeting should in any event occur prior to making a contested application for ancillary relief (or for first appointment under the new scheme).

[12] Ann Halpern, *Negotiating Skills* (Blackstone Press, 1992), pp. 35–6.

9

Conclusions: Family Law Practice – A Business or a Profession?

DAVID HODSON AND Lisa Dunmall[1] begin a text offering guidance about good practice to family lawyers by proclaiming:

> Family law practice as a business? Certainly, it provides an essential legal service to a community. Occasionally, it is regarded as one of the caring professions. Cynically, it is sometimes seen as a firm's pro bono work. But viewed as a business? Moreover, as a business making a profit, efficiently managed and methodically organised? Very rarely.

The text therefore proceeds to offer guidance as to how a family law practice might be run as an efficient business. But is it right to see family law practice as a business? If we do, does this defeat the values which are supposed to underpin the activities of lawyers and which are associated with "professional" conduct? For, if it does, are family lawyers not open to the criticisms that they are more concerned about their own interests than those of the public?

In posing these questions we seek to relate our examination of the work of family lawyers to the larger question of the *nature* of the occupation undertaken by family lawyers. If we start with the paradigm of a profession as an occupation which requires "a demonstrated mastery over a body of formalized knowledge"[2] and one which has control over entry to this knowledge and regulation of its practitioners,[3] it seems fairly clear that family lawyers at first sight qualify as professionals. If a profession is to retain its power, it must claim some kind of unique access to the knowledge in question and special expertise in its use for

---

[1] David Hodson, with Lisa Dunmall, *The Business of Family Law* (Bristol: Family Law), p. v.

[2] Richard L. Abel and Philip S.C. Lewis, *Lawyers in Society: An Overview* (UCLA Press, 1995), p. 40.

[3] See generally Terry Johnson, *Professions and Power* (Macmillan, 1972).

the benefit of its clients. It must maintain public confidence in its ability to provide it. One can see that any claim of family lawyers to be unique providers of information is being challenged. There is the prospect of information meetings under the Family Law Act 1996, and other developments, such as the Internet.[4] Others, such as mediators, may claim a competing role in using the knowledge to achieve the same results sought by the lawyers. Furthermore, the adverse perception of their role by policy-makers could begin to undermine public trust in their work. These pressures could inject an element of commercialisation into family law practice, which, together with the element of competition encouraged by the development of contracting for public funding,[5] might be thought more consistent with business than with professional practices.

We do not, however, think it is particularly fruitful to consider how far family law practice, or legal practice in general, may now be departing from a specific historical paradigm.[6] As we will argue below, it may be possible to combine elements which are characteristic of business practice with those associated with professionalism. The starting point in considering the nature of the family solicitors' occupation must be the solicitors' role in making the law a reality for their clients. For the primary commodity they have to offer is their legal knowledge. A person can ask anyone to help to resolve a conflict, and, indeed, that is part of the lawyer's function as well. But the special point about the fact that the task is performed by a lawyer is that the lawyer has a duty to try to resolve the matter in accordance with the norms of the law. We have no difficulty in stating, as our accounts above make very clear, especially when we discuss the way in which solicitors negotiate a "position" with their clients,[7] that this is exactly how the lawyers do operate. We do however note that on occasion they adopt positions at variance with their view of the relevant legal norms on the instructions of their clients (pp. 95–101). We return to this issue later (p. 188). The greater problem which lawyers have encountered is the perception that, *by the very fact that they do operate within a legal framework*, they have a

[4] See "Couples log on to the Internet to log off from their marriages", *The Independent*, 8 November 1999.
[5] P.S.C. Lewis, *Assumptions about Lawyers in Policy Statements: A Survey of Relevant Research*, above p. 6, note 24; pp. 31–2.
[6] For discussions see John N. Adams and Roger Brownsword, *Understanding Law* (Sweet & Maxwell, 1999), pp. 229–31; Abel and Lewis, *Lawyers in Society*, above p. 181, note 2, ch. 2.
[7] See Chapter 5, section B.

deleterious effect on all affected by the issue by inflaming conflict and running up unnecessary costs. Supplemental to this picture is the notion that lawyers are using the law *for their advantage* rather than for the benefit of their clients. Both allegations seriously undermine the professional values which require the legal knowledge to be used for the benefit of the clients.

This is, therefore, an opportune moment to recall the assumptions which Lewis identified as being made by government policy-makers about the activities of family lawyers (above, p. 6). They were that the practice of arms-length communication reduces communication and often increases tension and conflict; that "translation" problems between client and lawyers cause misunderstanding and anger in the other client; that negotiating through lawyers is associated with "getting the best deal" at the other party's expense; that lawyers only give legal advice; that third parties are not involved; and that lawyers will "unpick" or "interfere" with agreements reached without their involvement. To this one might add the Lord Chancellor's observation that legal negotiation involves "scoring points and settling wrongs, real or imagined".[8] If at least some of these consequences are inherent in the legal process, the service which lawyers provide (bringing to bear their knowledge of the law to the issue) may be being bought at too high a price.

The Lord Chancellor's point appears to reflect a perception of a barrister's rather than a solicitor's role in the legal process. We found only two cases where some element of "scoring points" may have been present. In Case 319 the husband suspected the wife was not making sufficient efforts to find employment. Our interviewee, the wife's solicitor, complained that the other solicitor was:

"exceptionally aggressive and caused a lot of distress to my client; some of the things that were written in letters about her – disrespectful comments that I would never ever write".

The lawyer felt the other solicitor (although a member of the SFLA) should not be doing family law work, and it seems likely the letters did not follow the SFLA Guidance on Good Practice on Correspondence. We will return to this matter below (p. 189). The other case (Case 315) was soured by the fact that the husband wanted the wife to return money he had given her in the course of an attempted reconciliation.

---

[8] Above, p. 7.

But the tit-for-tat element here was client-driven; the lawyers sought to discourage it. Of course lawyers bargained, and sometimes put pressure on the other side, but that does not amount to "scoring points and settling wrongs, real or imagined".

We did not find an example of misunderstanding resulting from a "translation" problem, though we did note the extent to which lawyers repeat explanations and advice to clients (p. 74) in an effort to avoid misunderstanding. We have shown abundantly that the lawyer's role is not confined to merely giving legal advice. It extends to providing reassurance and practical support for many clients during a particularly stressful period. It often extends to dealing with third parties. With respect to reducing communication and increasing tension, we had no evidence about how far the experience of using lawyers aided or hindered clients from communicating with one another. But lawyers standardly encouraged clients to discuss matters between themselves, especially those concerning children and the household contents, although they did tend to warn some clients against entering into agreements with the other party over finances unless they checked with the solicitor. There were moreover a number of cases where the parties were only able to communicate *through* the solicitor, so in those circumstances the lawyer was the only channel of communication which worked. It is also impossible to measure the tension which may or may not have been generated by the use of lawyers. Our evidence does, however, show the lawyers consciously taking many measures to try to *reduce* tension. The most notable was the reluctance to mix disputes about children with financial matters, or to take formal steps which would raise the temperature. We give further examples from our observational data later in this chapter. In view of the often highly emotional state which many of their clients were experiencing when they came to see the lawyer, it is difficult to see how the lawyers could have worked with the client at all unless they succeeded in reducing the level of distress. The extent to which negotiation through lawyers results in settlement (p. 16) is perhaps a testament to their success.

The question whether lawyers seek to achieve the "best deal" at the other parties' expense is problematic. Of course in a sense any improvement in the outcome for the client will generally correspondingly reduce the benefit to the other party, though this overlooks benefits which may be given to other family members (such as children). But that is true for any form of negotiation, or even mediation, through lawyers or anyone else. The question is rather whether lawyers push for the maximally optimal outcome for their client, regardless of any other matter. This is clearly not the case, on our evidence. The lawyers sought to achieve the best deal for their clients *within the normative standards of the law*. Hence lawyers discouraged clients from pursuing unreasonable claims, either because they would risk running excessive costs, or were beyond what they were entitled to, and were therefore unlikely to be acceptable to the other side or to succeed in litigation (pp. 92–5, 125–8). The point is related to the one about "unpicking" agreements. We have seen that our lawyers have advised clients not to proceed with *informal* arrangements made without advice (though one discouraged, unsuccessfully, departure from a *formalised* agreement: p. 98). But it depended on how reasonable the lawyer believed the agreement to be (p. 94), and in any case, the lawyers were careful to make it clear that the ultimate decision was that of the client.

Yet cases where decisions which one party had thought had resolved the matter were abandoned as a result of legal advice, did appear to leave the other party with a deep grievance, sometimes making subsequent settlement more difficult. The lesson we draw from this is that informal agreements made without legal advice can be dangerous, for they might promise what they cannot deliver. But the matter raises a wider question altogether. How far are parties entitled to pursue their legal rights, even at the risk of appearing disruptive? The pejorative connotation which the expression *adversarial* has attracted conjures the image of the troublesome, selfish, individual, unwilling to settle for what the existing dispensation delivers. Yet it can sometimes be only by challenging that dispensation that justice is promoted. It is salutary to remember that, in 1945, the then President of the Divorce Division, Lord Merriman, proposed that all undefended divorces should be referred to tribunals of lawyers and social workers who would try, first, to bring about reconciliation or, if that failed, to secure agreement on future arrangements by consent. One might wonder whether the legal rights of women on divorce would have developed as they have done had that proposal been implemented.[9] We therefore feel it is important to reaffirm the importance of the principle that proper respect for individual rights requires recognising that people should have the opportunity to pursue them.

---

[9] See Stephen Cretney, *Law, Law Reform and the Family* (Oxford University Press, 1998), chapters 5 and 6.

However, we also recognise that no rights are unrestricted, and even that not every claim to a right can, or should be pursued *in all circumstances and at all costs*. But this is to say little more than that other people's rights must be respected, too. The tensions between these rights lies deep within family law itself. Take, for example, the legal position regarding the enforceability of agreements regarding post-divorce financial and property adjustment reached prior to consent order. As Hoffmann LJ explained:

> . . . It does seem to me that the law is in an unsatisfactory state. There are in theory three possible answers to the problem. One might be that an agreement between the parties, at least where each has independent legal advice, is binding upon them subject only to the normal contractual remedies based on fraud, misrepresentation, undue influence etc. At present, the policy of the law . . . is against such a solution. The court retains its supervisory role and only its order gives finality. Another answer might be that when the parties are negotiating with a view to agreement which will be embodied in a consent order, everything should be treated as without prejudice negotiation until the order is actually made. In the latter case, the parties would know that until the court had given its imprimatur, nothing which they had negotiated was legally binding or even admissible. If one of them changed his or her mind, they would have either to go back to the negotiating table or litigate the matter de novo. This may be tiresome . . . (b)ut the parties would at least know where they stood. The result of the decision of this court in *Edgar* v. *Edgar* [1980] 3 All ER 887 . . . is that we have, as it seems to me, the worst of both worlds. The agreement may be held to be binding, but whether it will be can be determined only after litigation and may involve, as in this case, examining the quality of the advice which was given to the party who wishes to resile. . . . The appellant's counsel . . . told us that he reckoned that in Northampton an agreement has an 80 per cent chance of being upheld but that attitudes varied from district judge to district judge.[10]

Hoffmann LJ's first option is one in which parties' interests, as legally defined, would be vigorously pursued and upheld; the second would be governed by extra-legal dynamics of moral credit and sensitivity to pragmatic and emotional elements. In fact, the course taken by the law gives scope for pursuit (and support) of self-interest *as well as* their subversion by responses to an appreciation of wider interests, especially those of children.[11] This fault line runs throughout family law. The very concept of divorce itself has been a battleground between

[10] *Pounds* v. *Pounds* [1994] 4 All ER 777, 792–3.

[11] See especially the judgment of Roch LJ in *N* v. *N (Consent Order: Variation)* [1993] 2 FLR 868.

the pursuit of individual self interest and the interests of other parties and communal values. Parents' rights v. children's rights (or welfare); family autonomy v. state supervision; short-term v. long-term; clean break or continuing obligation: all these dichotomies reflect the inherent conflict between the individualistic values of the contemporary Western world and an aspiration for protection and cultivation of the benefits of caring, co-operation and communality. It is therefore quite wrong to present the conflict only, or even primarily, as one between law, rights, or legal processes on the one hand and non-legal discourses, duties or "alternative" resolution processes. They are tensions within the law itself.

Since these tensions exist within the law, it is not surprising that they are reflected in legal practice. Lawyers can both pursue the interests of their clients *and* observe the wider interests at stake. The picture of family lawyers' work in a variety of settings which emerges from our observational data is one of informed guidance, support, and expert facilitation through the divorce transition process within the legal frame. This involves, indeed requires, a certain commitment to the client's viewpoint. There is a sense in which it is perverse to expect lawyers to put the interests of other parties, especially the State, above that of their clients. Whether they are paid by the client or by the State on behalf of the client, it is the primary role of the solicitor to protect the client's interests. However, this does not mean that the solicitor acts within a vacuum. The normative standards within which the solicitor must shepherd the client's interests are there not only to protect the client, but also other parties and the common interest. The client's interests can be pursued only insofar as they are consistent with these standards. In recognising this, it may be said that the solicitor acts as a professional rather than as a person of business, but such a characterisation is perhaps not very helpful, for "business", too, must be conducted within legal and ethical standards.

But we had five cases where clients pressed lawyers to take positions which the lawyer believed did not coincide with the client's legal rights, four of them being private clients (pp. 96–7). We have seen that the lawyers tended to resist proceeding in this fashion but that ultimately the lawyer felt bound to respect the client's instructions. These are not cases of lawyers acting *contrary* to the law, but of lawyers reluctantly pressing claims they think are unlikely to prevail. The lawyer who adopts such a course after warning the client does not act unprofessionally; lawyers "need not impose a screen on the client's case before litigating".[12] But Boon and Levin also say that solicitors should not send letters or make demands which "they know have no foundation in law", and give as an example a demand summarily to force a wife out of the matrimonial home.[13] The Good Practice Committee of the SFLA's Guide to Good Practice on Correspondence draws attention mainly to the manner and style of correspondence, and does not address this issue, but the general principle of the SFLA Code that solicitors should "conduct matters so as to encourage and assist the parties to achieve a constructive settlement to their differences" would seem to preclude such demands. The lines between inflated claims for payment (as an opening to a bargaining process), hopelessly low offers and (unreasonable) insistence that a party gives up the children, the house, or some other asset may not be easy to draw, and while it is clear that the solicitor should advise against such extremities, the problem remains of what to do if the client insists. There are of course incentives against pursuing such conduct, in particular the possibility of penalties in costs (which the client may not be able to meet), or even a "wasted costs" order against the solicitor personally. The solicitor also stands to lose reputational credit.

Nevertheless, it might legitimately be asked whether lawyers should be *obliged* to discharge such a client. Where the client is publicly funded, the "success" criteria (see p. 25) could lead to a withdrawal of funding, or even risk the firm's contract with the Legal Services Commission. In private client cases, the solicitor might be justified terminating the retainer on the ground that there is good cause.[14] The argument that the clients should be free to spend their money as they please is mitigated by the fact that they are probably causing the other party unnecessary expense. Yet sometimes clients did better than the solicitor anticipated when they persisted against their advice. While the matter warrants further discussion, it is our view that the solicitor discharges the professional duty in advising against the course of action, but that she should be entitled to put the client's position, even if she thinks it a bad one. To do otherwise would be to give lawyers too much power to prejudge outcomes. Of course, the lawyer should put the case in a moderate way, signalling, perhaps, that the issue is client-driven, and being receptive to constructive proposals from the other party.

---

[12] Andrew Boon and Jennifer Levin, *The Ethics and Conduct of Solicitors in England and Wales* (Hart Publishing, Oxford, 1999), p. 203.

[13] Ibid.

[14] Ibid., p. 183.

After all, the norms in this area are not static, and what might be considered to be a weak case at one time might later become incorporated into the law's norms. But lawyers should also be aware of the risks of proceeding in these circumstances, and could legitimately deem them too considerable to retain the client.

B WHAT IMPROVEMENTS MIGHT BE MADE?

The preceding discussion draws attention to one issue where consideration might usefully be given to ways in which current practice might be improved: how to pursue a case which the solicitor believes to be seriously misguided. We have also mentioned other areas where we think improvements in practice might be considered, notably whether the guidance on disclosure might be re-examined with a view to determining whether it might include criteria for seeking disclosure,[15] encouraging constructive use of inferences which may be made from non-disclosure in the negotiation process,[16] and development of a practice where, in cases where extensive negotiations seemed likely, the solicitors agreed a timetable which would include a round-table meeting between them.[17] But perhaps the most important is suggested by the case mentioned earlier in this chapter[18] where the solicitor interviewed expressed the view that the opposing solicitor, a member of the SFLA, had clearly breached the Association s Guidance on Good Practice in Correspondence. The solicitor gave no indication that anything would be done about this. We are left wondering how frequently members of the SFLA fail to live up to the standards to which they subscribe, and how effective are the mechanisms for policing these standards. At the very least, solicitors should be encouraged to report deviations from the standards by SFLA members, and some form of appropriate response ensured.

[15] Above Chapter 8, p. 166.
[16] Above, Chapter 8, p. 165.
[17] See Chapter 8, p. 179.
[18] Above p. 185.

C   DO FAMILY LAWYERS CREATE WORK TO MAXIMISE PROFIT?

We have referred earlier[19] to the criticism often either made or implied with respect to the legal process that practitioners are motivated solely, or at least primarily, by the profit motive and have thereby compromised their professional integrity, which requires the promotion of the client s interests within the normative context as stated above.

In considering this issue, we must return to the new system of publicly funding family law work which will restrict the providers of such work to firms who have entered contracts with the Legal Services Commission. The process of franchising has been in operation for some years, though hitherto it has operated more as a measure of quality control than as a means of determining an exclusive source of publicly funded legal service. Many of the firms in which our interviewees worked had secured a franchise. The process of securing it was described as time consuming and difficult, but was appreciated for its impact on efficiency. The lawyers we observed who did legal aid work were beginning to prepare cash flow projections, to audit each other's cases and to accept the Board auditors. They were beginning to move on from the situation described by Hodson and Dunmall[20] in which they suggested that family law was seen not so much as a profitable business but as an essential legal service to the community, sometimes as work done pro bono within the firm, and linked with the work of the caring professions. It was now coming to be seen as a branch of practice which could be run profitably. However, among the lawyers we saw, who had made great efforts to become more efficient and business-like, we heard a number of complaints that they were now being criticised for following this route and being out to make large profits from client misery. What kind of creature were they: entrepreneurs or a caring profession?

Our observations indicate how both of these views can be held. We saw our solicitors treating their firm as a business organisation, thinking about marketing, about collecting unpaid bills for work done, cutting costs, being aware of changes in demand for services and local variations in the organisation of family work. Solicitors' firms are businesses which need to make profits in order to survive. Thus marketing the firm, looking out for new clients, worrying about cash flows, chas-

[19] Above p. 59.
[20] Above p. 181, note 1.

ing up unpaid bills, refusing to incur further costs until bills are paid, worrying about taxation of legal aid bills were all part and parcel of their daily work. The solicitors engaged in marketing activities such as occur in many other businesses. Practitioners with both high and low income clients were active in finding new business. For example, we saw a provincial solicitor who worked with predominantly legal aid clients and a middle-income private client practitioner in London both organising drinks parties and making donations to local charities for marketing purposes. We also observed these two solicitors trying to secure other work from a divorce client. For example, the legal aid lawyer offered to obtain a quote from her firm's conveyancing department for one of her clients who had been given bad advice on selling a property by a sole practitioner. And we observed a "big money" solicitor in a provincial firm targeting other firms in the area for the introduction of private matrimonial work. Another middle-income solicitor gave advice through an employee advice scheme which gave £240 free advice paid for by the employer. She saw this as a useful source of new business. A legal aid practitioner in a small country practice ran a free legal advice clinic one afternoon a week, which he saw as another way of bringing in potential new clients.

Again, like any other business, solicitors' firms were concerned to minimise cash flow problems arising from late payment or failure to pay bills. So, for example, one solicitor was worried about a middle-income private client who had not yet paid anything and owed £15,000. She had started billing him monthly instead of quarterly, and began a meeting with him by asking whether he had brought a cheque with him. When he said that it was in the post, she said "It's just that this is an important issue – it's a matter of trust. I need to trust you and you need to trust me to do a good job for you". We observed two solicitors, one with middle-income client private practice and one dealing with "big money" cases, refuse to do more work on cases where large bills were outstanding, and in both of these firms clients were asked for an initial down payment which is kept until the final bill. So we saw lawyers behaving like entrepreneurs in the context of the firm's policy on attracting business and getting accounts settled.

Did we also see profit maximisation in individual cases? Although firms set out to make profits, our observations suggested that this did not translate crudely into maximising fees for individual clients, but quite the reverse. We observed numerous instances where the lawyer would suggest strategies explicitly designed to keep the client's legal costs down. We observed this kind of behaviour in both legal aid and private client work. For example, it was common to advise clients to take on simple tasks for themselves in order to keep their costs down. One London solicitor advised a middle-income private client to fill in the Statement of Arrangements form herself, rather than waste the solicitor's time and her own money. The same lawyer advised another client who had approached her about transferring the family home to her sole name to check first for herself whether the building society would be prepared to transfer a mortgage to her, before starting to incur legal costs by transferring the property. We observed similar behaviour in a partner in a small specialist firm dealing mainly with legal aid work. The latter gave some initial advice to a client about divorce procedures and filling in forms, and then advised her that she should deal with her own non-contentious divorce to avoid paying high legal costs, either directly or following a legal aid certificate issued for ancillary matters.[21]

A second strategy for keeping costs down for the client was to avoid escalation of disputes and to avoid chasing up every minor point which emerged during the divorce process. For example, we observed a legal aid solicitor talking to the other side's solicitor on the phone when trying to come to a financial settlement. She said "It's not worth fighting over this amount of money . . . so far these clients have been immensely sensible and haven't wanted to pay lawyers to sort this out, a very sensible approach if you ask me". We observed this strategy being used even with "big money" cases. For instance, the lawyer dealing with a multi-million pound divorce said to his client. "It's not worth paying us to worry about dividing the house contents". And when a dispute was emerging we observed serious attempts by solicitors to limit the conflict between the parties. For example, a legal aid family specialist in a country practice left it up to one of his clients whether or not to pursue her claim against her estranged partner for £600 for leaving her property out in the rain. He did not encourage her to engage in seeking compensation. Instead he suggested gently that she might be well advised to "put it down to experience". He discouraged her from going round and "thumping" the husband. He told her that litigation might give her "short term gratification" but it would lead to "long term hassle". We saw attempts to defuse potential conflicts in private client cases. For example, in a "big money" case, we saw a solicitor advise a client

---

[21] See also above pp. 96–7.

against making a financial threat towards the wife. In another case the same lawyer wrote to the other side about a list of household possessions saying "We wish to avoid a prior exchange of lists of possessions. These matters can become very acrimonious and that is not the spirit in which the request is made".[22]

When matters relating to the children arose, every lawyer without exception tried to persuade the parties to negotiate directly with their spouse rather than involve lawyers. We have mentioned earlier in our case studies the strategy of separating the emotionally charged decisions to be made about children from the decisions to be made about property, which they called the "commercial decisions", best made without undue emotional influence. This was apparent also from our observational data. The preference for the separation out of issues may be another point of differentiation from mediation practice, where all issues are dealt with together, since it is held that in mediation the more aspects of a case that are on the table, the more the room for manoeuvre and thus hopefully settlement. In one case we observed, when a dispute about arrangements for children had developed, the solicitor made strenuous efforts to calm down the father who was seeking more extensive contact than his wife or the court welfare officer recommended. She first explained that he would have a stronger case for contact if he accepted a lower level as an interim measure, then she suggested various different contact arrangements, and finally that frequent contact might exacerbate the wife's negative feelings which would be counterproductive. Only when the client threatened to go to another firm did she reluctantly accept his instructions and proceed to a contested hearing. In another case the solicitor attempted to reduce conflict by getting the parties to look ahead . . . saying "think of your daughter's graduation in ten years' time. You'll both want to be there, won't you? And you can't be at each others throats then". This lawyer said that by focusing the party's minds on future events like this it was easier for them to see why they must try to sort things out in a reasonable way and avoid court battles.

We observed far more discussion of ways of limiting client costs than of puffing out work in both legally aided and private client work. For example, one practitioner with middle-income clients said to us that if she used an experienced barrister on a legally aided case that she would balance the costs by sending a cheap trainee solicitor to court, in order

[22] See also p. 71.

to keep within costs which would be acceptable to the Board. And a solicitor with high income clients in a provincial firm explained that in his firm partners were charged out at £150 per hour, so that in cases handled by partners, counsel were used for advocacy in court because this was considerably cheaper. A legal aid firm on the other hand pointed out that solicitors are not paid for sitting behind counsel in the magistrates' court, and therefore in these cases it is more cost effective for the solicitor to do his own advocacy. We saw no exceptions to the general practice of encouraging clients to carry out simpler tasks for themselves, of trying not to pursue fruitless avenues of dispute, and of encouraging clients to talk directly to each other particularly about the children and the contents of the family home. All of these examples indicate the link between trying to reduce and contain the episodes of conflict which erupt during even the most amicable divorces, and trying to encourage the parties to do what they can for themselves and keeping costs down.

The busy solicitor with more work than he can handle has every incentive to act in this way, whether the Legal Aid Board or the private client is meeting the bill. For the Board, the solicitor is given authority to carry out certain pieces of work and would not be paid for doing unnecessary work. And for the private client, a happy client is the one with the lower bill which he is more likely to pay quickly, thus helping with the firms cash flow situation, which seems to be a universal matter of concern to the profession. Such a client would also be likely to recommend the firm to others, and goodwill is as important to solicitor firms as to all businesses. Legal aid work which involves relatively low hourly fees together with restrictions about the nature of the work which can be charged for, was almost universally regarded as requiring considerable amounts of unpaid or poorly paid work. As a result, solicitors in firms doing legal aid work generally felt that they needed to increase the amount of private work which they did relative to the legal aid work. This was seen in extreme form in one "big money" firm which had decided not to take on any more legal aid work . . . not even for old clients on hard times, or for the children of clients. They simply did not see it as financially viable as a result of strict taxation by local district judges and the prohibitive cost of appealing against taxation decisions. They had found that often a judge would tax off what was seen as excessive time spent on a case regardless of the circumstances of the case, or the characteristics of the client who might be particularly vulnerable and therefore time consuming. We have observed solicitors having to explain the same point many times to clients who were either too stressed or not intellectually able to grasp what was happening. They felt also that legally aided clients tended to spend a long time with the solicitor, whom they used as a therapist, or sounding board, and while the firm was able to refer private clients to a counsellor, it was very hard to do so for legal aid clients as it was rarely possible to find state funded counselling. "It costs more to sit here than the Board will pay". As another predominantly legal aid solicitor explained to us, with Green Form cases only two thirds of his time could be charged so he usually ended up billing for only two thirds of his time. The hourly rate under the Green Form scheme was £41, while for private clients it was £135; and the overheads remained the same. He had seen a client on a fixed fee first appointment who could not pay the fee, worked on cases before the legal aid certificate was signed and therefore could not charge, and also found that former clients often phoned up for advice and that time could not be charged for. Another lawyer told us that even when a certificate is granted, where a client is inadequate he has to spend a great deal of time talking to social services and other professionals trying to work out what his client's wishes are. Clearly this time is not chargeable. All our legal aid practitioners reported financial problems arising not only from the low hourly rate but from the amount of time which could not be charged. The economics of legal aid work from the lawyers' point of view depend on fast throughput and not on taking a case to extreme lengths. The lawyers did however point out that the way legal aid was paid gave the client, but not the lawyers, no incentive not to escalate or protract the case as they do not have to think about the costs of every procedure, and therefore the client rather than the lawyer may go for more drastic options than a private client facing a monthly invoice.

We therefore conclude from our observation that the lawyer thinks about the firm as a business, in terms of attracting custom, increasing turnover and cutting costs. But the lawyer's behaviour as a member of a firm differs from the lawyer's approach to individual clients. We did not see lawyers approaching their clients other than by way of what might be called a "professional" manner, concerned with discovering what the client's wishes were and guiding them towards achieving as much of the game plan as possible within the legal framework. We did not see short-term profit-driven escalation of conflict or costs. The lawyers were preoccupied with returning tasks wherever feasible to the client, especially routine administrative jobs and anything to do with the children. They were busy avoiding costly and pointless disputes especially over household contents. They were working hard to keep down their own costs which may or may not be paid by the client or by the Legal Aid Board. Increasing private client business, however, was a major concern for the legal aid lawyers as legal aid work was seen to be becoming increasingly unprofitable.

D. FINAL THOUGHTS

The policy question may not be how to control the shoals of sharks waiting to exploit the system, but how to ensure that enough lawyers are willing to bid for whatever kind of contracts the new Legal Services Commission is offering to provide the expert advice and assistance in managing family transitions which the good family solicitor can offer. We have endeavoured to demonstrate that the perception of the work of family solicitors entertained and encouraged by policy-makers bears little relation to reality. These misconceptions raise the danger of creating a demoralised sector of the profession, uncertain of its role and doubtful about its true value. Had a fuller and more up-to-date picture of their work been available, it must be uncertain whether actual and proposed reforms would have taken their present form. We have also given reasons to doubt whether the cost-savings objectives of some of them will be achieved, or, if they are that they will be very great, and, even if they do occur, whether the risks to the client in losing protection of his or her interests should be taken. However, we are aware that the changes are in their early stages, and that many of the problems raised by them have been recognised by the Legal Aid Board and the Lord Chancellor's Department. We hope that further implementation of reform will be undertaken flexibly, and with a sensitive understanding of the impact on existing family law work. Since the research associated with monitoring projects has been of exceptionally high quality, we have every hope that this will occur.

Whether the new divorce framework set out in the Family Law Act 1996 is eventually enacted in its entirety or not, it is evident that in publicly-funded cases the work of family law solicitors will be heavily affected by the changes connected with mediation and with the new contracting system for family law work. At the very least, this will entail a good deal of additional record keeping. While it has been clear to us, as it would be to anyone observing such work, that there is always room for improvement in practice, and we have made some suggestions about this at appropriate points in this book, there must be a concern that the additional workload which will arise will impose severe strains on some practices. It is inevitable that fewer firms will offer publicly-funded family law work. Yet, as we hope readers of this book will conclude, family law work has a very important part to play in the lives of many adult citizens and their children.

Appendix

1. Outline of the methodology and general issues

There were three stages to this study. In the first, Law Society and Legal Aid Board statistics were examined in order to identify the characteristics of the workforce of family specialists. The next stage involved the researchers spending time in the offices of ten such family specialists, observing and recording in detail their daily activity. This produced the "observational data". In the third stage, we conducted forty depth interviews with family solicitors in four areas of the country. These solicitors were selected at random from the Law Society Regional Directories and were interviewed in detail about the progress of one recent divorce case to give us a picture of the work done on a case by case basis (producing our "case studies").

In devising our methodology, we were conscious of the arguments for and against various methods of data collection. We wanted to collect information about the progress of individual divorce cases, from the first contact the client had with the solicitor through to decree nisi and decree absolute, and through what might be complex and lengthy negotiation and settlement of any associated financial and children matters. Because of the complexity of the subject matter, we chose to adopt primarily a qualitative rather than quantitative approach. We were aware that every divorce case is different; and that while obviously the same themes would come up in different interviews, the order of events, the circumstances and motivations of the divorcing parties and their representatives would differ. We felt that a qualitative approach would allow us the flexibility during the interview to explore these events and motivations in an order that suited the solicitor and the case, rather than imposing a rigid structure or "grid" on the interview (Cicourel, 1964). With a quantitative interview, the researcher pre-defines the subject matter in his or her own words, but by adopting a less structured approach, the solicitors would be able to describe their experiences and practices in their own words. The flexibility inherent in a qualitative approach would also allow us to follow up any new themes and ideas as they emerged (Britten, 1995).

We also felt that this form of in-depth interview would enable a better relationship to develop between the researcher and the solicitor. As Oakley (1981) has written, a qualitative approach allows a more reciprocal relationship to develop between researcher and respondent than is possible through a standardised interviewing technique. In a quantitative interview, the only one to gain from the interview is the researcher, who is in complete control of the interview questions. With a qualitative approach, both parties gain something from the interview, with the respondent able to ask the researcher questions of his own, and to play a part in the direction of the discussion. Certainly, in both the observational stage and the depth interviews, we found that some solicitors said that they had enjoyed the experience and the opportunity to consider and discuss their work with us.

In-depth interviews were chosen over observation of solicitors as the main method of data collection, because one of our key aims was to chart the progress of a sample of divorce cases. Observation of a solicitor over eighteen months to two years (the average amount of time taken to resolve a divorce case) was clearly not practical either in terms of resources or acceptability to the solicitors. In-depth interviews, based on a divorce case file, could be scheduled at the convenience of both the researcher and the solicitor (Denscombe, 1983). Moreover, while observation, enabled us to observe *what* a solicitor was doing, it would not enable us to see *why* she was doing it. Qualitative interviews would have the advantage of giving us access to the solicitor's thoughts and motives (Patton, 1980; McCracken, 1988), and would enable us to gain the solicitor's point of view in addition to our own understanding of events (Marshall and Rossman, 1989).

However, we could see that there were problems inherent in relying on qualitative interviews alone. There is a danger that data can become skewed in qualitative interviews when the researcher makes an unwarranted assumption that she shares a common perspective with her respondents (Denzin, 1970). For these reasons, we decided to precede the depth interviews with an observation exercise. By observing the day to day activity of family specialists, we were able to familiarise ourselves with the setting in which divorce cases are dealt with by solicitors, the terminology used, and to make sure that we had made no unrealistic assumptions or pre-conceptions about a family solicitor's work.

Another common reason for not relying on qualitative interview data alone is that respondents themselves may not give an accurate description of reality: they may be looking through "distorted lenses" (Becker and Geer, 1960). They may be under considerable pressure to present themselves as competent individuals during the interview situation, and therefore, rather than simply describing reality, give an account of events which presents such a front (Scott and Lyman, 1968; Goffman, 1983; Dingwall 1997). Some ethnomethodologists have taken the extreme view that, for these reasons, qualitative interviewing should be abandoned altogether in favour of observation. However, we felt that the problem of participants "putting on a front" was similarly applicable to observation studies. Indeed, during our observation exercise, a number of solicitors mentioned to us that for at least the initial part of the exercise, they had been self-conscious and more thoughtful about what they were doing and saying than they would have been in our absence. Nevertheless, as they became more accustomed to the researcher's presence, the pressures of their work environment were such that any response conditioned by the observation must have been much reduced.

That of course does not argue against the possibility of distortion of the truth as a potential problem in our in-depth interviews. In this study, we were aware not just of the pressure on the solicitor to appear competent as an interview respondent, but also of a considerable pressure to present as a competent professional. We needed to be aware of this, both during the conduct of the interviews and in the analysis of the data. However, in our view this potential feature was reduced by the fact that the interviews were so closely focused on the case files. We asked solicitors to have the relevant case files in front of them during the interview, and to use them as a resource for information about the chronological order of events. We believed that this gave solicitors less opportunity or inclination to re-construct history in their accounts.

2. Solicitor observation exercise

2.1 Review of observation literature

Before embarking on our solicitor observation exercise, we reviewed literature on observation techniques. As well as recent socio-legal observations, the literature covered a diverse range of fields – among them, the study of the doctor-patient relationship, workplace case studies, ethnographic studies of heroin addicts and biker gangs, and cultural anthropological studies of remote jungle tribes. The studies reviewed included both participant and non-participant observation, and the techniques used included simply sitting silently in a corner with a pen and paper, a combination of direct observation with interviews, the viewing of group sessions through a hidden mirror window, and the use of video – or audio – equipment.

A number of themes emerged from the literature review:

• Knowing what you are looking for
• Making field notes
• Coding and analysis of the observations
• Effect of the presence of an observer

Knowing what you are looking for

If the researcher does not have a clear idea at the outset of the observation study what the focus of the research is, there is a danger that (s)he will miss the wood for the trees. Observations must be concentrated on the issues of importance to the research. ". . . observation, if it is to be at all scientific, must be guided by a working hypothesis which enables the observer to make active discriminations in the complex interplay of factors before him. Without such guidance he is likely to miss much of significance and become lost in a welter of irrelevance". (Roethlisberger, 1939).

In Roethlisberger's 1939 study of factory working practices, observers were briefed to focus on a number of themes in their observations, rather than trying to record absolutely everything that was going on. Naroll and Naroll warn that at least initially an observer may be disposed to "exotic data", that is, behaviour or events or speech patterns which are different from his/her own culture or experience (Webb et al, 1981). Over time however, the observer will become more accustomed to the setting and will be less and less affected by these differences from his/her norms.

Jorgensen (1989) describes an observation study as a continual process of observation – analysis – refocusing – observation, repeated until the researcher is clear exactly what the observations should be focused upon. As the study progresses, the researcher's note-taking will become more refined as (s)he learns to concentrate on the important issues. Jorgensen suggests that debriefing by other researchers during the course of the project can be a useful method of identifying the key issues and patterns emerging.

Making field notes

The importance of making field jottings while in the field and then writing them up without delay as detailed field notes is strongly emphasised throughout the literature. Lofland (1971) recommends that full field notes should be a more or less chronological log of what is happening to and in the setting, and to and in the observer. The final notes should include a running description of observed events, people, conversations, times and places, analytic ideas and inferences, personal impressions and feelings, and notes to look up or ask for further information about specific events or issues.

In the studies to which Lofland is referring, the observers write down phrases, quotes, and key words in the course of their observations, in order to jog their memory for writing later field notes. In others there is a more structured method of note-taking. For example, Prebble and Miller studied methadone maintenance programmes for heroin addicts. They kept a record of very specific things decided upon before the study (e.g. age, ethnicity, habit of addicts) while also keeping additional notes to record emergent unanticipated findings (Jorgensen, 1989). In Roethlisberger's (1939) observation of workers assembling telephone relays, a number of different types of record were kept, including a mechanical log of time taken to complete each relay for each worker, a log sheet which was a chronological account of each partner's activities, a quality of output record, a daily history record, a temperature and humidity record and physical examinations of the workers. In Geraci and Geraci's (1994) study of triage nurses, the observers were given a form on which to record their data. Columns were provided on the form to record patient registration time, activity rating, onset and end times of the triage function, pre-defined categories for emergency, clinic or other disposition and pre-defined categories for marking anticipated telephone / physical triage activities. A separate sheet was available for recording unanticipated functions and for documenting any special notations.

Coding and analysis of the observations

In any observational exercise, it is important to develop a category system by which to record the behaviours of the people being observed. This category system can be used during or after fieldwork, or a combination of the two. There is an established and extensive code frame called the Outline of Cultural Materials (OCM), which is often used for coding ethnographic materials. For instance, code 586 is divorce, 701 is military organisation, 674 is crime and so on. The researcher goes through his/her field notes marking the appropriate codes in the margins or at the top of the pages. Another established code frame is Bales' Interaction Process Analysis coding, which has been used in many observation studies to record the content of speech acts in small group situations. In this system, each person in the room is given a number and the speech acts are recorded in terms of who initiated it, and to whom it was addressed; and then the type of speech act is allocated to one of twelve distinct categories. This system can be used at the time of the observations by trained observers, or it can be used to later code the speech acts from transcripts or recordings of the group session.

Many other project-specific code frames have been devised for individual observation studies. For example, a study of the doctor-patient relationship by Byrne and Long (1976), which involved coding the observations after the event, was based on listening to tape recordings of doctor-patient consultations to discover what sorts of behavioural phenomena were occurring. The researchers initially used Bales' 12-factor system of examining group behaviour, but felt that it was not sensitive enough for analysis of the doctor-patient relationship because so many of the doctor's activities fell into a limited number of categories – asking for and giving information and opinion. So, Byrne and Long developed more detailed categories to code the doctor's approach to opening the discussion, gathering information about the patient's condition and suggesting treatment/further investigation.

Another project-specific code frame was that used in the Geraci and Geraci (1994) study, which involved coding triage nurse functions as they were observed. Two trial observations had been conducted before the main study in order to develop a code frame for recording the data. Lay observers were then trained to complete specially designed forms using the code frame as they observed the nurses. Similarly, in some elements of the Roethlisberger study of factory workers, the categories of relevant behaviour were identified in advance, and observers recorded their data directly onto pre-designed log sheets.

Effect of the presence of an observer

Another theme, which pervades the literature on participant observation, is the need to be aware that the behaviour of the observed may be affected by the presence of the observer. For instance, in the Roethlisberger study, workers' murmuring tended to stop when the observer approached, in much the same way as with the foreman or supervisor. However, this effect lessened with time as workers got used to the presence of the observer.

2.2 Selecting a sample of solicitors for observation

A sample of ten solicitors was selected through personal contacts, and designed to reflect the variety of firms in which family work is carried out. We sought a geographical spread, and observed solicitors in the North West, the Midlands and the South East (including London). We also wished to observe a wide range of types of firm, from those doing mainly legal aid work to those with wealthy clients.

Three of the solicitors were men, seven were women. All were family specialists, and were aged between thirty-five and fifty-five. All but one were partners. In more detail, we observed:

- A family partner in a London firm, dealing mainly with private work; observed for three days
- A family partner in a provincial firm, dealing mainly with legal aid work under franchise; observed for two days
- Two partners in a small specialist matrimonial firm, dealing mainly with legal aid work under franchise; each partner observed for one day
- A divorce specialist, working as a sole practitioner, mainly for private clients; observed for one day
- A partner and his assistant in one of two branches of a small country practice, dealing mainly with legal aid work under franchise; partner observed for two days, assistant observed for one day
- A family partner in a city centre office of a major national firm, dealing only with private clients; observed for one day
- A partner in a specialist matrimonial practice, one of two branches, dealing mainly with private work; observed for one day
- A partner in a London firm, a qualified mediator; observed for one day.

2.3 Conduct of solicitor observations

The researchers spent a total of fourteen working days alongside ten family specialists in eight different firms. This yielded over one hundred hours of observation. As far as was possible, the researchers shadowed the solicitors throughout the day, including sessions with clients (where permission was given by the clients) and attending court hearings, meetings with counsel and so on. Sequential field notes were kept, which were then written up in full. As a check on their reliability as observers, the two researchers observed the same solicitor on subsequent days in one firm, and two different solicitors within another firm, and then compared and discussed their experiences.

2.4 Development of code frame, and analysis of observation data

A code frame of solicitor activities was drawn up based on the full observation transcripts. This code frame of activities is appended. Each activity was allocated a code – contact with clients, counsel, other solicitors within the firm, other professionals (this contact coding being similar in principle to that used in Bales' Interaction Process Analysis); the mode of that contact, and its content, such as establishing information from a client, discussion of fees or other procedures, provision of advice, negotiation, comfort or therapy and so on. Once the code frame had been drawn up, the activities of each solicitor were coded and the resulting observation summaries were used to draw up case studies and to compare the contents of the solicitors' days.

3. Depth interviews with solicitors

3.1 Selecting a sample of solicitors for depth interviews

A sample of individual solicitors was selected from four areas in England and Wales. The sample was drawn from the Law Society Regional Directories in which solicitors are listed for each region. Solicitors are listed (within alphabetically ordered firms) with their position – partner, assistant, consultant – and up to six specialisms in order of importance. In each of the four areas, two samples were drawn: "specialists" – defined for this project as solicitors who put family work as their first or second specialism, and "non-specialists" – solicitors who put family work as their third to sixth. Selections were carried out using a random start fixed interval method from the solicitor lists, as ordered in the directories. In a number of cases, where the original selected solicitor had left the firm for which (s)he was listed, or was unable to take part, interviews were conducted with a substitute solicitor at that firm.

3.2 Conduct of depth interviews

Interviews were conducted with forty solicitors in the four selected areas. Of these, twelve were substitutes for the originally selected solicitor. The interviews lasted between forty-five minutes and one hour, and fieldwork was conducted during late 1998, early 1999. A further twenty solicitors had been contacted by letter, but had not been interviewed. Of these, four had no longer been working at the firm or did not do matrimonial work, and there had been no suitable substitute solicitor at the firm; for five solicitors, despite repeated attempts, no telephone contact was made; broken appointments were not rescheduled for two solicitors; four solicitors refused to take part because of pressure of work; and five solicitors did not take part for other reasons.

The selected solicitors were contacted first by letter, then (where possible) by telephone in order to make appointments for interview. They were asked to select a divorce case using the following criteria, in order to avoid a biased sample caused by solicitors choosing their most interesting cases: *Please select the first divorce case for which a petition was filed on or after 1 March 1997, and for which at least a decree nisi has been obtained.* Prior to the fieldwork, a topic guide was drawn up (this is appended). The researchers started every interview by collecting some background information about the solicitor and firm, and some basic details of the selected divorce case. The intention was to ask the solicitor to talk through the selected divorce case from their first contact with the client to the current situation. We were aware that the order in which various issues arose would vary from case to case; so we used the topic guide as a checklist of issues to probe, rather than as a chronological guide to the interview.

If there was sufficient time at the end of the interview, solicitors were also asked for their views about recent and forthcoming legal aid changes, and the debate surrounding the possible introduction of property division rules and pre-nuptial settlements. All interviews were taped and transcribed by the researchers. They were allocated a number (used in the main text of this book). The initial number identified which of the researchers carried out the interview.

3.3 Analysis of depth interviews

Rather than a simple transcription of the taped interviews, a data sheet was devised on which to record the content of each depth interview. The data from each interview (including direct quotes from the interview) were organised into themes, in such a way as to retain the individuality of each case, and also allow analysis by broad themes:

- Background information about the solicitor and firm
- Basic details of the selected case
- Situation at first contact with the client
- Issues arising in connection with the divorce petition
- Financial issues (details of marital assets, establishing financial information, advising or giving information to client about finances, process of negotiating the financial settlement, involvement of other professionals, details of any hearings)
- Children issues (establishing information about the children's situation, advising or giving information to client about children, process of negotiating the children issues, involvement of other professionals, details of any hearings)
- Current state of case
- Final bill
- Checklist of important dates (e.g. date of petition, decree nisi, decree absolute, hearings)
- Solicitor's impression of case and client
- Attitudes towards property division rules, pre-nuptial settlements and legal aid changes.

In addition, for each interview, a full chronological account of the divorce case was recorded, charting in detail the development of the case from first contact with the client to outcome of the case, or the current position. From these chronological records, one page "time lines" were produced for each case which marked the timing of each key event from month one (first contact with client) to the end of the case. Comparison of these time lines allowed analysis of the time taken to reach various stages, and the factors which affect the course of a divorce case.

References

Bales, R.F. (1950) *Interaction Process Analysis*, Cambridge MA: Addison-Wesley.

Becker, H.S. and Geer, B. (1960) Participant observation: the analysis of qualitative data. In: Adams, R. and Preiss, J. (eds), *Human Organisation Research: field relations and techniques*, 267–89, Homewood, Ill: Dorsey.

Britten, N. (1995) "Qualitative Research: qualitative interviews in medical research", *British Medical Journal* 311, 251–4.

Byrne and Long (1976) *Doctors talking to Patients*, London: HMSO.

Cicourel, A.V. (1964) *Method and Measurement in Sociology*, New York: Free Press.

Denscombe, M. (1983) Interviews, accounts and ethnographic research on teachers. In: Hammersley, M. (ed), *The Ethnography of Schooling*, 107–28, Driffield: Nafferton Books.

Denzin, N. (1970) *The Research Act*, 1st edn, Englewood Cliffs NJ: Prentice Hall.

Dingwall, R. (1997) Accounts, interviews and observations. In: Miller, G. and Dingwall, R. (eds), *Context and Method in Qualitative Research*, 198–205, London: Sage.

Geraci and Geraci (1994) "An observational study of the emergency triage nursing role in a managed care facility", *Journal of Emergency Nursing*, 1994 Jun, 20 (3).

Goffman, E. (1983) "Felicity's Condition", *American Journal of Sociology* 83, 1–53.

Jorgensen, D (1989) *Participant observation: a methodology for human studies*, London: Sage Publications.

Lofland, John (1971) *Analysing Social Settings: a guide to qualitative observation and analysis*, Wadsworth Publishing Company.

Marshall, C. and Rossman, G. (1989) *Designing Qualitative Research*, Newbury Park, CA: Sage.

McCracken, G. (1988) *The Long Interview*, Newbury Park, CA: Sage.

Murphy, E., Dingwall, R., Greatbatch, D., Parker, S. and Watson, P. (1998) *Qualitative research methods in health technology assessment: a review of the literature*, University of Nottingham.

Oakley, A. (1981) "Interviewing women: a contradiction in terms", in Roberts, H. (ed), *Doing Feminist Research*, 30–61, London: Routledge and Kegan Paul.

Patton, M.Q. (1980) *Qualitative Evaluation Methods*, Newbury Park, CA: Sage.

Roethlisberger, F.J. (1939) *Management and the Worker: an account of a research program conducted by the Western Electric Company, Hawthorne Works, Chicago*, Cambridge MA: Harvard University Press.

Sarat, A. and Felstiner W.J. (1995) *Divorce Lawyers and their Clients*, Oxford: Oxford University Press

Scott, M. and Lyman, S. (1968) "Accounts", *American Sociological Review* 33, 46–62.

Sherr, A., Moorhead, R., and Paterson, A. (1992) *Transaction Criteria*, Legal Aid Board.

Spradley, James P. (1980) *You owe yourself a drunk: an ethnography of urban nomads*, Boston: Little Brown.

—— (1980) *Participant Observation*. New York: Holt, Rinehart and Winston.

Webb, E.J. (1966) *Unobtrusive measures*, Chicago: Rand McNally.

Webb, E., Campbell, D., Schwartz, R., Schrest, L. and Grove J. (eds) (1981) *Non-reactive Measures in the Social Sciences*, Boston: Houghton Miffling.

OBSERVATIONAL STAGE

CONTACT

Contact with
01 Client
02 (Solicitor for) spouse or ex-spouse
03 (Solicitor for) other party

Within firm
04 Other solicitor within firm
05 Secretary
06 Other professional within firm

Other professionals
07 Counsel (for client)
08 Counsel (for other party)
09 Guardian
10 Social worker
11 Court/court admin. staff
12 Court clerk
13 Court welfare officer
14 Legal Aid Board
15 Financial adviser/accountant/pension adviser
16 Other solicitor (outside firm, unconnected with a particular case)
17 Taxation draftsman
18 Immigration adviser
19 Professional association (e.g. SLSA, AWS)
30 Mediator/mediation service
31 Benefits Agency
32 Client's employer

00 Other professionals

Mode of contact
20 Face-to-face
   (A—solicitor initiated contact/meeting; B—other person initiated contact; C—court attendance)
21 Telephone
   (A—solicitor initiated contact; B—other person initiated contact)
22 Writing or dictating a letter, fax or email
23 Reading a letter, fax or email

CONTACT WITH CLIENT

Admin.
100 Provides client with documents, copies of correspondence etc.
101 Acknowledges receipt of document, cheque, letter etc.
102 Asks client to complete or sign document   **
(likely to be linked to appropriate code below re establishing story/information)
103 Leaves telephone message
104 Arranges meeting/suggests client makes appointment

Fees/Billing
110 Advises about the likely cost of the proposed work
111 Explains billing procedures or charges to client
112 Bills client
113 Chases client for payment
114 Suggests tactics which would keep costs down (purpose of tactics expressed explicitly)
115 Advises client that solicitor will come off the record, or do no further work if no further contact made or fees paid

Discovery/Establishing story/Seeking information
120 Probes for facts/establishes client's story
121 Asks client to provide specific documents or information (e.g. indicating value of assets)
122 Works out (or offers to work out) client's finances
123 Checks client's story again
124 Asks client to check accuracy of the solicitor's draft affidavit, petition, letter etc.
125 Asks client to comment on other party's story/affidavit/CWO report etc.

Giving "information"/Explanation of procedures (as opposed to "advice")
130 Explains procedures/next steps (e.g. form to be sent off to LAB, other party to sign affidavit, solicitor to contact other party's solicitor, hearing coming up)
131 Provides other information (as opposed to advice)
132 Asks client whether (s)he has any questions
133 Apologises for mistake/delay
134 Updates client on current state of case (e.g. current standpoint of other professionals or parties)
135 Explaining terms of order/making sure client understands terms

Advice strategy

140 Recommends course of action (various discussed)
141 Recommends course of action (only one discussed)
142 Encourages client in his/her proposed action/takes instructions willingly
143 Discourages client's proposed action
144 Explains likely outcome of course(s) of action
145 Points out the important issues to focus on
146 Issuing a disclaimer where advice ignored
147 Explains various options to client without recommending one in particular
148 Takes instructions reluctantly

Negotiation/Coming to a settlement

150 Advises direct contact between client and other party
151 Use of "court" as a negotiation tool
152 Use of "the needs of the children" as a negotiation tool
153 References to "other people in this situation"
154 Tries to dampen client's expectations/encourages realism
155 Tries to raise client's expectations
156 Advises client that current terms (s)he is offering is too low
157 Advises client that current terms (s)he is offering is too high
158 Advises client that other party's offer or current terms are reasonable
159 Advises client that other party's offer or current terms are <u>un</u>-reasonable
160 Communicates terms offered/suggested by other party
161 Advises client to proceed without representation
162 Advises use of solicitors in drafting legal documents, in otherwise unrepresented case
163 Confirms settlement
164 Suggest practical solutions (e.g. place for contact, opening new bank account)
165 Advises client to stay away from other party
166 Represents client in court

Involvement of other professionals or parties

170 Tells client that solicitor will seek advice from another professional
(*A=mediator; B=counsellor; D=another solicitor; E=pension adviser; F=immigration adviser; G=LAB; H=counsel; J=financial adviser; K=court; L=social services; M=bank; N=doctor/hospital; O=police; P=expert witnesses; Q=school; R=Ombudsman; Z=other*)
171 Advises client to contact other professional
172 Advises client to contact 3rd party (not professional) (e.g. friends/relatives)
173 Suggests words to be used in approach to other professional/party
174 Obtains (or offers to obtain) quote for other professional services (e.g. conveyancing, life insurance)

Dealings with counsel
180 Champions client's cause in front of counsel
181 Backs up counsel's opinion
182 Disagrees with counsel

Non-legal action advised
185 Advises client to keep a diary of events/communication
186 Advises client to read literature (e.g. on coping with divorce)
187 Other non-legal action advised
188 Solicitor offers to help with non-legal issues (e.g. moving house)

Comfort/Therapy
190 Offers comfort/acknowledgement of difficult feelings or situation
191 Listens quietly/lets client "get it off their chest"
192 Gives impression of being on client's side (e.g. agreeing with views about other party)

Other
195 Other issues

CONTACT WITH (SOLICITOR FOR) SPOUSE OR EX-SPOUSE

Admin.
200 Leaves message
201 Arranges meeting
202 Sends copy of document
203 Asks him/her to complete or sign a document, or to confirm service of documents
204 Acknowledges receipt of document
205 Explains next steps (e.g. waiting for client to sign document, details of forthcoming hearing)
206 Apologises for mistake/delay
207 Asks for petition/order etc.

Discovery/Establishing story/Seeking, updating and sharing information
210 Provides information about client's assets/situation
211 Asks for/obtains information about spouse's assets/situation
212 Checks client's story with other solicitor
213 Update each other on current state of case (e.g. current standpoints of various parties/professionals involved)

Negotiation
220 Advises direct contact between client and other party
221 Use of "court" as a negotiation tool (e.g. "no court would grant your party that . . .")

222 Use of "the needs of the children" as a negotiation tool
223 References to "other people in their situation"
224 Communicates (revised) terms offered or suggested by client/client's wishes
225 Disagrees with other party's proposed terms
226 Makes a final offer
227 Accepts a final offer
228 Warns of future action if other party continues to flout terms of agreement
229 Advises that parties should proceed without representation
230 Expresses a desire to avoid a court hearing/litigation
231 Discusses keeping parties' costs down
232 Suggests action to be taken by other party (e.g. insurance of maintenance payments)
233 Agree to leave counsel to come to an agreement
234 Explains will seek advice from other professional/organisation (e.g. Benefits Agency)
235 Discourages involvement of other professional/organisation (e.g. CSA)
236 Agrees to set down for contested hearing

Chat
240 Chat

CONTENT OF CONTACT WITH OTHER SOLICITOR IN FIRM

Contact about specific case
300 Gives advice or 2nd opinion about case
301 Receives advice or 2nd opinion about case
302 Gives update on particular case (inc. briefs other solicitor before hearing)
303 Receives update on particular case (inc. is briefed by other solicitor before hearing)
304 Refers client to another solicitor within firm
305 Accepts referral of client from another solicitor within firm
306 Asks for quote for related services (e.g. conveyancing, making will)
307 Gives quote for related services (e.g. divorce for commercial client)
308 Gives other solicitor papers to read

(Other) management of junior staff
310 Delegates task to junior staff member
311 Signs time sheets/leave forms etc. for junior staff member
312 Other general supervision of junior staff

Internal management or office issues
320 Staff recruitment (interviewing, discussion of applicants etc.)
321 Discusses networking/marketing of firm (inc. day at races with clients, client parties)

322 Discusses computer/IT issues
323 Discusses finances/taxation/billing
324 Arranges internal meetings
325 Discusses other management or office issues (e.g. timetabling)

Other issues

330 Discusses attendance at conferences/seminars
331 General discussion of current state of law/legal profession
332 Other

335 Leaves message

Chatting

340 Chats

CONTACT WITH COURT STAFF

Admin.

400 Sends documents to be filed at court (e.g. petition, marriage certificate, legal aid declaration)
401 Apologises for error in document
402 Transfers case to another court
403 Pays/is asked to pay court fee
404 Swears affidavit

Hearing

410 Makes application for hearing
411 Arranges/asks for/reschedules date(s) or time(s) for hearing (or filing evidence)
412 Arranges/confirms/changes other details of hearing (e.g. who will be attending, purpose of hearing)
413 Vacates hearing
414 Is hurried by clerk, magistrates waiting to start hearing

Other

420 Checks court/legal procedures (e.g. re asking for expert for consultation only, not report; when will order be ready)
421 Provides info about client or case/updates court on case/answers district judge's query
422 Other activity/subject

CONTACT WITH OTHER FAMILY LAW PROFESSIONALS:
(COUNSEL/OTHER SOLICITOR/SOCIAL WORKER/COURT WELFARE OFFICER/GUARDIAN)

Admin.

500 Leaves message
501 Arranges meeting
502 Arranges/agrees/reschedules date(s) or time(s) for hearing (or filing evidence)
503 Arranges/agrees/confirms other details of hearing (e.g. who will be attending, purpose of hearing)
504 Sends document/letter
505 Acknowledges receipt of document/letter
506 Sends cheque/arranges payment on account by LAB
507 Discusses/explains delay

Information

510 Gives information about client's situation/concerns
511 Asks for/receives information or 2nd opinion about client's situation
512 Asks for/obtains information about other side's situation/concerns/ proposed arrangements
513 Update each other on current state of case (e.g. current standpoint of various parties, professionals)
514 Discusses/asks for/receives advice about legal procedures (e.g. court procedures, legality of order)
515 Asks for/obtains quote for related services (e.g. conveyancing, insurance)
516 Explains next steps

Negotiation

520 Suggests (revised) action/terms of order to other professional
521 Asks whether suggested terms agreeable to party represented by/known to other professional
522 Asks whether suggested terms agreeable to other professional
523 Discusses or suggests terms/proposals which would be acceptable to all parties
524 Discusses with counsel (or other prof. working for same client) offer to be made to other side
525 Agrees terms/proposal with other professional
526 Argues or disagrees with other professional's views or proposals
527 Leaves other professional to sort out an agreement directly with client (e.g. re finances)
528 Discusses/suggests practical solutions to situation (e.g. location for contact visits, attendance at parenting programmes, phoning grandmother to get baby ready for contact visit while mother delayed, counselling etc.)

Interaction with counsel

530 Champions client's cause in front of counsel
531 Backs up counsel's opinion in front of client
532 Works together with counsel to dampen client's expectations

Other

540 Discusses law in general (e.g. implications of recently reported family law cases)
541 Chat
542 Other activity/subject

CONTACT WITH OTHER PROFESSIONALS OR ORGANISATIONS
(e.g. Legal Aid Board, Benefits Agency, accountant, immigration adviser, taxing draftsman, expert witness, charity, professional association)

Admin.

600 Leaves message
601 Arranges meeting
602 Arranges/agrees/reschedules date(s) or time(s) for hearing (or filing evidence)
603 Arranges/agrees/confirms other details of hearing (e.g. who will be attending, purpose of hearing)
604 Sends document/letter
605 Acknowledges receipt of document/letter
606 Sends cheque/arranges payment on account by LAB
607 Discusses/explains delay

Information

610 Gives information about client's situation/concerns
611 Asks for/receives information, advice or 2nd opinion about client's situation
612 Asks for/obtains information about other side's situation/concerns/proposed arrangements
613 Update each other on current state of case (e.g. current standpoint of various parties, professionals)
614 Discuss/asks for/receives advice about legal procedures (e.g. court procedures, legality of order)
615 Asks for/obtains quote for related services (e.g. conveyancing, insurance)
616 Explains next steps

Practical solutions

620 Tries to sort out practical ways of solving client's financial problems (debt/benefits etc.)
621 Tries to sort out practical ways of solving client's other problems

Legal Aid
630 Asks for advice about eligibility for a client
631 Re-applies for legal aid for client
632 Checks on outcome of appeal for legal aid

Other case-specific contact
635 Other case-specific contact

Contact related to the firm
640 Discusses firm's financial situation
641 Asks for advice about bills/fees
642 Marketing of firm/networking
643 Other contact related to the firm

NON-CONTACT ACTIVITIES

Drafting/Reading
700 Dictates or writes attendance note
701 Drafts legal document/fills in legal form
702 (e.g. Schedule of Finances/legal aid application/Green Form)
703 Reads legal document/looks through client file
704 Reads magazine articles, professional association newsletter etc.
705 Legal research (e.g. looking up law on judicial separation)

Fees/Billing
710 Processes incoming cheque
711 Processes incoming bill
712 Checks accounts/billing situation on current cases
713 Preparing bills for taxation

Time management/Case management
720 Makes a "To Do list"/checks diary/makes note of future meetings/
hearings/deadlines
721 Fills in time sheets/dictates time allocations
722 Fills in case plan for a file (key dates)
723 Puts note on file for later action
724 Opens new file
725 Fills in internal forms (e.g. to send file to storage)

Other activities
730 Travel
731 Checks/signs post
732 Other activity

733 Looks through post

Type of case
750 Private work
751 Legal aid work
752 Green Form work
753 Pro bono work

754 *Divorce or separation* case involving:
755 Money/property disputes or settlements
756 Disputes or issues arising from the presence of children (e.g. residence and contact)
757 Domestic violence

758 Child protection case
760 Parental responsibility case
761 Inheritance
762 Pre-nuptial agreements
765 Other family case

759 Non-family case

CASE STUDIES

BACKGROUND INFORMATION ABOUT THE SOLICITOR
Partner or assistant
Date of admission
SFLA membership
Whether specialist (defined as spending more than 50% of time on family law, including public children law)
Proportion of fee-earning time spent on Legal Aid family work

BACKGROUND INFORMATION ABOUT THE FIRM
Number of partners in firm
Structure of firm (e.g. separate family law department within large firm)
Specialisms of firm (family, and others)
Number of solicitors (partners and assistants) who deal with/specialise in family work
Proportion of firm's gross fee income from family work
Proportion of firm's fee-earning time spent on family work
Whether or not firm has Legal Aid franchise for family work
Proportion of family work which is legally aided

The rest of the questions in the interview refer to one of the solicitor's recent divorce cases, selected according to the following instructions:
Select the first divorce case, which you personally handled, for which the divorce petition was filed on or after DATE [18 months ago], and for which at least a decree nisi has now been granted.

BASIC DETAILS OF CASE:
Date of opening file/first instructions
Public **funding** of client
—Green Form? Legal Aid applied for? Legal Aid granted? Other side legally aided?
Was other party represented?

Details of parties/children (identified during interview by Christian names only)

Length of marriage

SITUATION AT FIRST CONTACT WITH CLIENT:
At what **stage of marital breakdown?** *(e.g. considering separation, already living apart (for how long?), already legally separated?)*

Was there any talk of **reconciliation?**
Did either party have a **new partner?**

Where were the **children living**?
Any **domestic violence**?

What sort of information/advice was client looking for from solicitor at initial contact? (*e.g. pre-separation advice about likely divorce settlement, advice as to how to respond to the other party's divorce petition etc, advice about domestic violence or about a dispute over children*)

DIVORCE PETITION ISSUES

At what stage was divorce discussed?
Who petitioned *for divorce*? On **what grounds**? How were these decided?
Any cross-petitions/threats of cross-petitions etc?

FINANCIAL ISSUES

- *Details of marital assets*
  —equity of house, other property, pensions, shares, savings, income of each client

- *Establishing information about the financial position of parties*
  Client
  —any **problems** establishing details of marital assets from client?
  —at initial contact, did client come with **prepared information**?
  —**was client reluctant** to reveal assets to solicitor (or to other party)?
  —did solicitor feel the need to check the **accuracy** of the financial facts?
  —were there any **delays** in establishing/providing information about *client's* finances? Why?
  —if so, what was the cause of these delays—client, solicitor or 3rd party?
  —how did solicitor deal with these delays/problems?

  Other party
  —were there any **delays or problems** in discovering information about *other party's* finances?
  —if so, what was the cause of these delays—other party, solicitor or 3rd party?
  —how did solicitor deal with these delays/problems?
  —was **full discovery** obtained in the end? If not, why not?

- *Advising/Giving information to client about finances*
  —had client **already agreed** financial settlement with other party?
  —if so, did solicitor advise against any part of that settlement, or advise any additional terms?

—if no agreement already made, **did client know the sort of financial settlement** (s)he wanted?

—if so, was it **realistic**? if not, how did solicitor go about raising or dampening client's expectations?

—had client sought **advice from other professional** about finances before contacting the solicitor? *(e.g. mediator, pension adviser, employer)*

—did you at any time suggest that the client seek such 3rd party advice, or seek advice yourself on his/her behalf?

—at what stage? For what reason?

—did client always **agree with and accept solicitor's advice** about finances?

—if no, why not? How was it resolved?

—did solicitor ever take instructions, against better judgment?

Did this case come under the **ancillary relief pilot**?

* *Negotiating financial settlement*

—summary of what financial **issues to be resolved**? *(e.g. sale of house, division of property and capital, spousal/child maintenance, pensions etc)*

—talk through the various **phases of the negotiation process**:

—**initial position** of parties?

—**offers** made/rejected?

—did solicitor ever try to **talk client out of making or rejecting an offer**? successfully? If so, how?

—was **counsel** involved in the negotiation? Did he/she meet with the client?

—were there any **directions hearings** about finances? Who asked for this? Why? At what stage?

—did you apply for a **contested hearing**? At what stage? Why?

—did hearing go ahead, or did you **settle out of court**? If so, at door of court?

—were there any further **enforcement hearings**? Why? When?

—any **difficulties** in negotiating the settlement? If so, what? Difficulties with the client or other party?

—general **atmosphere of negotiation** friendly or hostile? Changes over time?

—did client/other party have **difficulty separating finances from other issues** *(e.g. children/violence)*?

—did solicitor ever suggest **direct contact** between client and other party about financial issues?

CHILDREN ISSUES

* *Establishing information about the children's situation*

—**ages** of children?

—any **social services** involvement?

—at time of initial contact with client, what were the arrangements for **contact/residence**, and were there any problems with those arrangements?

- *Advising/Giving information to client about children*
    —had client **already agreed** a contact/residence plan with other party?
    —if so, did solicitor advise against any part of that plan, or advise any additional terms?

    —if no agreement already made, did client **know the sort of contact/residence plan** (s)he wanted?
    —if so, was it **realistic**? If not, how did solicitor go about raising or dampening client's expectations?
    —did the client ever suggest action which the solicitor didn't think was in the **children's interests**?
    —had client sought advice from **other professional** about children before contacting the solicitor?
    —did you at any time suggest that the client seek such 3rd party advice, or seek advice yourself on his/her behalf?
    —at what stage? For what reason?

    —did client always **agree with and accept** solicitor's advice about the children?
    —if no, why not?
    —did solicitor ever take instructions, against better judgment?

- *Negotiating children issues*
    —what children issues needed **to be resolved**? *(e.g. contact/residence, other specific issues)*

    —talk through the various **phases of the negotiation process**:
    —**initial position** of parties?
    —**offers** made/rejected?
    —did solicitor ever try to **talk client out of making or rejecting an offer**? Successfully? If so, how?

    —was **counsel** involved in the negotiation? Did he/she meet with the client?
    —was there any **court welfare officer** involvement? Did (s)he meet the children? Was a welfare report written?
    —was there any **expert witness** involvement? Who?
    —were there any **directions hearings** about arrangements for children? Who asked for this? Why? At what stage?
    —did you apply for a **contested hearing**? At what stage? Why?
    —did hearing go ahead, or did you **settle out of court**? If so, at door of court?
    —were there any further **enforcement hearings**? Why? When?

—any **difficulties** in negotiating the settlement? If so, what? Difficulties with the client or other party?

—general **atmosphere of negotiation** friendly or hostile? Changes over time?

—did solicitor ever suggest **direct contact** between client and other party about the children?

—did solicitor handle the **children and finance negotiations** in **different** ways?

CURRENT STATE OF CASE
—decree absolute granted?
—still in touch with client? If so, about what?

—how much was the **final bill**?

CHECKLIST OF IMPORTANT DATES
—date of petition
—date of affidavits of means (client/other party)
—date of statement of arrangements for children
—date(s) of directions hearing(s)
—date(s) of consent order(s)
—date of decree nisi
—date of decree absolute
—date of final/contested hearing
—date of subsequent enforcement hearing

SOLICITOR'S IMPRESSIONS OF CASE
—**impressions of client?** *(e.g. needy, aggressive, difficult, generous)*
—how much advice or explanation did this client need? More or less than other clients? Why?
—**impressions of case** Easy or difficult to sort out? Why?

ATTITUDES
—solicitor's attitudes towards the development of **rules for property division/pre-nuptial settlements**
—would it have worked in this case? How?

—attitudes towards **legal aid changes** (franchising, block contracting, fixed fees)?

SOLICITOR'S NAME
DATE OF INTERVIEW
INTERVIEWER:

Partner   ☐
Assistant   ☐

Date of admission:

SFLA membership?
Yes   ☐
No   ☐

Family specialist?
Yes   ☐
No   ☐

Proportion of solicitor's fee-earning time spent on family work?

Proportion of solicitor's family work that is legally aided?

BACKGROUND INFORMATION ABOUT THE FIRM

Number of partners in firm?

Structure of firm (e.g. separate family law department within large firm)?

Specialisms of firm (family, and others)?

Number of solicitors (partners and assistants) who deal with/specialise in family work?

Proportion of firm's gross fee income from family work?

Proportion of firm's fee-earning time spent on family work?

Proportion of family work which is legally aided?

Legal Aid franchise for family work?
Yes   ☐
No   ☐

BASIC DETAILS OF SELECTED CASE

Date of opening file/first instructions _____

Husband ☐
Wife ☐

Funding of client?
Private ☐
Green Form ☐
Legal Aid ☐

Funding of other party?
Private ☐
Green Form ☐
Legal Aid ☐

Was other party represented?
Yes ☐
No ☐

Details of parties/children (ages, number of children etc.)

Length of marriage: _____ years

SITUATION AT FIRST CONTACT WITH CLIENT

At what stage of marital breakdown?
(*e.g. considering separation, already living apart (for how long?), already legally separated?*)

_____

_____

Was there any talk of reconciliation? Did either party have a new partner?.

_____

_____

Where were the children living?

_____

_____

Any domestic violence?

_____

_____

_____

What sort of information/advice was client looking for from solicitor at initial contact?
(e.g. pre-separation advice about likely divorce settlement, advice as to how to respond to the other party's divorce petition etc., advice about domestic violence or about a dispute over children)

_____

_____

_____

DIVORCE PETITION ISSUES

At what stage was divorce discussed?

_____

_____

Who petitioned for divorce?
Husband   ☐
Wife   ☐

What were the grounds for divorce? How were these decided?

_____

_____

Any cross-petitions/threats of cross-petitions etc?

_____

_____

_____

_____

FINANCIAL ISSUES

• *Details of marital assets*
  —equity of house, other property, pensions, shares, savings, income of each client

  _____

  _____

• *Establishing information about the financial position of parties*
  Client
  —any problems establishing details of marital assets from client?
  —at initial contact, did client come with prepared information?
  —was client reluctant to reveal assets to solicitor (or to other party)?
  —did solicitor feel the need to check the accuracy of the financial facts?
  —were there any delays in establishing/providing information about client's finances? why?
  —if so, what was the cause of these delays—client, solicitor or 3rd party?
  —how did solicitor deal with these delays/problems?

  _____

  _____

  _____

  _____

  _____

  _____

  Other party
  —were there any delays or problems in discovering information about other party's finances?
  —if so, what was the cause of these delays—other party, solicitor or 3rd party?
  —how did solicitor deal with these delays/problems?
  —was full discovery obtained in the end? if not, why not?

  _____

  _____

  _____

  _____

  _____

Did this case come under the ancillary relief pilot?
Yes   ☐
No   ☐

_____

_____

_____

- *Advising/Giving information to client about finances*
    —had client already agreed financial settlement with other party?
    —if so, did solicitor advise against any part of that settlement, or advise any additional terms?

_____

_____

_____

    —if no agreement already made, did client know the sort of financial settle-ment (s)he wanted?
    —if so, was it realistic? if not, how did solicitor go about raising or damp-ening client's expectations?

_____

_____

_____

    —had client sought advice from other professional about finances before contacting the solicitor?
    (*e.g. mediator, pension adviser, employer*)
    —did you at any time suggest that the client seek such 3rd party advice, or seek advice yourself on his/her behalf?
    —at what stage? for what reason?

_____

_____

_____

    —did client always agree with and accept solicitor's advice about finances?
    —if no, why not? how was it resolved?
    —did solicitor ever take instructions, against better judgment?

_____

---

* *Negotiating financial settlement*
   —summary of what financial issues to be resolved?
   (e.g. sale of house, division of property and capital, spousal/child mainte-nance, pensions etc.)

   —talk through the various phases of the negotiation process:
   —initial position of parties?
   —offers made/rejected?
   —did solicitor ever try to talk client out of making or rejecting an offer? suc-cessfully? if so, how?

   —was counsel involved in the negotiation? did he/she meet with the client?

---

   were there any directions hearings about finances? who asked for this? why? at what stage?

—did you apply for a contested hearing? at what stage? why?

_____

_____

_____

—did hearing go ahead, or did you settle out of court? if so, at door of court?

_____

_____

_____

—were there any further enforcement hearings? why? when?

_____

_____

_____

—any difficulties in negotiating the settlement? if so, what? difficulties with the client or other party?

_____

_____

_____

_____

_____

_____

—general atmosphere of negotiation friendly or hostile? changes over time?

_____

_____

_____

—did client/other party have difficulty separating finances from other issues? (*e.g. children/violence*)

_____

_____

—did solicitor ever suggest direct contact between client and other party about financial issues?

_____

_____

_____

CHILDREN ISSUES

• *Establishing information about the children's situation*
  —ages of children?
  —any social services involvement?
  —at time of initial contact with client, what were the arrangements for contact/residence, and were there any problems with those arrangements?

_____

_____

_____

• *Advising/Giving information to client about children*
  —had client already agreed a contact/residence plan with other party?
  —if so, did solicitor advise against any part of that plan, or advise any additional terms?

_____

_____

_____

  —if no agreement already made, did client know the sort of contact/residence plan (s)he wanted?
  —if so, was it realistic? if not, how did solicitor go about raising or dampening client's expectations?

_____

_____

_____

—did the client ever suggest action which the solicitor didn't think was in the children's interests?

_____

_____

_____

—had client sought advice from other professional about children before contacting the solicitor?
—did you at any time suggest that the client seek such 3rd party advice, or seek advice yourself on his/her behalf?
—at what stage? for what reason?

_____

_____

_____

—did client always agree with and accept solicitor's advice about the children?
—if no, why not?
—did solicitor ever take instructions, against better judgment?

_____

_____

_____

• *Negotiating children issues*
—what children issues needed to be resolved?
  (e.g. contact/residence, other specific issues)

_____

_____

_____

—talk through the various phases of the negotiation process:
—initial position of parties?
—offers made/rejected?
—did solicitor ever try to talk client out of making or rejecting an offer? successfully? if so, how?

_____

_____

_____

_____

_____

—was counsel involved in the negotiation? did he/she meet with the client?

_____

_____

_____

—was there any court welfare officer involvement? did (s)he meet the children? was a welfare report written?

_____

_____

_____

—was there any expert witness involvement? who?

_____

_____

_____

—were there any directions hearings about arrangements for children? who asked for this? why? at what stage?

_____

_____

_____

—did you apply for a contested hearing? at what stage? why?

_____

_____

_____

—did hearing go ahead, or did you settle out of court? if so, at door of court?

_____

_____

_____

—were there any further enforcement hearings? why? when?

_____

_____

_____

—any difficulties in negotiating the settlement? if so, what? difficulties with the client or other party?

_____

_____

_____

_____

_____

—general atmosphere of negotiation friendly or hostile? changes over time?

_____

_____

_____

—did solicitor ever suggest direct contact between client and other party about the children?

_____

_____

_____

—did solicitor handle the children and finance negotiations in different ways?

_____

_____

_____

CURRENT STATE OF CASE

—Decree absolute granted?

Yes ☐
No ☐

—Still in touch with client? if so, about what?

_____

_____

_____

_____

_____

_____

—How much was the final bill? £ _____

CHECKLIST OF IMPORTANT DATES

—Date of petition

_____

—Date of affidavits of means (client/other party)

_____

—Date of statement of arrangements for children

_____

—Date(s) of directions hearing(s)

_____

—Date(s) of consent order(s)

_____

—Date of decree nisi

_____

—Date of decree absolute

_____

—Date of final/contested hearing

_____

—Date of subsequent enforcement hearing

_____

SOLICITOR'S IMPRESSIONS OF CASE

—**impressions of client?**
  (e.g. needy, aggressive, difficult, generous)
—how much advice or explanation did this client need? more or less than other clients? why?
—impressions of case (easy or difficult to sort out? why?)

_____

_____

_____

_____

_____

_____

ATTITUDES

—solicitor's attitudes towards the development of rules for property division/pre-nuptial settlements
—would it have worked in this case? how?

_____

_____

_____

_____

_____

_____

—attitudes towards legal aid changes (franchising, block contracting, fixed fees)?

_____

_____

_____

_____

_____

_____

OTHER ISSUES

_____

_____

_____

_____

_____

_____

_____

_____

CHRONOLOGICAL SUMMARY OF DIVORCE CASE

Index